W9-BIK-324

# YOUR ENVIRONMENT, YOUR HEALTH AND YOU

# YOUR ENVIRONMENT, YOUR HEALTH AND YOU

## Donald E. Waite, D.O., M.P.H.

**VANTAGE PRESS**
New York ● Los Angeles

FIRST EDITION

All rights reserved, including the right of
reproduction in whole or in part in any form.

Copyright © 1991 by Donald E. White, D.O., M.P.H.

Published by Vantage Press, Inc.
516 West 34th Street, New York, New York 10001

Manufactured in the United States of America
ISBN: 0-533-08834-8

Library of Congress Catalog Card No.: 89-90505

1  2  3  4  5  6  7  8  9  0

To Kris Lee Waite, who never had the opportunity to live life to its fullest, nor to demonstrate his full potential; and to my parents, Sidney B. and Louise A. Waite, whose labor, sacrifices and dedication to family so enriched their progeny.

# Contents

# Foreword

Medicine is changing rapidly, and the general public is kept well informed. In fact, the latest research is often published in newspapers and magazines before many physicians have an opportunity to read the reports published in the traditional professional journals. A well educated and interested public can learn a great deal by keeping informed. On the other hand, there are conflicting scientific claims and legitimate controversies which may confuse people and create a lot of doubts. The environment, including nutrition, chemical toxins, natural dangers, and accidents are critical factors in one's health and well being. *Your Environment, Your Health and You* contains the background and fundamental information to understand principles of personal health. That is why this book is important. It is practical and avoids sensationalism. In a clear and succinct style the reader samples a variety of pertinent environmental and natural influences on family and individual health.

A balanced view on current issues can be found in this well-written work. Practical advice as well as background scientific information on nutrition, exercise, common and uncommon environmental hazards, and inherited conditions are discussed clearly and understandably.

Physicians and medical educators have been criticized, often justifiably, for their emphasis on treatment of illness rather than prevention. I am enthusiastic about this book because it provides clear information to the general public to become interested and knowledgeable about preventive medicine. They in turn will stimulate the professionals to do likewise.

—Manuel Tzagournis, M.D.,
Professor of Internal Medicine,
Dean of the College of Medicine and
   vice president for health sciences,
Ohio State University

# Preface

The goal of this book is to bring together in one source all of the references that the average family needs to guide them in protecting their health from environmental exposures that they are likely to encounter. This is a lofty goal. The subject is vast. The information is constantly changing, almost on a weekly basis, as new knowledge is acquired. We are discovering with alarming frequency that substances we have long regarded as benign do indeed pose a risk to our health and well-being. These new discoveries are transmitted to the professionals through various journals and publications, as well as through the multitude of continuing-education meetings throughout the nation. The general public has no such source of information, and must rely upon the news media, a most unreliable source as far as objectivity and accuracy are concerned. This project attempts to fill that void, at least for a time. The reader must bear in mind that the information conveyed herein will be altered or modified by ongoing discoveries.

This book addresses many medical problems and potential problems, but only in a very general manner. The individual's personal physician should always be consulted for all medical needs. Only a well-trained physician, dedicated to remaining current, can accurately assess an individual's complaints and medical problems. This book in no way attempts to circumvent that absolute necessity.

# YOUR ENVIRONMENT, YOUR HEALTH AND YOU

# I

# Hazards of Pesticides and Herbicides

## PESTICIDES

Those of us who are in our fifth or sixth decade can well recall the fly-laden screens of our homes when we were growing up. Keeping these pests out of the house was a constant and frustrating task. This was a particularly urgent problem in the 1940s since flies were considered to be one of the chief vectors of poliomyelitits, a prevalent and dread disease of the time. Then came DDT to the rescue. It had been used during World War II to dust populations and cities to control lice and diseases such as plague, which could have invoked death and destruction upon our troops. It was a godsend to our troops and to our war effort.

After the war, I recall vividly the war surplus jeeps fogging the neighborhoods in my hometown with DDT, and the flies (and mosquitoes) disappeared. Although DDT was to fall into disrepute, it was a great blessing at the time. The era of chemical control of pests that transmit disease and destroy our crops was thus ushered in. These weapons are, of course, a two-edged sword. They cannot be used indiscriminately with impunity, and careless handling and application have resulted in illness among humans. Fortunately most of these instances in the United States have resulted in temporary illness and few fatalities. Far more serious incidents have occurred elsewhere. More than a hundred people died in India after eating wheat that had been contaminated with parathion from spillage during shipping. Fewer deaths occurred, but more than three thousand people were poisoned by hexachlorobenzene in Turkey after they ate seed grain that had been treated with this fungicide. Numerous similar tragic incidents have occurred worldwide from eating seed grain treated with organic mercurial compounds and other fungicides.

The United States experience has demonstrated that these chemicals can be utilized with relative safety if handled and applied with intelligence and care. Significant risk exists during the handling and application of chemicals. The individual who loads the materials aboard aircraft for aerial application of pesticides, and the flagman on the ground who marks the flight path and signals the end of the row to the pilot are especially at risk. Agriculture in general is the area where the greatest risk exists, and particularly in commercial agriculture. The organophosphate pesticides, which in general are limited to commercial and farm use, are by far the most frequently involved in poisoning. While they are among the most potent toxic pesticides, good treatment for poisoning is available if it is promptly administered. Most of these agents should not be used in or around the home. Regulations controlling their application are designed to minimize residual on fruits and vegetables. Washing of all fruits and vegetables before consumption is advisable, however.

There is little excuse for events such as the poisoning of over one thousand individuals in 1985 when aldicarb (Temik) was illegally applied to melons commercially grown in California. The Centers for Disease Control reported that poisoned individuals who ate these melons were seen at medical facilities in Alaska, Arizona, Colorado, Hawaii, Idaho, Nevada, Oregon, Washington and in two provinces in Canada. Several previous episodes of poisoning resulted from consumption of cucumbers and mint that had been treated with aldicarb.

Aldicarb, which is a very effective systemic pesticide, is taken up by the plant and stored in the fruit or vegetable. It is not licensed for such application. During that period its use was limited to citrus groves and potato fields. Its use is currently limited to greenhouse applications. Even in that setting it must be handled with great care because it is absorbed through the skin. It is very toxic through this route as well as by ingestion. Deaths have occurred from such skin contact among workers in the field. Aldicarb is capable of causing sickness and death at the lowest concentration of any registered pesticide in the United States. Fortunately, poisoning is amenable to treatment if medical care is sought promptly. Deaths have occurred, however. Individuals who have other medical conditions or who are on certain medications are at an increased risk. No long-term harmful effects are known, and it is not a suspected carcinogen.

Much progress has been made in the development and control of pesticides during the past forty some years. Much more needs to be done, particularly in the education of the general public. These substances have produced great benefits to us, both in the reduction of disease and in increased crop yield. Every precaution must be taken, however, to prevent entry to the body through breathing, eating or application to the skin.

Several categories of pesticides exist. DDT belongs to the group classified as chlorinated hydrocarbons. Also in this group are methoxychlor, chlordane, aldrin, dieldrin, endrin, toxaphene, heptachlor, kepone, lindane, mirex and benzene hexachloride. These compounds as a group are much more persistent in the environment than most other pesticides, because they are resistant to breakdown. They thus tend to accumulate in the soil and in the beds of lakes and streams. They also tend to accumulate in biologic systems, being transmitted up the food chain from lower species to higher species, including humans. It is for this reason that they have fallen into disfavor. As a class they have less acute toxicity than the organophosphates or carbamates, but a greater potential for chronic toxicity. They are poorly absorbed through the skin and are most efficiently absorbed by ingestion. They are not very soluble in water. They are therefore commonly formulated in petroleum distillates, such as kerosene, so vomiting should not be induced following ingestion.

## DDT

This was first introduced for commercial use in 1947. It was the most effective of all the synthetic insecticides, and the least costly to produce. As mentioned previously, it was widely used during World War II to control lice by dusting on humans. It is poorly absorbed from the skin (unless formulated in petroleum distillates). No evidence has emerged over the past forty-five years that any harmful effects resulted from this application. On the other hand our troops were spared the disease and pestilence that could reasonably have been expected. There is no evidence of any fatal poisoning in humans from DDT in spite of such widespread and intimate application. In fact all recorded attempts at suicide where DDT was used failed.

Virtually everyone who lived in that era, and indeed since, has demonstrable residues of DDT in the body fat tissues. No health hazards have become evident as a consequence of this long-term storage. DDT was reported to cause liver tumors in laboratory animals (rats and mice) as early as 1947. Extensive use of this pesticide

3

worldwide ever since that time has failed to demonstrate similar effects in humans.

Fish, on the other hand, are extremely susceptible to the acute toxicity of DDT. Behavioral changes were among the most obvious evidence of accumulation of DDT in fish. Birds have demonstrated an equally strong susceptibility. The threat to the survival of certain species of wild birds through the thinning of their egg shells has had widespread publicity. This occurred primarily among those birds that consume fish in their diet. These toxic effects on fish and birds were enhanced by the fact that DDT was very persistent in the environment and thus accumulated there. It was also stored in the fatty tissues of fish and most animals including humans. The higher up the food chain that these stores of DDT were consumed, the greater became the concentration stored in fat. The predatory nature of fish-eating birds assured a higher concentration of DDT in these creatures. Similarly, a higher level of DDT was concentrated in predatory fish than in those lower down the chain with different dietary preferences. These toxic effects on fish and the thinning and breakage of eggshells of birds have been reversed with the decline in the usage of DDT.

As a consequence of its toxicity and the impact of DDT on the environment, its use has been virtually banned in the United States and markedly curtailed in some other countries. By virtue of its low cost and the absence of an effective substitute, it continues in wide use internationally. Millions of lives have been saved and continue to be saved by the control of mosquitos, flies and lice that transmit such diseases as malaria, yellow fever, dengue fever, filariasis and plague.

## METHOXYCHLOR

This is a chlorinated ethane, the same chemical class as DDT, and it is the designated hitter for DDT in the United States. It is virtually nontoxic to mammals and demonstrates little persistence in the environment or in animals. It is stored in body fat at about 0.2 percent the extent of DDT. The half life in the rat is about two weeks compared with six months for DDT. It is not as effective as DDT, however, and cannot be substituted universally in the control of the diseases mentioned above. It is somewhat effective against fleas, ticks, flies, and mosquitoes, but malathion and chlorpyrifos are more commonly used for these pests today. Methoxychlor is commonly incorporated into home orchard sprays.

4

# LINDANE

This pesticide has been the mainstay in the treatment of head and body lice, as well as scabies. It is absorbed through the skin and is toxic to the brain and other sections of the nervous system, however. It is also toxic to the liver. Although it remains the most widely used drug for lice and scabies, it should never be used on infants and young children, where convulsions have been associated with its use. Crotamiton, which is also very effective, has been substituted in young patients with these parasites. More recently the development of the synthetic pyrethroid permethrin (Nix) has provided an effective agent of low toxicity for the treatment of head and body lice (see pyrethroids, p. 11). Fatal cases of aplastic anemia due to skin absorption have resulted from prolonged use of lindane in adults. The directions for the use of lindane instruct the user that it should be left on for a specified period of time, then washed off thoroughly. Significant absorption can occur during this period, however. Repeated applications carry an even greater risk, and this practice is discouraged.

# ALDRIN, DIELDRIN, ENDRIN

These are all closely related chemical substances whose use has been markedly restricted due to their toxicity and suspicions of carcinogenicity. Subsequent studies regarding carcinogencity have yielded conflicting reports, as is frequently the case. Dieldrin has been shown to cause liver cancer in mice, but the extrapolation of such data from mice to men has never been clearly established. This continues to be the subject of intense debate. Endrin has been shown to cause serious birth defects in the offspring of hamsters fed a single dose.

There is no dispute about the toxicity of these three compounds, however. Several incidents of accidental ingestion of endrin from contaminated flour have been reported, and these events have resulted in severe convulsions and many deaths. In 1956 forty-nine people became ill after eating bakery foods prepared with flour that had been contaminated with endrin. The bags of flour had been shipped in a railway car that had previously been used to ship leaking containers of endrin. Several instances of this type of contamination of food products with toxic chemicals have occurred worldwide. Over 1200 cases of illness with 45 deaths were recorded as a result of consumption of food contaminated with endrin in Wales, Qatar, Saudi Arabia and Pakistan prior to 1970.

In 1988 six residents of Orange County became acutely ill after eating frozen taquitos, all purchased from the same store during the same week. Five of these individuals suffered multiple seizures. One seventeen-year-old boy was diagnosed as having epilepsy and was placed on anticonvulsant medication until the true cause of the seizures was discovered. Examination of the remaining taquitos from the first family revealed endrin contamination of several of them. Samples taken from the store and tested by the U.S. Department of Agriculture were negative for endrin. The USDA also inspected the plant where the taquitos were produced and found no evidence of pesticide. It is suspected that the packages were deliberately contaminated somewhere in the distribution chain.

Dieldrin was incorporated into aerosol sprays for home use and was available after DDT was banned. In contrast to DDT, aldrin, dieldrin and eldrin are all absorbed through the intact skin, increasing the risk to individuals involved in their manufacture and handling. They also are very persistent in the environment, and they undergo bio-magnification in the food chain, as was the case with DDT. Ingestion of solutions of dieldrin can result in severe convulsions and death if not treated promptly and aggressively. Children are particularly at risk given their propensity for drinking just about any substance regardless of its taste. A number of fatalities have been attributed to these agents and the use of aldrin and dieldrin was banned in the United States in 1974.


## CHLORDANE

This potent and effective pesticide was introduced for commercial use in 1945 and gained widespread use in agriculture, in the household and in the garden. Being in the same chemical classification as aldrin, dieldrin and endrin (cyclodienes), it shares most of their properties and toxicity. Abnormalities reflecting its toxicity to the brain and nervous system in general are among the most serious. It is readily absorbed through the intact skin, making its handling and application hazardous. The use of adequate and proper clothing and skin protective devices during application is imperative. Any contaminated clothing must be removed immediately and the skin should be cleansed carefully. Chlordane is also readily absorbed when ingested or inhaled. One fatality occurred when a worker spilled chlordane on the clothing and did not remove the clothing immediately. Convulsions ensued forty minutes later, followed by death. Recovery can be effected following such exposure if prompt and vigorous treatment is instituted.

Chlordane has served a very valuable role in the control of ants and termites. No other substance has proven as consistently effective over an extended period of time. Because of its toxicity its use has been restricted to licensed exterminators since 1975. Surface application is not approved even by licensed personnel; it must be injected into the soil. Its persistence in the soil for as long as five years enhances its usefulness in this application. Recently it has been linked to illness in homes where it was improperly applied to interior surfaces, or where it leaked into the home through cracks in the foundation. In some instances it found its way into heating and ventilating ducts.

The marked reduction in the usage of chlordane has been accompanied by a concomitant decrease in manufacturing facilities, so that at present less than 100 employees are engaged in its production in the United States. As a result of the strict control measures that have been maintained since 1979, no health problems have been identified in this group of workers. Its was banned for use in agriculture and most general applications effective in 1976. Its use for the control of termites was exempted from that ban.

## HEPTACHLOR

This substance is closely related to chlordane chemically, and shares many of its properties and toxicities. It is only slightly less persistent in the environment. The half-life of chlordane is one year, and that of heptachlor about nine to ten months. Both have been shown to cause liver cancers in mice, and both have been tested in the National Cancer Institute's carcinogen program, not only for this reason but also because of their resistance to degradation. Heptachlor was included with chlordane in the EPA ban in 1976.

## MIREX

This substance is closely related to **kepone**, and probably is degraded to kepone in the environment. It has been used extensively to control the fire ant in the southern United States. Mirex and

7

kepone are very toxic and are carcinogenic. They are bioconcentrated in the food chain several thousand fold. This is a matter of grave concern in the Chesapeake Bay area. Gross contamination of the soil surrounding a kepone manufacturing plant in Hopewell, Virginia in 1978, and the subsequent run-off into the James River resulted in the curtailment of fishing and shellfish harvesting in this area. This contamination has extended to the Chesapeake Bay, an important commercial fishing body. This substance has been deposited in the bed of the James River and the Chesapeake Bay in significant concentration. No means of decontamination has been devised.

Whereas many pesticides undergo degradation by bacteria in water and soil, mirex and kepone show little or no such tendency. They are very persistent in the environment, and will remain in these bodies of water for decades, contaminating the shellfish and other aquatic life. They are very toxic to the liver and nervous system and are carcinogenic. This incident, one of the most serious and most irresponsible by an industry in the United States, resulted in serious illness in seventy-six workers.


## ORGANOPHOSPHATES

This group of pesticides blocks the enzyme, cholinesterase, that maintains the normal balance at the nerve endings throughout the body. This results in an excess accumulation of acetylcholine in the nerve endings, not only in the muscles throughout the body, but in the heart and nervous sytem as well. The result is a tightness in the chest with wheezing, increased sweating and salivation, nausea, vomiting, diarrhea, severe cramps, slowing of the heart, headache, anxiety, insomnia, nightmares, confusion, slurred speech, tremor and convulsions. This blockade tends to be persistent, in some cases lasting for days. The onset of symptoms occurs rapidly, usually within two to three hours, in less time with heavy exposures. Death can occur in an acute exposure within twenty-four hours if untreated, usually from asphyxia as a result of respiratory paralysis.

Treatment of these disorders of the nervous system is available at medical centers that are equipped for such poisonings. Measurement of the pseudo-cholinesterase level in the red blood cell helps to confirm the diagnosis, but a baseline level should be established prior to exposure in workers. A more ominous finding has been the delayed neurotoxic effects of some of these compounds. This is a sometimes permanent degeneration of the nerve cell with a resultant weakness in the muscles of the legs. In most of the cases these problems begin insidiously, becoming progressively worse, then subsiding. Recovery is not always complete. An electromyogram and muscle biopsy will reveal the pathology.

The organophosphate compounds are readily absorbed through the intact skin as well as by inhalation, which fact makes them more hazardous. Re-exposure is possible from contaminated shoes and clothing days after the original exposure. Several instances of significant poisoning of pet groomers and handlers from organophosphate flea dips have been reported. Health officials have only become aware of these events since about 1986, and the full extent of the problem is not known. Certainly some residual pesticide is carried home on the pet and transferred to the carpet and furniture. No infant or young child should be permitted to play where this has taken place.

It is from this group of compounds that most of the commercially applied insecticides are selected. Parathion was the first organophosphate to be utilized as an insecticide (1944) and it continues to be used extensively in commercial agricultural applications. It is the pesticide most frequently involved in fatal poisonings, partly due to this widespread use and partly due to its toxicity. It is ten to two hundred times more toxic than most of the commonly used organophosphate pesticides. Parathion should not be used around the home. Its use on the farm carries a significant risk. They should be used only after a thorough study and awareness of their properties and toxicity.

Other organophosphates include **abate**, the least toxic agent in this group, and **malathion**, a substance with very wide application, frequently incorporated into home orchard sprays. Malathion is also seen in lawn and shrub sprays, and has been utilized in aerial application to control fruit flies and mosquitos, even in populated areas. No toxic reactions have been observed in these applications. Malathion carries one of the lowest toxicity levels of all of the organophosphates, including skin contact. It may be used outside around the home with relative safety. In spite of the relatively low toxicity, when applying this substance, as with all pesticides, clothing should cover the entire body. A washable cap should cover the head, and all clothing should be well laundered when application is completed. If clothing should become contaminated during application through spillage or wind drift, it should be removed immediately and the skin should be carefully cleansed by showering.

Thorough showering and shampooing should, of course, be completed as soon as possible after any application of pesticides.

**Dursban** (chlorpyrifos), another organophosphate, has been used in neighborhood mosquito control programs. It is also used in products sold to control fleas and ticks on dogs, both as an application to the pet and as a spray for the carpet. In these applications it carries a risk to the inhabitants and to pets. It has been marketed recently in a polymer base to prolong its effectiveness in flea control on dogs to a period of weeks. The binding of dursban in the polymer is presumed to render it less toxic by decreasing the amount released at a given time. **Diazinon**, which is widely used to control ants and grub worms in lawns, belongs to the same chemical family as dursban, phosphorothioates. They carry a toxicity through the skin that is about ten times less than parathion. Malathion, on the other hand, is about 220 times less toxic than parathion through the skin. It is apparent that malathion carries much less risk to animals and humans. Others in this group with a relatively high toxicity include **disulfoton (Di-Syston)** and **mevinphos (Phosdrin)**.

## CARBAMATES

Unlike the organophosphates, MOST of the carbamate ester insecticides have a very low toxicity when applied to the skin. **Carbaryl (Sevin)**, in particular, has developed widespread use around the home in the control of aphids, gypsy moths, leaf miners and Japanese beetles. It is useful and effective on shade trees, ornamentals and flowers. It is also effective in controlling fleas. These agents do not share the broad spectrum of the organophosphates, however, and some household pests such as the house fly and cockroach may not succumb following their application. Bees on the other hand are extremely sensitive, and their populations suffer from the application of this as with most pesticides. This occurs particularly when pesticides are applied to fruit trees and other honey-producing crops. The pesticidal activity of the carbamates is enhanced by the addition of pyrethrin or piperonyl butoxide.

At the other end of the spectrum, **aldicarb (Temik)**, which is structurally different from the other carbamates, has an extreme toxicity when ingested or applied to the skin. The poisoning of over one thousand individuals when this substance was inappropriately used on melons, was described previously (see p. 2). Its use is restricted to applications in greenhouses, and skin contact must be restricted.

The carbamates are the substances that were being manufactured in Bhopal, India when the release of a toxic cloud of methylisocyanate (MIC) resulted in the tragic suffering and death in that community. This disaster was not caused by the pesticide, but by the MIC that was being used in its production.


## PYRETHROIDS

**Pyrethrum**, an extract from chrysanthemums, has been recognized for its insecticidal properties since the 1930s. It possesses a low order of toxicity for humans, except for the annoying allergic reactions. These include a contact dermatitis as well as respiratory reactions after inhalation, including hay fever and asthma. Ragweed sufferers are particularly sensitive. Several synthetic pyrethoids have been developed in an effort to create substances more stable to heat and light than the naturally occurring pyrethrum. These seem to evoke less allergic response. **Permethrin (Nix)**, which has been marketed for the treatment and control of head and body lice, is even less sensitive to breakdown by light and heat than the other synthetic pyrethroids, which include **allethrin**, **cypermethrin**, **fenvalerate**, **phthalthrin** and **resmethrin**. These substances are the common ingredients in aerosol sprays marketed for the control of insects such as flies and spiders in the home. They are effective and relatively safe, but they should not be used in the kitchen or around food, drink and utensils. Permethrin also has been marketed recently for use as an aerosol to spray onto clothing for protection against ticks. It has proven virtually 100 percent effective when used along with DEET and the proper clothing (see also chapter VII, Recreation).

We are currently in our third generation of these synthetic analogs. As the efforts to create more potent insecticides progress, so will their toxicity increase. Individuals with known allergies or asthma should be particularly careful to avoid breathing the aerosol spray from any of the pyrethroids. None of these substances should be sprayed in the home indiscriminately, and none should be inhaled. Such aerosols generally remain airborne for approximately twenty minutes, so no one should be in the room for about a half hour after spraying in order to minimize any health risk. A fly swatter entails even less risk, and a smaller cash outlay.

11

## ROTENONE

This substance is also a plant extract, derived from the roots of plants such as **derris**. It is more toxic than pyrethrum, particularly when applied as a powder. The dust causes irritation of the eyes and skin, and inhalation causes irritation of the lungs. It has been used in garden applications in the past, but has been largely supplanted by other agents today. It was "discovered" by the Indians of South America, who would spread it on the waters of likely fishing spots, then harvest the immobilized fish.

## NICOTINE SULPHATE

This ancient garden spray has been used to control insects on vegetables and flowers alike. It is one of the most toxic of all of the insecticides, and has been supplanted for the most part by the newer agents. Nicotine is absorbed through the skin as well as by ingestion and inhalation, and has a rapid onset of symptoms. Death usually occurs within four hours. Many unpleasant symptoms are produced in the interim. It has been responsible for many human deaths through accidental ingestion or suicide attempts. Nicotine sulphate is occasionally used in a futile effort to control moles. For the lice in the chicken house the pyrethroids or malathion would seem a safer substitution. Unfortunately, from a public health standpoint at least, most of the nicotine in cigarettes is destroyed by the heat of burning, and the smoker is spared most of the more extreme side effects of this drug.

## PIPERONYL BUTOXIDE

This substance will be found on the label frequently, particularly with the pyrethroids and carbamates. It is not an insecticide of itself, rather it inhibits the metabolism of the pyrethroids and carbamates in insects, thus increasing the effectiveness of the insecticide. It accomplishes this role by inhibiting the enzyme in the insect that normally inactivates the pesticide. It has a similar effect on liver enzymes in humans, and thus it influences the metabolism of many drugs. This is a classic demonstration that even though a substance may not be particularly toxic of itself, it can nonetheless have significant effects on the body, and should not be inhaled casually.

## HERBICIDES

These chemicals are weed killers, used not only to keep our lawns beautiful, but to control weeds and undesirable plants along highways and railways and on the farm among crops. They exert their effect by accelerating the growth of the plant, thus compressing its life span into a few days rather than weeks. The most widely used herbicides are the chlorophenoxy agents, **2,4-D** and **2,4,5-T**. These substances previously were felt to pose no hazard to man, and indeed the pure compounds without contaminants are still known to be of low toxicity.

Considerable interest has been aroused by the widespread claims of Vietnam veterans of serious health hazards resulting from exposure to **Agent Orange**. This substance, which was a mixture of 2,4-D and 2,4,5-T, was widely used as a defoliant in the jungles of Vietnam. Some troops were sprayed during aerial application. Many health problems that have subsequently evolved in these veterans and in their offspring have been blamed on this previous exposure. Retrospective studies on exposed veterans have not substantiated any increased incidence of nervous system disorders, heart, liver or kidney disease, sterility or birth defects among offspring. These studies included those who loaded the substance on the planes and thus suffered the heaviest exposure. A study by the Veterans Administration of 13,496 Vietnam era veterans revealed no increased incidence of soft tissue sarcomas (cancer) among those individuals serving in Vietnam nor among those exposed to Agent Orange. Similar studies with similar results have been done on other exposed populations.

The agent 2,4,5-T was first marketed for commercial use in 1948. In 1949 a plant manufacturing this substance in Nitro, West Virginia experienced an accident that resulted in illness among the workers who were cleaning it up. The symptoms initially were irritation of the skin, eyes, nose and throat. These symptoms subsided by the end of two weeks. Nervousness, irritability, muscle pain and general weakness persisted, and chloracne developed. Enlarged livers and abnormal liver function tests were also noted. The enlarged liver and abnormal function tests returned to normal. This group of workers was monitored and by 1953 all of the symptoms had cleared except for chloracne.

In 1957 it was discovered that **TCDD (tetrachlorodibenzo-dioxin)** had been produced as a contaminant in the manufacture of 2,4,5-T, and that it was the substance that was responsible for the production of chloracne. Such contamination occurs when the 2,4,5-trichlorophenol used to produce 2,4,5-T, reacts with itself to produce TCDD. At that time virtually nothing was known about the health risks of exposure to TCDD. Since then, considerable data has been collected in the laboratory, and we now know that it is a very toxic substance. We know that it is a potent carcinogen, mutagen and teratogen in laboratory animals. It is known to have been present in Agent Orange in significant quantities.

References to "dioxin," which has become almost a household term, frequently evoking near hysteria, invariably mean TCDD. TCDD is only one of some seventy-five chlorinated dioxins, but it is of far greater significance than all of the others because it is one of the most toxic substances known. It is important, therefore, to make this distinction between TCDD and "dioxin."

In 1979 a study was undertaken of some two hundred workers from the plant in Nitro, West Virginia who had been exposed during the manufacture of 2,4,5-T from 1948 to 1969. This group of exposed workers was compared to a control group of 163 individuals who had worked at the plant during the same period, but who had had no exposure to TCDD. No evidence of birth defects, cancer, nervous system disorders, heart, liver or kidney disease or sterility was found among the exposed workers. Chloracne was found in approximately one half of the exposed group, and none was found in the control group. Evidence of an increased susceptibility to ultraviolet radiation (sun) damage in the form of elastosis of the skin was present in those who demonstrated chloracne.

A far more extensive and more serious accident occurred in 1976 in Italy. An explosion at the ICMESA plant near Seveso sent a toxic cloud into the air spreading TCDD over an area of about 700 acres. The plant was manufacturing 2,4,5-trichlorophenol for use in making both the herbicide 2,4,5-T and hexachlorophene, a surgical bactericide. The contaminated area included parts of the towns of Seveso (population 17,000), Meda, Cesano, Maderno and Desio. Seveso, which was to gain worldwide notoriety, is about twelve miles north of Milan. Two hundred fifty acres were sealed off and seven hundred people were evacuated. No human fatalities occurred, but thousands of animals, including rabbits, chickens and birds, perished. The trees and vegetation over a wide area were destroyed. The entire plant was contaminated. Workers who were in the plant during and shortly after the accident were found to have abnormal liver function tests, but these had returned to normal two weeks later.

Prompt and decisive actions were taken by the Italian authorities. The area surrounding the plant was divided into three zones,
based upon the concentration of TCDD found in each zone. A fourth
zone, outside of the area of contamination and thus with no TCDD
exposure, was added to serve as a control population. The residents
of the three zones contaminated with TCDD, a population of over
36,000 people, were examined thoroughly throughout the period
from 1976 to 1985. Over 30,000 blood samples were collected and
measured for TCDD during this period. The only significant abnormal finding in this exposed population has been the development
of chloracne. This has occurred in only a small percentage of the
population, as contrasted to the cleanup workers following the plant
accident in Nitro, West Virginia. There was a higher incidence of
chloracne among the maintenance workers at the ICMESA plant
subsequently.

TCDD has a strong association with the production of chloracne
and porphyria in humans. It appears to have a relatively low toxicity
in man otherwise, compared to certain species of animals, especially
the guinea pig. In the guinea pig it is an extremely toxic chemical,
causing degenerative changes in the liver and thymus gland and
fetal abnormalities. It also suppresses the immune system, and non-
Hodgkin's lymphoma is known to occur more frequently in im-
muno-deficient states in humans. This relationship has prompted
several studies to establish a relationship between exposure to TCDD
and the subsequent development of lymphomas. No such association has been seen in the populations who have had significant
exposure. Furthermore, TCDD is a potent animal carcinogen, inducing cancer in the lung, nose, mouth, tongue, liver, thyroid and
skin in the guinea pig. No such propensity has been shown for 2,4-
D in animals.

The accident at Seveso provided a large population of people
who had been exposed to significant levels of TCDD. The health
authorities have monitored and carefully evaluated this population.
Valuable data has been collected on the impact of acute exposure
of humans to high levels of TCDD. The TCDD levels in the blood
collected from these people are the highest ever reported in humans.
No adverse health effects other than the chloracne have been found.
Not all of the individuals with a high blood level of TCDD developed
chloracne. Those who did develop this skin problem appear to be
at increased risk of skin damage following ultraviolet (sun) exposure.
No increased incidence of skin cancer has evolved as yet. Since

TCDD persists in the body tissues for many years, these individuals will need to exercise great care to avoid exposure to the sun.

Chlorinated dioxins are formed in wood-burning fireplaces and on the grill whenever steaks are prepared. They have been with us at least since fire was discovered. Recent advances in analytical techniques permit us to measure substances that are a thousand times weaker than what we could measure just a few years ago. In those days we didn't know that they existed. We may have been better off for the ignorance.

It is true that TCDD is the most toxic chemical that has ever been synthsized by man. In spite of acute toxic episodes where humans were exposed to large doses, no evidence of cancer, mutagenesis or teratogenesis has appeared. In this respect it appears to cause less harm in humans than some other substances, one such being thalidomide. The fact that a chemical is toxic does not mean that it automatically is hazardous to our health. The human organism is a far more sophisticated creature physiologically than the animals that we study in the laboratory. Toxic effects seen there cannot be directly extrapolated to humans. These findings should provoke thoughtful study, but not panic.

A Kansas study suggested that farmers who spent more than twenty days per year applying 2,4-D experienced a six-fold increase in the incidence of non-Hodgkin's lymphoma. No such risk was found in exposures of lessor length. A Swedish study yielded similar findings. The possibility that a toxic contaminant existed in the 2,4-D used by these farmers earlier (1946) has been postulated. No similar risk following exposure to 2,4-D has been seen elsewhere in spite of worldwide use.

Aside from the industrial accidents, poisoning resulting from use of the chlorophenoxy herbicides has been rare. Both 2,4-D and 2,4,5-T that has not been contaminated with TCDD during manufacture, have a low order of toxicity for all animals including humans. Use of 2,4-D in particular appears to be reasonably safe for the control of broadleaf weeds such as dandelions, plantain and chickweed on lawns, parks, campuses, golf courses and among crops. Skin contact should be avoided as with all pesticides and herbicides. These substances in themselves do not accumulate in animals and thus pose no threat to the food chain. In 1979 the Environmental Protection Agency banned 2,4,5-T from use around homes, in parks and around most food crops because of the past contamination by TCDD. It had been totally banned in Italy in 1970.

# BIPYRIDYL COMPOUNDS

**Paraquat** is the best known and most widely used substance in this group of herbicides. Unfortunately its use is expanding. It is used in harvesting cotton by spraying the cotton plant to eliminate the leaves prior to processing. It is extremely toxic to the lungs whether ingested or inhaled, resulting in acute pulmonary edema and death by respiratory failure. These dire consequences do not require massive nor repeated dosing. A single dose has preceded most of the deaths that have resulted from smoking marijuana that had been contaminated with this substance. Even with low levels of contamination, pulmonary fibrosis may occur over time. Several hundred deaths have occurred as a result of accidental or suicidal exposures. Numerous deaths have resulted from smoking contaminated marijuana.

Paraquat has been the herbicide used by the United States authorities to spray illicit marijuana fields in an effort to control the use of this drug. Approximately twenty percent of the marijuana in the Southwestern United States has been found to be contaminated with this agent. This practice by the authorities has been strongly criticized because of the serious consequences and the fatalities that have resulted.

Agricultural workers who have been exposed to paraquat spray over extended periods of time have developed irritation and inflammation of the mouth, throat and lungs with a resultant cough. Skin and eye irritation have also been noted, as well as damage and deformity of nails, even the loss of nails in some instances. Minimal skin absorption occurs, but even these small quantities can produce serious damage to the lungs and kidneys. Additionally, workers in the field frequently have minor scratches on the hands and arms that permit significantly greater absorption. One worker who mistakenly took a mouthful from a container, and immediately spit it out, nonetheless developed severe dyspnea and cyanosis fourteen days later. Survivors of acute lung reactions from paraquat exposure may develop chronic obstructive lung disease and respiratory failure later in life. Studies in laboratory animals regarding the inhalation of dust from soils that had been sprayed with paraquat were unable to demonstrate any harmful effects from this exposure.

## DIQUAT

This related compound does not produce the acute toxic effects in the lung that are seen with paraquat, but both compounds produce serious destruction in the liver and kidney.


## PENTACHLOROPHENOL

This substance is used as a herbicide, as well as a fungicide and as a wood preservative, to protect against termites and other wood-boring insects. It also provides protection against wood rot caused by fungus. Wood pulp used in the production of paper and paperboard is treated with pentachlorophenol to prevent the growth of slime producing organisms. It is also used to defoliate plants prior to harvest. It is readily absorbed through the intact skin and it accumulates in the body. A number of cases of acute poisoning in man have occurred, including a number of deaths. Cattle have also suffered poisoning as a result of rubbing against timbers that had been treated with this preservative. Twenty infants in a hospital nursery were poisoned as a result of diapers that had been contaminated with pentachlorophenol in the laundry where it had been used as a fungicide. Two of the infants died.

Some commercial pentachlorophenol has been discovered to be contaminated with dioxins other than TCDD, and with dibenzofurans, both of which are toxic substances. These substances produce chloracne and liver damage, including porphyria. Even when pure, pentachlorophenol is toxic in its own right. The use of pentachlorophenol as a soil fumigant and wood preservative in structures in contact with the ground has resulted in contamination of surface and drinking water in some locations. This has raised serious concern about the health threat produced by the toxicity of pentachlorophenol as well as the chlorinated dioxins.


## AMINOTRIZOLE

Amitrole (aminotriazole) produces cancer in animals, even though it is lacking in acute toxicity. It is a very potent antithyroid agent, suppressing the function of the thyroid gland, and it can produce goitre. This substance provides an important lesson for us in that an agent that does not demonstrate acute toxicity nonetheless can invoke significant harm in humans through other mechanisms. Many of the pesticides and herbicides have an influence on the function of the enzymes, particularly in the liver. These alterations are not always apparent, and they are not readily discovered by laboratory studies commonly performed in most laboratories. A Swedish study suggested that railway workers who had been exposed to amitrole experienced an increased incidence of cancer. Few other studies regarding this risk have been completed. Amitrole is not permitted as a herbicide on food crops.

## DINITROPHENOL

This group of compounds includes several different substances that are very toxic. They interfere with cellular metabolism producing anoxia in the cells (lack of oxygen) even though abundant blood and oxygen are present. Death or recovery usually occurs within twenty-four to forty-eight hours. They are marketed for the control of weeds.

Dinitro-orthocresol causes cataracts in some individuals subjected to chronic exposure. It was sold without a prescription from 1935 to 1937 as an antiobesity agent. Cataracts developed in several hundred of the people who tried this remedy. Interestingly, cataracts do not show up in studies on laboratory animals, except for rabbits. Acute poisoning may produce a marked increase in metabolism, with temperature elevation and death due to hyperthermia. Chronic poisoning produces anxiety, sweating, thirst and weight loss. The risk is much greater in hot weather.

Nitrocresol compounds have similar uses and similar toxicity. All contact with these substances should be avoided.

## CARBAMATE DERIVATIVES

These substances are less commonly used but have a relatively low order of acute toxicity. **Propham** is a typical example. (See previous discussion of carbamate pesticides, p. 10.) **Barban** is somewhat more toxic than propham and is a potent sensitizing agent, provoking skin rashes and other allergic reactions.

19

## ORGANOPHOSPHATE

Some agents in this class have been used as herbicides in special application. **Merphos** and **DEF** (**S,S,S-tributylphosphorotrithioate**) are used as defoliants to faciliate the harvesting of cotton. These are usually applied through aerial spraying, and the greatest risk is to the mixers, pilots and especially the flagmen. These agents carry the customary risks of the organophosphates, and additionally the delayed neurotoxic effects, both of which have been discussed above under the pesticides.

## TRIAZINE

**Atrazine** and **simazine** are marketed as herbicides and for weed control. They also have a low level of toxicity, but are not as widely marketed to the general public.

## DINITROANALINE

**Trifluralin** and **benefin** possess a low toxicity and have demonstrated no ill effects in dogs and rats in laboratory studies.

## ARYL ALIPHATIC ACIDS

**Dicamba** is a pre-emergence weed control and has a low order of toxicity.

Substances used to control vegetation such as ivy require more caution in handling. Some of these are used in commercial farming, where the residue is of some concern, specifically any potential for a cancer risk. Some of these substances have not been as extensively studied.

## DALAPON

**2,4-dichloropropionic acid** has been proposed as a substitute for some of the more toxic herbicides described above because it has a low order of toxicity for all animals, including humans. It, along with trichloracetic acid, have been used in the control of perennial weeds, but they are of limited usefulness.

In summary, 2,4-D is the only herbicide commonly sold for general use by the public to control dandelions and other broadleaf weeds in the lawn. There is no TCDD nor any other dioxin in 2,4-D. It can be used with relative safety if skin contact is avoided. The major risk to health from the remaining herbicides resides in their application in agriculture, where residues in foods such as rice pose a threat. It must be kept in mind also that walking through areas where these substances are used to control weeds and brush growth carries a very real risk of skin and clothing contamination. In general people will be unaware of such contact, unless a rash occurs. Even with the occurrence of a rash the association is seldom made.


## RODENTICIDES

These are substances marketed to control mice, rats, gophers and sometimes rabbits. Rat poisons have produced numerous deaths in man, and these lethal products are still available. Fortunately, however, the most widely used agent today, warfarin, carries little risk for man or pets unless consumed as a regular diet, for it requires repeated dosing. This does not rule out children as victims, of course, since they have repeatedly demonstrated that they will consume anything, especially if not placed on their dinner plate. Warfarin destroys rodents by inhibiting blood clotting mechanisms and thus causing internal hemorrhage. Repeated feeding is necessary before an adequate blood level is reached to accomplish this event. Hopefully, when the animal takes his last meal he will retire to quarters well removed from one's household.

The difference in dosages, based upon animal weight, required to produce fatal bleeding is used in South America to control vampire bats. Warfarin can be safely fed to cattle, but the vampire bat, after extracting a sufficient quantity of blood, succumbs due to internal hemorrhage.

The **indandiones** are similar in action to warfarin, producing hemorrhage by interfering with Vitamin K metabolism in the production of prothrombin. This group of agents has an advantage over warfarin in that they are water soluble, and thus are easier to formulate in baits without arousing the suspicion of the dinner guest. Other products in this category are marketed under the following

21

names; **Diphacin, Fumarin, Pival, PMP, Valone, Pindone** and **Triban**.

Bleeding in humans who had handled bait containing these substances has occurred after repeated skin contact and the resultant absorption. Individuals who are on cimetadine for an ulcer are particularly sensitive to this risk. Since the substance can be absorbed through the intact skin to varying degrees, such contact should be avoided when handling toxic agents. Appropriate gloves can help avoid this risk.

## FLUOROACETATES

These are among the most potent rodenticides and are highly toxic to humans. Poisoning can occur not only by ingestion but also by absorption through the skin and by breathing the dust. There have been a number of fatalities in humans as a result of contact with these agents. Convulsions and heart irregularities leading to cardiac arrest are the usual causes of death. Their use is for the most part restricted to licensed pest control personnel, and extreme caution is required in handling them.

## RED SQUILL

The bulbs of this plant have been used as a rodenticide for many years. They kill mainly by inducing irregularities in the heart with resultant cardiac arrest. The bulbs also contain a substance that induces vomiting in animals other than the rodent, a fact that contributes to its relative safety in humans. The inability of the rat to vomit accounts, in great measure, for the effectiveness of this product.

## PHOSPHORUS

Used as a paste, this substance is spread on bread for rats, and it has poisoned man on several occasions. Because of its severe toxicity to humans it has been supplanted by safer and more selective substances.

# THALLIUM

This metallic element is extremely toxic and is absorbed through the intact skin. The powder is toxic when it is inhaled. It resulted in poisoning of hundreds of individuals, including many fatalities, until it was banned in 1955. Its use was restricted to licensed personnel, but it is no longer available in the United States as a rodenticide. It is very effective for that purpose, however, and continues to be widely used in Mexico, South America and abroad. Serious cases of poisoning continue to appear among immigrants who obtain it from relatives or other sources in those countries. Other than these imported cases, toxicity in the United States occurs chiefly as a result of exposure in industry, where thallium compounds are widely encountered (see also Workplace, chapter VIII). No effective treatment is available.

# STRYCHNINE

Known as extract nux vomica, this is perhaps the most widely known poison. It has been used as a rodenticide since the sixteenth century. It has been marketed as a bait (on peanuts) for gophers and moles. It produces severe convulsions in man, leading to death by asphyxia. Symptoms of muscle stiffness and excitability may occur as soon as fifteen to thirty minutes after ingestion. No effective treatment is available.

# HYDROGEN CYANIDE

This gas, with the smell of bitter almonds, is a potent rodenticide and pesticide, and is used to fumigate ships and buildings. Its severe lethality has had wide publicity in recent years through deliberate contamination of food and drugs by sick and perverted individuals. It is readily absorbed by all routes and death can occur a few minutes after ingestion of a small quantity. Cyanide is released when certain plastics used in furniture (i.e., polyurethane) are burned. Fires on airplanes and in public buildings have resulted in numerous deaths. Efforts are currently underway to substitute safer materials. Needless to say, plastics should not be burned in the fireplace, backyard nor around the campfire.

**Amygdalin**, the chief ingredient in **Laetrile**, releases cyanide in the intestinal tract through the action of bacteria. Several instances of human poisoning have resulted from this "therapy." Amygdalin occurs naturally in apricot and peach pits as well as in sweet almonds.

## HYDROGEN SULFIDE

The well-known sewer gas is occasionally used by exterminators. It produces symptoms similar in almost every respect to cyanide. It is present in some natural gas deposits and in volcanic gases. It is produced by the putrefaction of organic matter. Numerous deaths have occured among workers in sewers. A worker in the City of Omaha waste treatment plant in 1983 was found unconscious after he had gone to collect routine samples from the area where the waste water enters the plant. He subsequently died from hydrogen sulfide exposure as a result of an excessive level of accumulation of the gas.

Rat poisons have produced considerable morbidity and mortality in man. As a general rule, any substance applied by professional exterminators for the purpose of eliminating rodents must be considered to be very toxic, and it should not be permitted to come in contact with food, utensils and certainly not the skin. The need for extermination can be greatly reduced by storing garbage and pet food in rat proof containers. Traps provide a much safer alternative to poisons in the control of rodent populations around residences.

The control of rats is a significant public health imperative. No other creature has contributed so greatly to the demise of populations. During the fourteenth century, plague transmitted by the rat flea killed half of the population of England and one-fourth of the entire European population. In the United States the risk of plague transmission currently resides more with the ground squirrel. The fleas of these animals carry the potential for disease in man in southern California and Arizona. The risk has been compounded by the expansion of housing into the hills where the squirrels have their burrows. Efforts to control the disease in this area center more on ingenious devices to dust the animals with a pesticide to eliminate the fleas, than in the destruction of the squirrels.

## FUNGICIDES

This is a diverse group of agents, used on plants, seeds and produce, to control fungus diseases. One or the other of these agents is usually incorporated into home orchard sprays and is customarily added to pesticide sprays for roses. They also have been used in formulations for housepaints and stains to inhibit mildew formation. **Captan** is frequently incorporated with the insecticides malathion and methoxychlor in home orchard sprays. It is structurally similar to thalidomide and is known to produce birth defects in animals. **Folpet**, another common fungicide, is incorporated into rose sprays along with insecticides. It also has structural similarities to thalidomide, and has been shown to produce birth defects in some animal species.

**Mercury**, a metal which is liquid at room temperature, and its compounds are effective fungicides and have been widely used to treat seed grains to prevent rot. It has also been used in paint and stain formulations to prevent mildew. They are extremely toxic and are potent teratogens. The organic mercurials such as methyl mercury and ethyl mercury are particularly dangerous. Several large poisoning events have resulted from the consumption of food that had been contaminated by mercury compounds. Most of these cases involved fish or seafood and grain that had been prepared for use as seed. These mercury compounds are severely toxic to the brain and nervous system as well as to the kidneys. The poisoning episodes have been particularly tragic in the cases where the contaminated food was consumed during pregnancy and severely retarded and defective infants were born. Organic mercury compounds such as methyl mercury cross the placenta into the fetal circulation. They also appear in the mother's milk, as do virtually all drugs and chemicals that gain access to the woman's body (see also mercury, chapter VI).

## DITHIOCARBAMATE

This group of fungicides includes **ziram, ferbam** and **maneb**. They have been widely used in agriculture and have a low level of toxicity in all animals. There have been no significant reports of toxic effects or of human illness following exposure to them. The breakdown of some of these compounds during cooking to substances which suppress the thyroid gland and may be carcinogenic, mutagenic and teratogenic mandates that a minimal residue in food be assured.

25

## HEXACHLOROBENZENE

This compound is a fungicide with serious toxic properties. It produced more than 3,000 cases of acquired toxic porphyria in Turkey when seed grain that was prepared for planting was treated with this substance and subsequently consumed as food. Hexachlorobenzene has also caused illness where it has been used as a disinfectant. This toxic substance should not be confused with lindane, which is frequently called gamma benzenehexachloride, but is more accurately described as hexachlorohexane.

## PENTACHLOROPHENOL

Commonly called penta, this substance is used as a wood preservative, as an insecticide and herbicide as well as disinfectant. Its action in protecting wood is similar to creosote, which is a mixture of phenols. Several instances of poisoning, both in man and in cattle, have occurred, including the deaths of several infants in a hospital nursery from inappropriate use, as described previously (see p. 18). This is a substance that should not be permitted to contact the skin, since it is readily absorbed and is toxic. In handling lumber and fence posts treated with it the worker must be aware that it will penetrate most gloves customarily used for such work.

## CREOSOTE

This mixture of phenols is derived from wood or coal by distillation. It is retained in treated wood for over twenty-five years. It has a similar action and toxicity as pentachlorophenol. Wood treated with either of these substances, or indeed any of the pressure treated wood that contains products such as copper arsenate, should not be burned. Serious illness has resulted from burning these products in fireplaces or stoves. Vapors from creosote are irritating and produce burning of the nose, throat and eyes. Corneal scarring has been reported among exposed workers. Caution also should be taken when sawing treated wood. The sawdust should not be permitted to come in contact with the skin.

# BIS

**Bis{tributyltin}oxide** is an organic tin compound sold in a 25 percent solution to be added to paint as a mildewcide. It was previously incorporated into marine paints to inhibit the growth of marine life on boats. This use has been discontinued due to its potent toxic effects and the dispersion of the compound into the marine environment. This substance and some other organic tin preparations, notable triethyltin, are very toxic when ingested, producing serious central nervous system (brain) symptoms. Great care should be exercised when adding this substance to paint. Skin contact should be avoided, from both the compound and the subsequently treated paint. Pronounced irritation can occur, even if washed immediately. Paint treated with BIS should be applied only with adequate ventilation and only in areas where no risk of human poisoning exists. The many cases of lead poisoning that have resulted from the lead pigments in paints should be kept in mind when applying this or any treated paint in the house. Whereas removal of lead from the body can be facilitated, no such remedy is available for these tin compounds.

# II

# Hazards of the Household

## ACCIDENTS

More than 20,000 people die as a result of accidents in or around the home each year. More than 6,000 of these deaths result from falls, many on stairs, ladders and in bathtubs. Most of these tragedies could be prevented by such simple measures as placement of non-skid mats in tubs, keeping stairs free of all toys and other materials, and more careful placement of ladders to assure a secure and firm base. Hand rails on stairways and in bathtubs are essential for the elderly and for those with arthritis or other afflictions that affect stability of footing.

About 160 people die in the home each year as a result of electrocution. This hazard has been greatly reduced by the modern electrical codes. Children remain at great risk, and solutions to this problem are discussed in chapter V. Accidents of an unusual nature continue to occur each year, such as dropping a hair dryer in the bathtub while standing or sitting in water. No electrical appliance should ever be brought near or placed in the proximity of the bathtub nor basin. This has been a repeated source of electrocution over the years.

The risks of electrocution while flying kites should have had enough publicity by now to eliminate this accident, but it continues to occur each year. The same can be said about the use of aluminum ladders and erection of radio, television and CB antennas. Other aluminum or steel devices that are bought into contact with overhead power lines are cleaning devices for outdoor swimming pools and masts for sailboats. Digging into an underground power line can be just as deadly. When cleaning up fallen trees and branches following a storm, fallen power lines must be observed and avoided.

Approximately 700 people drown at home each year, in swim-

28

ming pools and in bathtubs. Swimming pools are a particular hazard for children. An adequate fence and secure gate reduces this risk, but small children must still be kept under constant vigilance.

## FIRE

More than 4,000 Americans die each year in residential fires, and some 20,000 additional individuals suffer injuries. The financial loss adds up to about 3.5 million dollars annually. Approximately three-fourths of all fire related deaths occur in the home. It is safe to say that the thought of a fire in the home, especially during the night when the family is asleep, evokes fear in just about everyone.

The first step to take to minimize the risk of this personal and financial disaster in your home is to methodically tour the entire residence room by room, then the basement and garage, and remove all obvious risks. Matches, candles and cigarette lighters with their fuel should not be stored where children can get their hands on them. Simply placing these items on a shelf that is high off the floor will not safeguard them, as has been proven on many occasions. These items, along with medications, cleaning agents and harmful chemicals, need to be stored under lock and key. It is neither difficult nor expensive to have an effective lock installed on a closet or storage cabinet door. This may seem inconvenient but it is one of the necessary sacrifices that must be made for the privilege of having children.

Moving to the garage, inventory all combustible items such as solvents (naphtha, paint and lacquer thinner), gasoline for mowers, and Coleman fuel. These items should never be stored in the basement, and never in the garage if any pilot lights exist there. It is far safer to store gasoline and flammable liquids in a storage shed, removed from the house. The quantity of these items that are kept on hand should be limited. They tend to accumulate, and need to be inventoried and disposed of periodically. Stores of gasoline should be limited to the smallest practical volume. Gasoline is a very explosive and dangerous substance.

Perhaps the next step to take is the installation of effective smoke detectors in strategic locations. One should be placed near the kitchen, one near the bedrooms and one near any room with a woodburning fireplace or stove. Notice that I say near. If a smoke detector is installed in the kitchen, it will sound the alarm every time a meal is prepared. It will prove more peaceful to install the detector in a room next to the kitchen. If properly located, it will still detect a fire early, but will not be set off by cooking a meal. An exhaust fan in the kitchen, used when cooking, will also help to eliminate false alarms. Similarly a smoke detector placed in the garage may be set off by the exhaust from the automobile. A detector placed in a room with a furnace may be set off by combustion ions from the furnace. Trial and error may be necessary to determine a location where this is not a problem.

In two-story homes detectors should be placed on each level. One unit on the second level should be sufficient to protect the bedrooms in most homes. If you are unfortunate enough to have a smoker in the house, a detector should be placed in that bedroom. One should also be placed in the basement, although it must be located far enough away from the furnace to avoid false alarms. In locating detectors near sources of combustion such as in the kitchen, and near fireplaces and furnaces it may be wise to try a temporary placement long enough to assure that false alarms will not be a problem, before drilling holes in the ceiling.

After the smoke detectors have been installed, it is important to check their operation periodically. Most have a test button, but this may not test for dirt accumulation. All of the units should be vacuumed regularly to prevent dust buildup and blockage by insects. One positive way to test the units is to light a match underneath each unit, blow it out and allow the smoke to drift into the detector. The length of the alarm thus evoked can be shortened by blowing fresh air across the detector with a small fan. The nine-volt batteries that power these units will last about one year, if they are fresh and of good quality. Most detectors emit periodic beeps for about a week when the battery needs replacement. This warning can easily be missed if it occurs while the family is away on vacation. The match test provides a more positive indication of battery integrity. Remember that a detector installed in the ceiling is nothing but an eyesore if it is inoperative.

After you have completed the installation of the smoke detectors, it is time to turn your attention to fire extinguishers. Better yet these should be purchased at the same time as the smoke detectors. This selection is more complex, because there are different types of extinguishers for different types of fires. The decision can be simplified by buying all purpose extinguishers that are effective against all three classes of fires, A, B and C. If price is no object, you can select one of the halon models, which have the added advantage of not leaving a corrosive residue that will damage whatever items

30

you save from the fire. If you choose a less expensive all purpose unit, it will contain a chemical such as ammonium phosphate, which does leave a corrosive residue.

The most important location for a fire extinguisher is in the kitchen, for about three-fourths of all home fires occur there. One should be accessible for any wood-burning fireplace or stove. One unit may serve this purpose as well as for the kitchen if they are not widely separated. A unit should be located in the basement, particularly if a workshop is located there, and one in the garage. These should also be all purpose types.

If you have a spare three or four thousand dollars left over after the above purchases, you can consider having a sprinkler system installed. New technology in recent years has resulted in sprinkler systems for private residences that are effective, if costly. In new construction such units add about two thousand dollars to the cost. Some fire officials are pressing to have these units included in building codes as required items. In making such an argument the cost of a human life invariably surfaces. While it is difficult to argue against saving lives, the cost of a new home already includes several thousand dollars mandated by building codes, licenses, plan inspection, foundation inspection, framework inspections, plumbing inspections, electrical inspections, final inspection, termite inspections, appraisal fees, credit checks, title searches, application charges, filing charges, realtor commission, and of course lawyer's fees. Mandatory radon inspection is on the horizon. And your irreplaceable congressman is complaining that houses are priced beyond the reach of the "average American," so more government subsidies are needed.

## THE KITCHEN

One of the most common hazards in the kitchen is that of burns. Most burns that are acquired during cooking or baking are not life threatening. More tragic are burns to children. These frequently occur as a result of the child pulling a pan of boiling water or hot food off the stove as a matter of curiosity. The inquisitive and exploring nature of young children is the major cause of accidents and injuries in this age group. Young children need constant supervision. Thousands are injured each year simply because they had a few minutes of unsupervised time.

These thermal burns have had wide publicity, and most people

31

are at least aware that they are a risk. Not so well known is the risk of chemical burns, and the many substances in the household that can cause them. There are several very potent substances found in the kitchen that are not encountered in most other walks of life, other than in chemistry laboratories.

One of the hazardous substances, and one that is a threat to adults and children alike, is household ammonia (ammonium hydroxide). This substance penetrates the eye particularly rapidly when accidentally splashed in it, and can produce severe, permanent eye damage after as short a time as three minutes. This can occur even if copious irrigation is undertaken immediately. Household ammonia should never be mixed with household bleach of the chlorine type, or with any household cleaner including wall and tile cleaner, and toilet bowl cleanser. Mixing these two substances causes a chemical reaction that releases hazardous gases. When a substance of this nature is poured from a container in an occupational setting, eye protection such as a face shield is required, and the operation is undertaken in a ventilated hood. One does not often see such a precaution taken at home.

Oven cleaners and drain cleaners are strong alkali substances that can produce severe chemical burns of both the skin and the eye. They contain sodium hydroxide, a very caustic substance. Durable rubber or plastic gloves must be worn when handling these materials, and the fumes must not be inhaled. A ventilating fan, **DUCTED TO THE OUTSIDE**, is helpful in minimizing inhalation of these irritating fumes. Many kitchen fans are not ducted to the outside, but merely recirculate the air through a filter. These are cheaper to install but they are of very limited usefulness. Strong alkali substances also can cause destruction of vision, and great care must be taken not to splash or spray this caustic in the eye. Particular care should be taken with the aerosol sprays to make certain that they are directed away from the body.

Drain cleaners are among the most heavily promoted household items encountered. A generous and diverse supply is available. One reason for this is that the members of households permit substances that will not readily flow through the drain pipes to enter the drains with remarkable frequency. In some instances inadequate or faulty plumbing contributes to the problem. Drains and sewers were basically designed to carry liquids for the most part, however. Another reason for the heavy promotion is that there is no magic bullet. Prevention remains the best remedy.

The chemicals that are available to unclog drains are very strong substances, either a strong alkali or a potent acid. These obviously are hazardous to handle, and hazardous to store under your sink, where the children play. These substances can cause severe burns to the mouth, throat and esophagus. If the child survives, he will require some serious surgery. In pouring these substances into the drain the danger of splashing them on the skin or in the eye are as severe as with ammonia discussed above. They should not be stored under the sink. If they are kept around the home, they should be stored under lock and key.

A safer and more direct approach to clogged plumbing is to use one of the mechanical devices available. The first tool to use should be a plunger or the hand auger. These will unclog most of the simple plugged drains. An electric auger can be rented at any of the rental agencies if the manual tool does not do the job. Various devices that apply pressure or a vacuum, or that attach to a hose and faucet for more pressure, have been introduced to deal with this ubiquitous household problem. Extreme caution should be taken in any instance where one of the strong chemicals has been tried first. It is far wiser to not get into that predicament.

In some instances, such as where the doll has been flushed down the toilet, there is no alternative to simply uncoupling the bowl and removing the culprit manually. In the case of the kitchen sink or bathroom basin, it is usually a simple chore to remove the trap and pour out the assortment of jewelry, beads, buttons and contact lenses. If the clog resides in the main sewer line it may well require a professional service. Consult the yellow pages.

Electric dish detergents are another strong alkali substance that has caused the loss of vision. When one of the small particles is accidentally splashed in the eye it adheres, produces a burn and penetrates the eye. Alkali substances such as this are much more damaging than acids. If the powder is spilled, you should never blow on it. With the new liquid preparations, the risk of splashing it into the eye is present, as when pouring any liquid.

Another source of eye damage and loss of vision that is present in the kitchen, that one would not ordinarily think of, is the disposal. Eye damage occurs when an object is ejected from the disposal. It is natural to look into the disposal during operation, but this temptation must be resisted. Objects sent into orbit from this appliance should strike the ceiling, not your eye.

Hand dish detergents generally contain surfactants, not strong alkali substances, and are less damaging to the skin. They are effective at removing the protective oils from the skin, nonetheless, and produce dryness, irritation and cracking. Secondary infections are always a risk when the skin defensive barrier is thus disrupted. This problem can be dealt with by wearing latex or vinyl gloves when prolonged or repeated immersion of the hands is necessary. Frequent applications of a good hand cream such as Lanolor help to restore the protective oils to the skin.

## THE LAUNDRY

The effectiveness of laundry detergents has been greatly improved by the addition of enzymes to faciliate the removal of stains and soil. The enzyme commonly used is alcalase, which is produced by the fermentation of the bacterium, Bacillus subtilis. Many people become sensitized to this enzyme, and allergic reactions are common. The reaction may vary from sneezing and cough to a severe asthmatic reaction. The latter is more likely to occur in individuals who have a history of asthma. This hazard can be minimized by exercising care when pouring the detergent to avoid disseminating the powder into the room. Using the liquid forms of the detergents eliminates the dust problem, but skin contact still should be avoided if sensitization has developed.

## TSP

Trisodium phosphate is normally incorporated into laundry detergents except in those states and municipalities where its use has been banned to lessen the phosphate buildup in lakes and streams. It greatly enhances the cleaning power of laundry detergents, but is a strong irritant to the skin. It is also incorporated into cleaners such as SPIC and SPAN, and is sold separately as a powder for the cleaning of walls and floors. Whenever these substances are used, latex or vinyl gloves must be worn to protect the skin, and care should be taken to avoid letting the solution run down the arm when cleaning overhead.

The goal of most people in doing laundry is to have the clothes come out looking clean. Many whiteners and bleaches have been marketed to make the laundry more pleasing to the eye. An equally important objective is to destroy the many microbial agents, the bacteria, fungi, viruses and protozoa that go along with the dirt. Good laundry detergents, used in adequate concentration, are effective in accomplishing this goal, but the temperature of the water has much to do with the level of success. The higher the temperature of the wash water, the more effective is the laundry process in killing microbial agents. Many spores, such as those that cause botulism and tetanus, are relatively resistant to destruction by high temperatures. High temperatures in conjunction with the surface acting agents found in laundry detergents greatly increase the destruction of these disease-causing agents. The addition of household bleach of the chlorine type will greatly increase the destruction of microorganisms.

It has become popular to lower the temperature of the water in laundry and dish operations in an effort to save energy. Laundry products are widely advertised for their cleaning ability in cold water. It is clear that clothes and linens can be made to appear bright and clean in cold water. There is no simple way to determine how many of the disease-producing agents have survived, however. The small amount of money saved by such false economy could better be saved by economies elsewhere in the household. This is especially true in the dishwasher. Nowhere in the household is cleanliness more important. Certainly one wants to destroy the Salmonella and other organisms that can produce diarrheal disease, and the virus that can transmit hepatitis, to mention only two. The temperature in the dishwasher should ideally be at least 160 degrees Fahrenheit, not the 120 degrees that some advocate. The practice of producing and marketing water heaters that deliver water at such low temperatures should not only be condemned, but should be banned as a public health measure.

The development of odors in towels and washcloths shortly after laundering is a clear sign that cleansing was less than desirable. The addition of a chlorine bleach, sodium hypochlorite, is effective in solving this problem for the reasons mentioned above. It must be used in accordance with the instructions on the package, however. These agents cannot be used on some fabrics. The so-called nonchlorine bleaches may be substituted to enhance cleaning in those fabrics that will not tolerate chlorine, but keep in mind that they do not possess the disease-killing powder of a chlorine bleach. Very hot water becomes all the more urgent in these circumstances.

Fabric softeners contain substances that neutralize the electrostatic charge on clothing. These substances do not carry a significant toxicity in normal use. The cloth fabric softeners produced a skin irritation in many people nationwide a few years ago, but this problem seems to have lessened. Presumably this irritation was due to a fiber in the cloth. The irritation was similar to that produced by fiberglass. The perfumes in these fabric softeners may present a problem to some individuals who are sensitive to them. These individuals should use the unscented packages that are available.

## THE BATHROOM

Toilet bowl cleaners contain the same stong alkali substances that are used in oven cleaners and drain cleaners. Great care must be taken to avoid splashing them into the eye. If they are accidentally spilled on the the skin, it should be washed immediately, flushing with water first, then washed thoroughly with soap and water. These products should not be mixed with ammonia for the reasons discussed above.

Several different aerosol sprays that present a health hazard are used in the bathroom. The propellent in all of these is a hazard. Freon was used in the past, and it was removed to satisfy the concern over the ozone layer in the atmosphere. Then vinyl chloride was used until it was discovered that it produces cancer. Following that, methylene chloride was substituted, and its toxicity is causing great concern. This substance, more accurately identified as dichloromethane, is very toxic to the liver and has recently been found to be carcinogenic. Butane is used in some products as a replacement for freon, but environmentalists now complain that butane is as troublesome as was freon. Carbon dioxide has been used recently as a propellent in some aerosol sprays, and does not present a toxic hazard. It also presents no hazard to the environment. It is a safe and effective substitute, and it's difficult to imagine why it is not the universal propellent today.

Of particular concern is the use of these toxic and hazardous substances in a small confined space such as a bathroom, where significant inhalation is assured. It has been demonstrated that these aerosols remain suspended in the air in bathrooms for at least fifteen minutes. Ideally, when these materials are used, one should have the exhaust fan on, should spray the hair as quickly as possible, and should vacate the bathroom as soon as possible. It should remain vacant for at least fifteen to twenty minutes.

In addition to the propellants in hair spray, other risks have been identified with components such as polyvinylpyrrolidone, the active ingredients in virtually all hair sprays. Thesaurosis, or storage disease in the lungs, was described in 1958. It has been the subject of some controversy since that time. Some investigators have not been able to substantiate the existence of this disorder as a separate entity. There is no question that a lung condition similar to sarcoidosis has developed in some individuals, many of them beauticians. Some authorities feel that the disease is indeed sarcoidosis, and not a separate entity. The role of hair sprays in producing this problem is unclear at present. It would be prudent to avoid inhalation of this or any other spray.

An additional problem with hair spray is contact lenses. Contact lenses should not be present in the bathroom, either in the eyes or in a container, unless it is closed, when hair spray, or any of the aerosol conditioners, are used. Once contact lenses have been contaminated with any substance, they should be taken to the optometrist or opthalmologist for examination and purging, if that is possible.

## GARBAGE AND WASTE

Proper management of garbage and waste is essential to the control of flies and rodents. Flies are the most common insect transmitter of disease in the United States. The habit of the fly of seeking out fecal material, manure or other rotting organic material to feed on and to lay its eggs on, brings it in contact with a diverse array of microorganisms capable of causing disease in humans. In feeding, the hairy body and sticky feet of the fly literally soak up these organisms. A single fly may carry over six million of them. The fly can also carry bacteria in its digestive system for the duration of its one-month life span, and can pass them on to subsequent generations through its eggs.

The fly that has fed on manure and sewage may next alight on the food in your household, or on your baby. Here it regurgitates its previous meal, and drops its feces, both of which contain the disease causing organisms. It also leaves behind some of the abundant supply of organisms from its body and feet. The black specks that are sometimes seen on the walls of restaurant kitchens represent dried vomit and fecal material. The diseases that are transmitted through this process include typhoid, paratyphoid and other Salmonella infections (the most common food-borne infections), polio, cholera, typhus and diarrhea from a host of different organisms including bacteria, viruses and amoeba. (See chapter VI for a discussion of food borne illnesses.)

Flies are attracted to the odor of food, garbage and other rotting organic matter. The most effective means that we have of controlling their growth and reproduction is to deny them food and breeding places. This can be done effectively in the city by adequate control of garbage, and by using screens. Screen doors should open outward, so that the flies are not swept into the house when they are opened. Garbage control has been rendered much easier and much more effective by the advent of the plastic garbage bag. These are very effective in denying access to breeding materials by flies.

The garbage bag still needs to be placed in a tight fitting, impervious container to deny access by rats (and dogs). Rodents are another important vector of disease transmission, and it is equally important to control them. Most people find them abhorrent, and accept this dictum of public health more readily than the control of flies, that are viewed, mistakenly, more as a nuisance. It has been amply demonstrated over the years that rats can be effectively controlled by denying them access to food, garbage and grain stores. They thrive and multiply in neighborhoods where food is abundantly available.

The purist in public health would like to see twice weekly pickup of garbage, but this is impractical and costly. Once weekly pickup is very effective in controlling flies. The fly eggs hatch in twenty-four to thirty-six hours. The larval stage exists for an additional five to eight days, and the pupal stage lasts for four to six days. The entire cycle takes about ten to fourteen days. If garbage is picked up once weekly, it is obvious that no flies will be hatching at your home from that batch. It is equally important, however, that no fly eggs nor garbage fragments that have eggs implanted in them be left adhering to the can. The plastic bags, again, are invaluable in avoiding this. If garbage is dumped into the can loose (which it should not be), the can must be scrubbed sufficiently each week to remove the residue and destroy any remaining eggs.

In the context of fly propagation, garbage includes all food scraps and residue, cooked or uncooked, including meat, fruit and vegetable. Dead animals are a prime incubator for flies, and these should be buried promptly. Most garbage pickup services refuse to handle this form of refuse. In that event prompt burial provides a safe means of denying flies access to the carcass.

Flies generally travel no more than about two miles, so effective control of garbage and waste at your site should markedly reduce the population, assuming cooperation from your neighbors. Pesticides can be used, judiciously, to further enhance control. This is especially important on the farm, where control of all organic material such as manure, or the droppings in the field, is impossible. In this setting, pesticides in residual sprays and in fly traps assist in controlling the population. These agents must be kept away from food and out of the house, for the agents commonly used for this purpose on the farm are organophosphates. Only the pyrethoids should be used in the home. (See pesticides, chapter I.) Flies have proven adept at developing strains that are resistant to a given pesticide, so one must be alert to the need to switch to a different agent when such resistance develops.

## SEPTIC SYSTEMS

A properly installed and maintained septic system presents no health hazard. For this we owe thanks to the public health departments and sanitary engineers who have designed safe, efficient and functional systems. Building departments of the state and local governments exercise their authority to approve designs for and supervise construction of these systems to safeguard our health. This protection breaks down when individuals violate the system, and the laws, and dump inadequately treated effluent into a stream or other body of water. Contamination also occurs when a drainage bed is installed too close to the surface on a hill so that the effluent seeps to the surface. In purchasing a used home with a sewage system, this is one of the many items to check out carefully.

A serious threat to health exists in communities where shallow wells (forty to sixty feet deep) have been installed in proximity to septic systems. This is particularly hazardous in sandy soil and in communities where residences are placed on lots of less than one acre. Such wells are almost certain to be contaminated by the effluent of the septic systems, with the resultant danger of disease transmission.

The most common such disease risk today is that of hepatitis. Whereas this illness used to appear only every seven or eight years, it is now with us year in and year out. It results only from eating or drinking food or drink that has been contaminated by human feces. Giardia is another disease, an infectious diarrhea caused by a microorganism, that has moved from the realm of the uncommon to that of a common infection in the United States today. It too is acquired from contaminated food or drink, frequently from wells that contain the organism.

Wells should always be drilled deep enough to assure against such contamination. This requires a depth of 350 to 400 feet in some localities. More commonly 70 to 160 feet is adequate. This depends on the particular geologic strata in a given locality. The key is to reach a water source that is protected by an overlaying layer of impervious clay that prevents seepage of contaminants into the water table. The well must be drilled and sealed in such a manner as to prevent contamination from being carried to the deep water source. Here again standards for wells are set by health departments in order to assure safe water supplies. These officials in your area will know the depth required for an adequate and safe water supply. They also issue the permits and license the well drillers to assure that safe standards are maintained.

Most people do not appreciate that septic systems do require maintenance. Neglect results in a clogged drainage bed, which necessitates replacement at a considerable cost. Common sense and maintenance can prevent this. First, it must be remembered that what goes into the septic system does not disappear by magic nor by evaporation. The system is capable of "digesting" most organic material. Cellulose fiber, on the hand, is not reduced to an effluent that can be disposed of in the drainage bed. Toilet tissue, facial tissue, vegetable fibers, egg shells, coffee grounds, seeds, pits and cigarette filters are examples of materials that tend to accumulate in the tank. Once a sufficient quantity of this nondigestible residue has accumulated, these substances move out into your drain field and clog it up. Prudence would dictate that these substances be sent to the septic tank in limited quantities if at all.

The septic tank should be pumped out every three to five years, depending on the number of residents and on the quantity of such nondegradable materials that is dumped into it. If all of the leftovers from the table are processed through the garbage disposal, this time frame should be shortened, perhaps to once a year or less. At any rate, the cleanout must be done before there is any evidence of backup in the plumbing. Once this occurs, the filter bed has become clogged by the overflow of nondegradable material, and it must be replaced. That is a costly procedure.

## HEATING

The skyrocketing cost of petroleum-based fuel products during the past decade has prompted many people to turn to alternate fuel sources for home heating. Wood-burning has been resurrected as a result, and new stove designs that offer greater efficiency than the fireplace have been introduced. One of the hazards associated with this means of heating is chimney fires associated with creosote build-up in the chimney. Such buildup occurs to a much greater extent in the airtight stoves designed to burn slowly in an oxygen starved atmosphere. Once this buildup of creosote ignites, it burns at 2,000 degrees F., threatening the integrity of the chimney and risking the spread of fire to the house. This event is best prevented by monitoring the creosote buildup, and removing it from the chimney before it accumulates to a dangerous level.

In a single-story home, it is a reasonably simple matter to look down the chimney with a powerful flashlight from the roof. Brushes to remove the buildup are widely available at hardware stores, but the creosote must be removed after it is brushed loose. It may be possible to do this from below in some instances, but it requires access to the chimney. This is frequently not possible with the fireplace inserts.

Chimney sweeps as a business have responded to this demand, and this service is available in most communities. More recently, catalytic burners have become available, both as add-ons and as integral units on new stoves. These burners increase the efficiency of combustion and reduce the quantity of creosote that is sent up the chimney. Secondary combustion chambers have also been added to new stoves recently in order to increase the efficiency of combustion.

## TREATED LUMBER

Lumber that has been treated with any preservative should not be used as fuel in any wood-burning device, nor in a campfire. The newer treated products contain chemicals such as arsenic that have caused serious illness and death when burned in fireplaces. Timbers, fence posts and railroad ties that have been treated with creosote or pentachlorophenol release very toxic chemicals when burned. These are hazardous when inhaled and upon contact with the skin. Care should be taken to avoid the smoke and fumes when these products are burned outdoors. They should never be burned in home heating devices, nor in campfires.

## ALLERGIES

One of the side effects of wood burning has been the extension of the allergy season. Individuals who in the past suffered allergic rhinitis, cough and itching eyes when the trees started to bud in April have found that these symptoms are now with them the year around. These individuals have found that whereas they could discontinue their allergy injections in the fall in the past, they now must continue them through the winter.

## CANCER

A further concern has been expressed over the fact that cancer causing agents are produced when wood is burned. The main culprit is benzo-*a*-pyrene, which is a known carcinogen, and is a byproduct of wood combustion. Studies have revealed that the use of a wood burning stove in homes increases the level of benzo-*a*-pyrene five fold. Nitrogen oxides are also produced by wood burning stoves, and increased levels of these have also been measured. These substances do not cause cancer, but they do cause respiratory problems through irritation.

In some neighborhoods, where wood burning is common, ambient air levels of all of these combustion products reach intolerable levels. Some communities, such as Missoula, Montana, with a population of 33,000, have enacted ordinances controlling or banning wood burning when ambient air levels reach a certain level. This problem is more common in geographic locations where air movement is restricted by mountains or other topography.

Periodically individuals will be seen with a rhus dermatitis (poison ivy, oak, sumac) in the winter as a result of contact with the vines that adhere to wood that has been cut for fuel. Obviously smoke from burning these vines should not be inhaled nor allowed to come in contact with the skin.

## SPACE HEATERS

Unvented kerosene heaters have also become very popular as an alternate heating appliance. These units have also been the object of engineering improvements to provide a cleaner burn. In spite of these changes, kerosene heaters produce significant volumes of carbon monoxide, carbon dioxide, nitrogen dioxide and sulfur dioxide, the quantity of the latter being in direct relationship to the sulfur content of the fuel. Good quality K-1 kerosene contains less than 0.05 percent sulfur and poses no problem. K-2 fuel contains a higher level of sulfur, produces a hazardous level of sulfur dioxide and gums up the wick. Any kerosene fuel turns yellow due to oxidation from one season to the next, and this also causes the wick to gum up, producing smoke and contaminants.

Even under the best of circumstances, with clean fuel and a clean, properly adjusted wick, all of the above listed gases are produced at levels that pose a hazard to health. Carbon dioxide in the room is measured at levels well beyond what is considered to be safe. Carbon monoxide has been found to be eight to ten times above safe levels, especially if the wick is less than perfect (and it usually is). Approximately 700 people die in their homes each year of carbon monoxide poisoning. These air contaminants cause greater problems in individuals with asthma or bronchitis, in children and older people, in individuals with emphysema or chronic obstructive lung disease, and in individuals with heart disease. Pregnancy presents a particular risk, and this is not the ideal atmosphere in which to cultivate a healthy, normally developed baby.

## GAS-COOKING STOVES

Some studies have shown that residents of homes where gas stoves are used for cooking suffer a significantly higher incidence of respiratory problems. Nitrogen dioxide levels in these homes have been measured at two to three times the level of that in homes where electric stoves were used. Elevated levels of carbon monoxide have also been measured. Both hazards can readily be removed by the installation of a range hood that exhausts to the outside. It has become popular to install hoods over the kitchen range in new homes that merely recirculate the air through a charcoal filter. This practice is done presumably to save the minuscule cost of installing ductwork to the outside. The charcoal filters do not accomplish what would be done by ducting to the outside, especially once the charcoal is exhausted.

## ASBESTOS

Many homes built in the fifties, and prior to that, contain furnaces and ductwork that are insulated with asbestos. Asbestos coated the exterior of the old gravity-feed furnaces, and was wrapped around the ducts. This material has a tendency to flake off, particularly where it has been struck by some object. Remodeling also poses the risk of disseminating asbestos fibers into the air. Asbestos fibers were routinely incorporated into spackling compound and drywall materials until 1975. In remodeling, tearing this material out or sanding materials applied in that era exposes one to asbestos fibers.

Asbestos is a significant cancer hazard. Workers exposed to it develop lung cancer eight times as frequently as nonexposed workers. Workers who are exposed who also smoke cigarettes can multiply this by a factor of at least ten, meaning that their risk is increased to eighty times or more. Prolonged exposure is not needed to face this risk. A latency period of twenty to thirty years makes it difficult to make the connection between the exposure and the development of the cancer. Individuals who worked in the shipyards of Philadelphia, Oakland and Richmond, California during World War II began showing up with lung cancer as a result of their asbestos exposure in about 1978. Many women joined the work force in these shipyards, and this was about the time when smoking also became popular among women. Working in the presence of asbestos increased their odds of getting lung cancer by a factor of six to eight, but smoking plus the asbestos increased the odds by eighty to ninety fold.

Mesothelioma is a cancer of the lining of the lung, and is a very rare tumor. It has been seen with alarming frequency in workers exposed to asbestos. A single exposure may be adequate to produce this incurable disease thirty years later. (See chapter VIII for more on asbestos.)


EXPLOSIONS

Volatile solvents (lacquer thinner, toluene, acetone, paint thinners) and fuels such as gasoline should not be stored in the house, basement or garage. This risk is increased when wood burning appliances are used. Fumes from these agents are easily ignited and may be explosive. Removal of ashes that contain hot coals can be disastrous if they are set in the garage alongside any of these volatile substances.

# III

# Hazards of the Home Workshop

In this chapter are included all of those activities around the home or farm that involve the use of tools. These include the myriad do-it-yourself projects that have become an important element in our society and economy. This latter area, around which a whole industry has evolved, has provided a great deal of gratification and recreation to thousands of individuals.

## EYE PROTECTION

One of the most serious risks involved in most of the activities in this realm is eye injury. Although the United States has the lowest incidence of blindness of all of the major nations of the world, far too much loss of vision results from injuries at home or on the job. Virtually all of these injuries could be prevented by the simple expedient of wearing proper eye protection. Such protection may range from a simple plastic face shield when grinding or working under the auto to prescription ground safety glasses. All prescription glasses in the United States are made from impact resistant materials, by law, but a greater impact protection may be advisable for some projects. Safety glasses provide protection around the periphery of the eyes that regular glasses do not. Information on eye protection routinely accompanies all power tools, such as saws, grinders, routers, drills, lathes and jointers, when they are purchased.

The most common injury sustained to the eye from these activities is the deposition in the eye of a foreign body, usually a fleck of wood or some other particulate material, or a metal fragment. The majority of these are removed at home with no complications. Far too often, however, a simple problem is converted to a more serious one when abrasion of the eye results from efforts to remove a foreign body at home. Such an event always raises the risk of infection in the eye, and should always be seen and cared for by a physician. An even more serious complication occurs when the object is forced through the surface of the eye. Such penetrating wounds must always be managed by a competent ophthalmologist, for it will require surgical removal. It must be kept in mind that a particle from a grinding wheel may be so imbedded, either from the force of impact or from the heat of the particle, that removal at home is impossible and often difficult even for the physician.

In any event where pain in the eye is present, examination by a physician is imperative. A variety of bacteria or viruses may gain entry to the eye through an abrasion or injury. This is the usual source of infection to the cornea. Such an infection in some instances can result in the loss of an eye when medical attention is delayed for as little as twenty-four hours. This risk has increased as a result of the emergence of bacterial strains that are resistant to antibiotics.

## WELDING

Welding, whether at home or on the job, carries two main risks. The first is to the eyes, from a "flash burn." This is a burn of the surface of the eye resulting from ultraviolet ray exposure. It frequently results from viewing the arc produced by an electrode before the face shield is put in place, or as a result of a bystander looking at the arc. It does not require a prolonged exposure. Flash burns have also resulted when welders have used a face shield that had a fine crack in the lens that was not detected. The same type of burn can occur with exposure to the sun, especially on snow, or to a sunlamp.

No change is noticed after such an exposure for several hours. Pain in the eye then evolves, severe enough to prevent sleep, perhaps for two nights. The eye feels as though it has sand in it. Light sensitivity and the production of tears are usually present. Healing takes place with no permanent damage, but the degree of pain usually requires medication. Ophthalmic anitbiotics should be used to prevent infection. Topical anesthetics give significant relief of the discomfort, but these **SHOULD NOT** be used. The cornea will not heal when it is anesthetized, and this increases the risk of infection as well as delaying healing. Pain relief must come from oral medications.

This painful affliction can be prevented by always wearing adequate eye protection while welding. One cannot see through the lens of an electric welding helmet before the arc has been struck, but the practice of delaying placement of the hood until the arc is struck runs the risk of this burn. The glasses designed for an acetylene torch cannot be used for electric welding. Bystander or passersby should always be protected from viewing the arc produced by welding.

The second risk associated with welding involves the lungs. Welding produces fume particles that are much smaller than particles that are produced by grinding or other mechanical means. As a consequence, these particles have access to the deepest reaches of the lungs. Some of the components of this fume, such as iron oxide, do not by themselves produce serious harm. Any dust inhaled over a period of time, however, can produce a bronchitis, and the risk is much greater in cigarette smokers. Cigarette smoke tends to paralyze the defense mechanisms that remove dust particles from the lungs and increases the production of mucus. The result is that welders who also smoke have twice the incidence of emphysema and chronic obstructive lung disease as do nonsmoking welders.

During the process of welding, both the welding rod and the material being welded are vaporized, producing the fume mentioned above. If the material in both of these sources is pure iron, little risk is involved. The significant risk comes from other substances in the metal rod. The presence of cadmium, either as an alloy or more commonly as a rust protective coating of the material being welded, produces a serious risk for the development of emphysema. Cadmium is often present in the coating on the rod, alloyed with copper or nickel. Cadmium is also virtually always present in the alloy of wire used for silver solder, and many disabling cases of emphysema have resulted from this process. Silica has also been incorporated in the coating on the rod, and inhalation of this substance produces one of the most serious and most disabling of all lung disorders, silicosis. Nitrogen oxides (the villain in auto exhaust pollution) and ozone are also present in the welding zone. Both of these produce irritation of the throat and lungs, and may lead to spasm, cough and bronchitis.

Adequate ventilation is essential in all welding, brazing and silver soldering operations. This means a properly designed booth with adequate exhaust and air replacement. Such a facility is never present at home, and all too often not on the job. Welding in the open results in significant inhalation of particles. Occasional welding of a pure iron based material with an electrode that does not contain silica or cadmium probably carries little risk. This ideal set of circumstances is rarely seen, however. One should avoid vaporizing materials that contain or are coated with cadmium (galvanized steel and plated screws) or spring brass that invariably contains beryllium.

## SOLDERING

Commercial solder sold for home use normally contains a mixture of tin and lead, usually 50 to 60 percent tin and 40 to 50 percent lead. This is the mixture that flows the best, provides the strongest joint and lasts the longest. Concerns regarding the risk of lead leaching into the water supply have prompted federal authorities to mandate the use of lead-free solder in residential plumbing. The degree to which lead is leached from the joints is related to the acidity of the water supply. The problem has been found in a few isolated regions.

One solder marketed to meet this new requirement contains 95 percent tin and 5 percent antimony. A more recent one contains zinc, silver and antimony in addition to the tin base. It is claimed that the latter product flows better. A eutectic mixture (that mixture which melts at the lowest temperature) of tin-lead (63-37) melts at 183 degrees Celsius (361 degrees Fahrenheit). The lead-free solders melt at 240 and 245 degrees Celsius respectively (464 and 473 degrees Fahrenheit). A significantly higher temperature will be needed in order to substitute these new solders. This may not be easy to achieve on three-inch copper plumbing joints. These new solder alloys cost about twice as much as conventional solder, and it remains to be seen how effective they are. For most of the soldering jobs, the conventional solder will continue to provide a stronger joint and will be easier to work with. If this transition proves to be a needed improvement it will be worth the added cost. It will also be a first for the federal bureaucracy.

## WOODWORKING

One of the most common activities in the home workshop, and one of the most widely enjoyed, is woodworking. These projects carry several risks. The most obvious risk when operating various power tools is the loss of fingers or other personal injury. I have seen individuals who have passed one to three fingers through a bench saw along with the wood being processed. This tragedy can be avoided by using blocks of wood rather than fingers to feed the work, and by keeping the hands well away from the the blade. These projects also should not be undertaken when you are tired. Eye injury, as previously discussed, must also be guarded against. The use of adequate eye protection when using power saws and the use of the anti-kickback device while ripping, are imperative.

A dust mask should be worn at all times when sawdust is being produced. The disposable paper masks are probably adequate for this purpose for most people, but every effort should be made to achieve a good fit. An efficient, well fit respirator is preferable, and is essential for asthmatics and individuals with a proclivity toward bronchitis. Inhalation of so called benign dust over a period of time can produce a bronchitis even in healthy individuals. Those who have a family history of bronchitis (parents, grandparents, aunts and uncles) should avoid inhaling dust at all times. Individuals who inherit a deficiency of the enzyme alpha-1-antitrypsin develop bronchitis as a result of dust exposure much more readily (see chapter V). A respirator, like safety glasses, is a nuisance when working, but the discomfort of advanced lung disease is more than a nuisance.

Asthmatics must face the added risk of an attack due to sensitization to western red cedar, mahogany and oak, in particular. Aside from bronchitis and asthma, inhalation of the sawdust of hardwoods and western red cedar can produce cancer of the nose and sinuses. Hardwoods carry five times the risk of producing cancer as do softwoods. Sawdust from treated lumber should never be allowed to come in contact with the skin. Lumber that has been treated with pentachlorophenol or creosote provides the potential for absorption of these very toxic chemicals through the skin (see pentachlorophenol and creosote, chapter I). Treated lumber that is popularly sold for decks contains copper and arsenical compounds that can cause serious illness and cancer. Death has resulted from burning these products in a fireplace.

Even more dangerous than bench saws and radial saws are chainsaws. Numerous serious injuries have occurred, including massive destruction of the face and jaw requiring extensive reconstructive surgery. Newer anti-kickback devices have lessened this risk some, but serious injuries still occur all too frequently. It is essential to have secure footing and a firm grip on the saw at all times. This is not always easy to achieve in a tree or on a ladder. Eye protection always should be worn, and hearing protection from noise is important here (see Hearing in chapter VII).

Some general safety rules should be strictly adhered to in the workshop, and whenever power tools are being used. These are included in abundance in the instruction sheets that accompany all power tools. These warnings are so voluminous at times that it is difficult to locate the instructions, and we thus tend to disregard them as superfluous. A few common sense precautions, however, may prevent the loss of a finger or hand and considerable suffering.

The worker in the home workshop should not wear loose clothing such as jewelry, a necktie, loose sleeves or any gloves while operating power tools. I have seen a finger pulled into a bench saw by a glove that became entangled. Similarly, the power cords should be disconnected before changing blades on power saws. All guards should be put back in place after servicing power tools. Remove all clutter, keep the work area clear to avoid stumbling and falling into a moving blade. Adequate lighting is important, and it seems that more is required as we age.

No one should ever operate an electrical appliance while standing in water or on a damp surface. Dry rubber soled shoes give an added measure of protection against electrical shock. In this same vein, all grounding devices should be retained. This means not cutting the ground prong on a three-pronged plug simply because an adapter is not at hand. Some of the newer double-insulated tools do not require grounding.

Children should be kept out of the workshop and away from all power tools (and soldering irons). The workshop should be locked when not in use to prevent exploring by young children. Switches that permit locking or disabling of saws and other tools are very desirable. When children are old enough to be taught the use of power tools, this should be done under strict supervision. As proficiency and maturity progress, strict supervision can be replaced by a watchful eye.

An additional risk from vibrating tools is Raynaud's phenomenon, a spasm of the small arteries in the fingers that results in a disruption of circulation. After prolonged use this can become permanent, and in the extreme can result in the loss of fingers. This problem develops more readily at some frequencies than at others, and work is underway to redesign tools to lessen this risk. Some individuals seem more prone to develop this problem than others. There appears to be some inherited predisposition. Once the disease has developed certain medications for blood pressure and certain eyedrops for glaucoma may make the symptoms worse.

## SOLVENTS

Organic solvents are used in the workshop and around the home and farm for many purposes. Cleaning of auto, tractor and machinery parts and removing paint and other residues are but a few of the uses. Some, such as acetone, naphtha and lacquer thinner, are highly flammable. An explosion may result from a nearby water heater or from a spark from the battery of a car while using these solvents. Even a dropped tool can produce a spark that can ignite the vapors (see Fire, chapter II). These solvents also can produce damage to the liver, kidney and brain and may produce a weakness of the skeletal muscles (solvent myopathy).

Other solvents, notably carbon tetrachloride, trichloroethylene and methylene chloride, are not flammable nor explosive, but they are toxic to the liver, kidney and nervous system (brain) when the fumes are inhaled. They are just as toxic when absorbed through the skin. Methylene chloride is also known to produce cancer. Some gasoline still contains lead, which is readily absorbed through the intact skin and causes damage to the nervous system and other organs. Gasoline also contains considerable benzene which should not be inhaled nor absorbed through the skin. It has been associated with the development of leukemia. Kerosene is a much safer cleaning agent and is less flammable than gasoline, and does not contain the additives that are present in diesel fuel.

## FURNITURE REFINISHING

Another very popular home workshop activity, one frequently undertaken by women, is the refinishing of furniture. Many of the solvents listed in the previous discussion are also used in these projects. Furniture strippers and sanding liquids usually contain such volatile and flammable agents as acetone, toluol, xylol and methyl ethyl ketone. These are the common constituents in lacquer thinner, and while they are effective in softening paint and varnish, they carry a serious explosive risk, particularly when used in a basement with a gas furnace and water heater. Methylene chloride is also incorporated in stripper and sanding solutions, sometimes without the other solvents, since a nonexplosive mixture can thus be marketed. Methylene chloride, even though it is not explosive, carries its own serious risks as mentioned above. None of these solutions should be permitted to come in contact with the skin.

I have not found a simple, effective way of accomplishing the task of applying these agents and avoiding all skin contact. The use of a paint brush to spread the solution over the surface helps to avoid exposure. Heavy duty vinyl gloves offer some protection, but these are not impervious to organic solvents. Reliance upon this protection should be limited to short periods at best. Only one glove provides adequate protection against these solvents, and that is Du Pont's Viton. Its cost renders it impractical for most home projects.

In refinishing furniture without the use of the above-mentioned solvents, sanding may expose the worker to the inhalation of paint pigments that contain lead or cadmium. Arsenic and mercury compounds have been used as wood preservatives in outdoor lumber and furniture. Sanding or scraping these carries the same risk of inhalation. All four of these substances are metals that are absorbed after ingestion, thus inhalation of their dust may result in toxicity after absorption in the stomach as well as in the lung. The use of an effective, well-fit respirator and showering afterward can help to protect from this hazard. Getting a good fit is impossible with a beard. In industry on jobs where respirators are required, beards are prohibited.

Needless to say none of the substances discussed above should be inhaled nor applied to the skin during pregnancy. This is a particular problem during early pregnancy, when uncertainty as to status still exists. The first three months of pregnancy is the period of most rapid development of the fetus and the most sensitive for the development of abnormalties. No one should be painting a room nor refinishing furniture during pregnancy, nor when pregnancy is a possibility.

## SANDBLASTING

This activity requires eye protection, but of equal importance is protection of the lungs. Most sandblasting in the United States is still done with silica sand, although other safer materials are available. Carborundum and aluminum oxide are not readily available from paint stores and builder supplies but they can be purchased in most cities at suppliers of sandblasting equipment. They are considerably more expensive, especially where used in systems that do not recover the abrasive. Silica sand carries the risk of development of silicosis when inhaled. The silica particle, when deposited in the lung, provokes a destructive process in the lung that leads to a very disabling and very unpleasant disease, silicosis and chronic pulmonary fibrosis. A high-quality respirator, not a simple dust mask, is required to filter out silica, and proper fit is critical. It is futile to spend the money for a quality respirator if it leaks around the seal. The presence of a beard makes it virtually impossible to obtain a good fit, as discussed above.

There is no cure, no treatment, for silicosis, and it may not make its presence known for many years. (See Silicosis in chapter VIII for a complete discussion of this risk.)


## PAINT SPRAYING

Projects that involve spraying of paint present a dual hazard of inhalation of the particles and pigments as well as the solvents. The latter are toxic to the brain and nervous system in general, as well as to the liver. A good, well-fit respirator protects against the inhalation of particles and pigments, but gives no protection against inhalation of the solvent vapors. Respirators with charcoal canisters that do provide protection for this hazard are available, but are not frequently used outside of industry, and seldomly around the home.


## THE WEEKEND MECHANIC

One of the most serious hazards associated with this activity is that of carbon monoxide. About 700 people die at home each year from this poison. Sources include furnaces, cooking stoves, charcoal grills and vehicles. The hazards of this gas are widely known, but its presence is never recognized nor suspected because it is invisible and has no odor. The most obvious risk is from leaving the engine of an automobile or tractor running in a garage, shed or other enclosed space. Flexible extensions are available to carry the exhaust outdoors, and these should be installed wherever these vehicles must be left running indoors.

The onset of a headache during or after working in these circumstances should always prompt immediate suspicion of carbon monoxide toxicity. This does not occur early, and headache is such a common occurrence that it usually is ascribed to "sinus trouble" or some other everyday cause. Kerosene heaters in such closed workplaces also produce significant levels of carbon monoxide. These heaters also present the risk of fire or explosion in such settings, since gasoline is frequently present.

The hazards associated with the use of gasoline as a solvent to wash parts in have been discussed above. Carburetor cleaner or Tyme solution contains phenol and methylene chloride, both of which are toxic. The risks associated with the use of methylene chloride, including its potential for causing cancer, have also been discussed previously. Phenol has the potential for causing cancer, particularly when present with polycyclic aromatic hydrocarbons, which are also present in Tyme solution. It is believed that this mechanism accounts for the increased incidence of skin cancer in workers exposed to cutting oils.

Phenol is also caustic, causing tissue destruction in a manner similar to acids and other strong chemicals. Although the seven percent in Tyme solution is only slightly higher than that used in some topical applications, in medical practice it is applied only to small areas, usually abnormal areas. This solution should not be permitted to come in contact with the skin, and the vapors should not be inhaled. Skin irritation frequently occurs following contact with phenol.

In repairing automobile radiators the mechanic should be aware that the manufacturers in the United States have reduced the tin content of the solder from the normal 50 to 60 percent to a mere 5 percent. As is the case in all such innovations, this has been done solely to increase profit. This change makes the manufacture more difficult and it makes the product develop problems sooner. In addition to assuring a repair sooner, it increases the risk of lead exposure during that repair. When these repairs are undertaken, great precautions should be taken to avoid inhaling the fumes generated. Even when the job is undertaken outdoors the worker usually has his nose close to the project and the smoke, because that's where his eyes are.

When doing brake jobs, the first task after removing the wheel has been to blow the dust out of the wheel and rotor, either with compressed air or with the mouth. This should **NEVER** be done. This dust contains asbestos particles which pose a serious risk of cancer or asbestosis (see Asbestosis, chapter VIII). Even if the manufacturers remove all asbestos from brakes tomorrow, asbestos pads will be rolling down the highways for some time. This dust should be vacuumed, preferably with a central vacuum system vented to the outside. Asbestos fibers pass through conventional vacuum cleaner filters, and a vacuum cleaner should never be used on brakes, then taken inside for use in the home.

# IV

# Hazards of Childhood and Adolescence

## CHILDHOOD

Accidents are the leading cause of death in children. More children die as a result of accidents than cancer, meningitis, congenital defects and heart disease all put together. There are over 3,000 deaths per year in infants under one year of age from falls, burns, drowning and suffocation. For every death, there are one hundred children seriously injured. Curiosity is the most common cause for most of these accidents and injuries. Young children demand constant attention and supervision. This is difficult to provide among the many other demands of a household, especially if other children are in residence. Accidents occur much more frequently when young children are left with a baby-sitter. They are also more frequent during an illness of the parent, during a pregnancy, or when the parent is occupied by other demands in general.

Blunt trauma may occur as a result of a fall, being struck by a motor vehicle, or by a baseball bat. The majority of the lesser accidents do not result in serious injury, but that possibility must always be considered. Certainly, whenever there is drowsiness or a visual change such as blurred vision or double vision, careful examination by a physician is imperative. Similarly, when a blow in the region of the eye is sustained, examination should be made to determine the extent of injury, if any. Blood in the anterior chamber of the eye is common in children following a contusion to the eye or the region surrounding it. This is a serious injury that requires prompt medical attention.

Dislocation of the lens of the eye, abrasion of the cornea, laceration of the eyeball and retinal detachment are other complications of blunt trauma to the eye that require medical attention. These are injuries that cannot be detected at home, and neglect can result in loss of vision. Cold packs can be applied following blunt trauma, but great care must be taken to avoid applying any pressure to the eyeball itself.

Burns of the retina as a result of looking at an eclipse of the sun occur every time we have this solar event, and permanent loss of vision results. There is no safe way to review a solar eclipse directly. An ophthalmologist should be consulted when this injury occurs. Ultraviolet burns of the eye (keratitis) resulting from looking at a welding arc are much more common in adults than in children, but they do happen. They can also happen on the ski slope as a result of the reflection of the sun on the snow, and as a result of a child looking at a sunlamp. Adequate eye protection will prevent it on the ski slope, and proper supervision will avoid the sunlamp incident.

Burns of the face frequently involve the eyelids. The threat here is secondary infections that are common with all burns. The most feared infection, and one that is common, is that of Pseudomonas. It is resistant to most antibiotics, and can destroy the eyeball.

Another threat to vision in children is that of a foreign body. These may be simple to remove, or they may penetrate the eye and require surgery. One such injury results from pounding on a metal object with a hammer, for instance. Another serious and common injury is that inflicted by an air gun or BB gun. About 35,000 individuals are injured by these each year, and about 2,000 of these involve the eye. The majority of eye injuries sustained in this manner (over 70 percent) occur in individuals between the ages of five and eighteen years. The loss of vision in this injury is the rule. No one should be permitted to handle these guns until they have a thorough understanding of their safe use. Children should not be permitted to handle these guns without supervision.

Electric shock is common in young children, resulting from insertion of metal objects or fingers into electric outlets, or from chewing on lamp cords. The latter results in burns of the mouth in addition to the other threats from electricity, frequently with destruction of tissue around the mouth that requires plastic surgery. Safety caps should be placed in all electric outlets in homes where children are exploring. Protecting them from lamp cords requires vigilance. Children and adolescents also are electrocuted as a result of flying kites, and climbing trees in the proximity of power lines. Death due to asphyxia, heart irregularities or respiratory arrest can occur within minutes if the child remains in contact with the electricity. In removing the child from the contact with electricity, care must be taken to avoid two casualties rather than one.

Approximately 20,000 children under the age of 5 years are hospitalized each year for having swallowed a potent toxic substance. Medicines account for about 45 percent of these cases and aspirin and other analgesics are the most common medicines involved. Medicines include both prescription and nonprescription drugs, and the latter are increasing in number and availability year by year. In 1985 the American Association of Poison Control Centers reported over 60,000 incidents of unintentional prescription medicine ingestion by children under the age of 5 years. In a review of 2,000 of these cases, the medicine was in a child-resistant container in 80 percent of the cases. The medication was in the original container in only 65 percent of the cases. Grandparents' medication accounted for 17 percent of the cases. The chief factors contributing to these poisoning were found to be:

Not replacing the cap securely
Not keeping the medication in a container
Keeping the medication in a container other than the original
Availability of medication in the kitchen and bedroom
Medication being left where it is accessible
The natural tendency of children to explore, and to put things in their mouths

Deaths resulting from accidental ingestion of these substances have declined by 70 percent since the enactment of the Poison Prevention Packaging Act in 1970.

In 1983, 110,000 children under the age of five years were treated in emergency rooms for the ingestion of a potent toxin. While accidents are the leading cause of death in children, poisoning is the fourth most common cause of death. The peak incidence occurs at age two years, most cases occurring under the age of five. Accidental poisoning is uncommon after the age of five. If poisoning is suspected, and if the poison is unknown, if the child vomits, the vomitus should be saved for analysis. In general, vomiting should not be induced after the ingestion of certain agents such as furniture polish, kerosene and hydrocarbons. The family physician should be called immediately. If unable to contact the family physician, the hospital emergency room or emergency medical team should be called.

There seems to be little excuse for accidental poisoning of children with medications in view of the use of mandated safety caps. The hazard of aspirin has long been known, and it should never be removed from safety cap containers. It should never be left where children can get their hands on it. The most toxic salicylate is methyl salicylate (oil of wintergreen), commonly used in liniments. Next to aspirin and other salicylates, caustics, lead and hydrocarbons are the most common poisons in children.

Strong alkali substances (caustics) produce more severe burns and greater damage, in general, than do acids. Caustics are seen in drain cleaners, toilet bowl cleaners, oven cleaners, fertilizers (potassium hydroxide, potash), electric dishwasher detergents and Clinitest tablets for diabetics. The newer liquid dishwasher detergents are much easier for children to swallow and are much more damaging. With the powder, the crystals stick to the lining of the mouth and burn, which discourages further consumption. There is a tendency to swallow much more of the liquid products. Severe burns of the mouth, throat and esophagus result from ingesting caustics, and the esophagus is frequently completely destroyed. Household bleaches, which are 3–6 percent sodium hypochlorite, are not corrosive and produce less damage.

Rust removing cleaners such as Zud and Barkeeper's Friend contain oxalic acid and result in damage to the kidneys in addition to burns. (See chapter II for information on kitchen, bathroom and household cleaners and their hazards.)

Lead-based paint pigments have not been used in homes since the sixties. Since 1977 legislation has restricted the lead content of paints used in households to no more than 0.06 percent (600 parts per million). Paints manufactured in the forties for indoor use contained as much as fifty percent lead (500,000 parts per million). This paint remains in 27,000,000 households today. This continues to be a major source of lead intoxication in children each year. In some cases the underlayers of paint are scraped off by children. Remodeling of these older homes is also currently popular, and children are poisoned by the particles produced by the scraping and sanding of these projects. Lead pigments are still used in paints on some objects, and this presents another source. Other sources of lead in cases of lead poisoning in children are:

Artists' paints
Lead shot, fishing weights, toys, curtain weights
Storage of acid foods such as fruits and their juices, tomatoes and tomato juice, pickled fruits and vegetables, wine, cider and soft drinks in improperly glazed ceramic utensils (usually imported)
Burning lead-painted wood in the fireplace
Inhalation or skin absorption of lead in gasoline

Casting lead bullets, sinkers or toys at home
Solder and soldered joints

Lead intoxication in children produces brain damage with de-creased intelligence and behavioral disorders. It is most harmful between the ages of one and six years. Periodically, an episode of gasoline sniffing results in lead toxicity among young people. There are hazards other than lead toxicity from this practice, the most serious being brain damage from the multiple toxic substances present.

Hydrocarbons include petroleum distillates, such as gasoline, kerosene, paint thinners, furniture polish and many pesticides and weed-killers. As strange as it seems, these continue to be among the most popular substances for children to experiment with and to drink. These substances are very toxic, especially in the lungs, where they are 140 times more toxic than in the stomach. They are fre-quently aspirated into the lungs when swallowed, and only a few drops in the lung can produce a serious pneumonia. Furniture polish (mineral seal oil) is particularly lethal. It produces damage to the kidneys and bone marrow in addition to the pneumonitis that it provokes.

Another group of hydrocarbons are the halogenated hydrocar-bons, which include carbon tetrachloride, trichloroethylene, trichlo-roethane and ethylene dichloride. These substances are used for general cleaning, including the dry cleaning of clothes, for degreas-ing and as solvents. They are found in many compounds in the home even if not present in their pure form. They produce severe damage in the liver, kidney and brain.

A list of some of the more common poisons in the home that pose a threat to children includes:

Nail polish remover (acetone): inhalation toxic to the brain
Household ammonia (ammonium hydroxide)
Ethyl alcohol (beer, liquors, wines)
Rubbing alcohol (isopropyl or denatured ethyl)
Methyl alcohol (paint solvents, shellac, canned fuel); causes blindness
Pesticides: virtually all are readily absorbed through the intact skin
Ant poison (thallium)
Rat and roach poisons; various agents; see chapter I.
Glues and cements, such as contact cement
Cleaning fluids (carbon tetrachloride, trichloroethylene)
Cosmetics
Hair removers
Permanent-wave neutralizers (high toxicity)

Permanent wave lotion
Lysol and other cresols such as creosote
Moth repellents (naphthalene, paradichlorobenzene):
   children's clothing should not be stored in napthalene, since this substance is
   absorbed through the skin; it is also very toxic when ingested
Floor wax (carbon tetrachloride)
Turpentine (paint thinners)
Antifreeze
Bath oil
Hair dyes
Hair tonic (alcohol)
Shaving lotion
Cologne, toilet water
Tobacco (ingestion and skin absorption)
Liniments and balms (methyl salicylate, oil of wintergreen)
Nitrates and nitrites in well water (and spinach); produce methemoglobinemia in
   infants
Artists' paints (lead and cadmium)

Many house plants are also toxic, and are commonly ingested by children. Those generally held to be toxic are philodendron and dieffenbachia (dumbcane), both of which contain oxalic acid, amaryllis, calla lilly and poinsettia. Symptomatic poisoning in children almost always involves the philodendron or diffenbachia. Castor beans are very toxic if chewed, or if the shell is cracked. Fava beans have also been responsible for poisoning in children.

Outdoor plants which are poisonous are: hemlock (respiratory paralysis), rhododendron, yellow jasmine, crocus, foxglove, oleander and larkspur.

A word about boric acid is in order. This substance was a popular home medicinal until about the fifties when a number of poisonings and deaths occurred from it. It remains useful in certain applications best left to professionals. It has no place in the home. Fatalities have resulted from mistaking boric acid eye solutions for a mouth wash. Fatalities also resulted from absorption of boric acid from baby powders when a diaper rash was present. It is no longer found in these products. Childhood poisoning is best prevented, rather than treated. This is done by:

1) Locking up all household cleaning supplies, medicines, pesticides, auto polishes
   and supplies, paints and paint supplies: it is not enough to place these on a shelf
   "out of reach"; children have repeatedly demonstrated that the top shelf is not out
   of reach
2) Not storing cleaning supplies with food
3) Leaving medicines and chemicals in original containers
4) Not storing household supplies under the sink

5) Not leaving medicines or chemicals available when answering the telephone or attending the dryer
6) Reading the name on the label prior to administration of any medication
7) Not taking medication in front of children; they are great imitators

Unfortunately, many medications have a very narrow safety margin, and even a moderate overdose in children can result in death. Iron tablets, even though they are available without prescription, are a medication, and many children have died as a result of consuming them. They are very lethal in overdose.

The telephone number of the family doctor, hospital emergency room or emergency squad, or all three, should be at the telephone, readily accessible. In any household with children, the family physician should be consulted regarding recommended procedures to follow in the event of an emergency, and what, if any, supplies such as ipecac should be kept on hand. In general when a substance such as a pesticide is spilled on the skin, it should be flushed with copious amounts of water, washed well with soap and water and then thoroughly rinsed. Never induce vomiting in the following circumstances:

If unconscious
If petroleum distillate has been swallowed
If a corrosive has been swallowed (lye, drain cleaner)

The family physician should be contacted immediately when a child has suffered a poisoning event. If there is inability to contact medical help, these guidelines may provide assistance while efforts to reach the doctor continue:

If medicine has been swallowed, give nothing
If a household product has been swallowed, give one glass of milk, water if milk is not available
Do not give the antidote listed on the label, they are frequently not current

If these measures seem onerous or unduly cautious, one should visit one of the large children's hospitals to view a child with a severely damaged esophagus, or other serious injury from poisoning. Remember, 20,000 children are hospitalized for such tragedies each year, and they suffer, many of them permanently.

The problem of methemoglobinemia produced in infants as a result of nitrates in the drinking water is discussed in Hazards of Food and Water, chapter VI. Botulism in infants as a result of using honey in the formulation is covered in the same chapter. Botulism in infants has also been traced to contamination of food by soil or dust from the vacuum cleaner. Botulism bacteria exist in the soil everywhere. Other cases in infants have resulted from breast feeding because the mother failed to cleanse the breast.

An environmental threat of a different nature is rheumatic fever. This disease, which damages the heart valves, has been under control for the past twenty-five years, thanks to vigilance and adequate treatment of streptococcal infections with penicillin. Recently, however, there has been a resurgence, with an increase in the number of cases reported. The reasons for this upsurge are not clear.

Rheumatic fever rarely occurs after age eighteen years. The disease itself is not an infection, but is a hypersensitivity reaction that follows the streptococcal infection. It occurs two weeks or more after the infection has cleared. It can be prevented by prompt treatment of any streptococcal throat or tonsil infection for a full ten days. Some individuals are carriers of streptococcus, showing no outward evidence of illness. Pets have also been shown to be carriers of this bacteria, and must also be considered as a source when repeated infections occur in a family. The role that the great increase in the number of household pets plays in the increase in the incidence of rheumatic fever has not been fully explored.

Inadequate or improper nutrition is a significant and common, although widely unrecognized, hazard of childhood. Growth and development continue through the teen years, and for this to proceed successfully the proper building materials must be available. A robust child does not guarantee a healthy child. Many obese infants and children are significantly malnourished. All individuals require an adequate quantity of and a proper balance between protein, fat and carbohydrates. Certain vitamins and minerals are required additionally. It is difficult for us in our land of plenty to visualize the serious nutritional deficiency states that are everyday occurrences in other lands. Vitamin A deficiency, for instance, is the leading cause of permanent blindness in the developing countries. It is easily preventable by dietary supplementation of Vitamin A, which is synthesized, and it is cheap. Protein, which provides not only essential building materials, but vital elements of the body's immune, protective and recovery processes, is widely deficient in the third world. This can be seen readily in the photographs of infants and young children with pot bellies.

It is not difficult to fulfill the nutritional needs of the body. The protein needs are readily supplied by one half to one third the quantity of meat that most of us consume on a daily basis. The requirements other than protein are normally supplied by a well-balanced diet. Some elements are not always present in the diet in adequate quantities, and these can be provided by supplementation. Vitamin C, for instance, is not abundant in most diets, and it is easily destroyed by cooking and by oxidation. It is easily and cheaply synthesized, however, and 250 milligrams per day readily supplies our needs. The two vitamins that can cause harm in overdose are A and D. Vitamin D should rarely be taken in supplementation, certainly not in doses exceeding 400 milligrams daily. Many foods such as breads and milk are universally "enriched" by vitamins A and D, ensuring their presence in our diets.

For the child who is allergic to cows' milk, calcium, which is essential for proper growth, can be supplemented by oyster shell calcium. Mineral sources of calcium such as dolomite contain other minerals which may be harmful. The most significant of these is lead. Animal sources of calcium (bone) carry the risk of containing other harmful substances. This was the case when strontium-90 was found in the bones of animals during atmospheric testing of nuclear weapons. Care must be exercised also with calcium to not overdose and risk damage to the kidneys.

There is overwhelming evidence that the administration of small amounts of fluoride to children from birth and throughout childhood virtually eliminates dental caries. Dental caries is caused by a destruction of the enamel of the teeth by acid that is produced by bacteria in the mouth. This is the most common cause of tooth loss up to about age 45 years. Fluoride alters the enamel in a fashion that it becomes almost impervious to this action. Fluoridation of municipal water supplies is the most efficient means of accomplishing this. Widespread and irrational public objections have prevented this from being done in many communities. In localities where the public water supplies are not fluoridated, the infants should be administered vitamins that contain fluoride. This should be continued throughout childhood. This simple practice will save the child much discomfort at the dentist and the loss of teeth. It will also save your pocketbook.

It is essential that supplemental fluoride not be administered in locations where an adequate fluoride content exists in the water. In addition to public water supplies where fluoride has been added, well water in some localities contains significant levels of fluoride. Your family physician or the Public Health Department can give you this information, and tell you whether or not administration of fluoride is advisable. Excess fluoride will damage the teeth by producing mottling. It also causes increased bone density with brittleness and neurological disturbances in high enough doses.

The objections to fluoridation of public water supplies have been based upon its toxicity and claims that it is a poison. These statements apply no more to fluoride than they do to other trace minerals in the diet, such as chromium, selenium, cobalt, nickel, copper and zinc. Iron overdose kills many children every year. Every substance is a poison if taken in overdose. This is true even of water. The point is that every substance taken into the body must be kept within the range dictated by genetics and physiology. Any substance that provides a benefit to health and well being should be supplied to the body within that range. Those of us who did not have the benefit of fluoride, and who suffered the dental consequences, can well be envious of today's generation.

## ADOLESCENCE

Accidents are the leading cause of death among adolescents also. In addition, many nonfatal accidents result in hospitalization of young people. In many of these cases, emotional disturbances are a significant underlying factor. This may be suspected where a history of running away from home, depression or truancy is obtained. In many cases, however, truancy is merely a reflection of a low priority for education on the part of the parents.

Approximately 15,000 to 18,000 of the accidents each year are due to automobiles, and many of these are alcohol related. Alcohol is the substance most frequently abused in this age group. Its use is reported in about three million adolescents each year. In addition to accidents, other risks associated with abuse of alcohol are cirrhosis of the liver and its sequelae, malnutrition and vitamin deficiencies. The malnutrition may be accompanied by increased frequency and severity of infections of all forms, including tuberculosis. In the presence of a family history of alcoholism there may be a genetic predisposition. Alcohol and other substance abuse may be purely recreational, or may be an indication of a deeper psychological disturbance. It may reach a level where it interferes with interpersonal relationships with family, friends and working cohorts, and may interfere with attendance at and performance on the job.

Suicide is the third leading cause of death among individuals between the ages of fifteen to twenty-four years of age (homocides rank number two). Suicide is the second leading cause of death among college students. The rate of suicide among young people has doubled since 1960. The majority of these people are depressed. Other psychological disorders prompt this drastic action in others. Signs are frequently in evidence when looked for in retrospect. Frequently these individuals have been withdrawn and have isolated themselves from friends and family. An increase in problems at home, at school and at work is frequently in evidence.

Some events that may precipitate the psychological trauma are loss of a family member or loved one, breaking up with a friend, or divorce or separation of the parents. Difficulty in coping with these traumas is usually apparent. Frequently suicide attempts are unsuccessful at first, a genuine wish to die may not exist. In some cases where the wish to die is not real, the suicide succeeds by accident or unexpectedly. The suicide attempt may reflect a desire to punish a parent or other person for a perceived injustice, or may represent an act of retaliation. It may represent self-perceived guilt.

## OBESITY

Obesity presents many hazards to health. One of these is represented in the increased incidence of elevated cholesterol and triglyceride levels in teenagers, and the early onset of atherosclerosis. Emotional and self image problems also accompany obesity frequently. Of equal importance is the poor nutrition that frequently accompanies this disorder. It is difficult to channel food intake toward the essential nutrients during this period, yet the fact that growth and development continue through these years makes it virtually as urgent as it is in the earlier years. Parents have much less influence over nutrition at this age today, since the combination of increased freedom, cash in the pocket and a fast food or ice cream facility on every corner almost guarantees consumption of these items. These are difficult obstacles to overcome, but neglect of nutrition during these formative years will almost certainly penalize the individual throughout the remainder of life.

Slipped capital epiphysis is a disorder of the femur. It is one of the more serious complications of obesity, at least from an immediate standpoint. The disorder is a separation of the upper portion of the femur (the bone in the thigh) at the growth plate of the head. It occurs more commonly in overweight individuals, and no hormonal imbalances have been found to explain its occurrence. It may follow a fall, but most cases present no history of trauma. Onset is insidious, with pain and limping. The pain may be referred to the knee, misleading the search for the cause. An x-ray reveals the diagnosis. In about one-third of the cases, the head of the femur is destroyed by necrosis (decay). Medical treatment is urgent, although it frequently does not prevent the unfortunate sequelae. There is a high incidencce of premature degeneration and arthritis of the hip joint in overweight adolescents even without this disease.

# V

# Hazards of Reproduction

The adverse effects of alcohol consumption during pregnancy on the fetus have been officially recognized since 1973. Low birth weight is the most common and most readily identified consequence. It appears to be dose related and a typical set of features in an infant with the fetal alcohol syndrome has been described. These include a set of typical facial features, and an I.Q. significantly below the mean, learning disabilities, short attention span and speech disorders. In addition to the risk to the developing fetus, alcohol places an added burden on the maternal liver. Any anesthetic presents some risk, but a liver compromised by alcohol greatly adds to that risk.

As with most poisons, no safe dose has been established, but two drinks per day have been associated with low birth weight. Cigarette smoking has also been associated with abnormal fetal development, and it appears to be synergistic with alcohol.

Spontaneous abortion prior to twenty-eight weeks occurs in ten to twenty percent of pregnancies diagnosed, and in approximately twenty to twenty-five percent of conceptions. Approximately one-third of these demonstrate chromosomal abnormalties, and about one-half of the remaining have malformations of one form or another. Thus about sixty-five percent of spontaneous abortions result from imperfect fertilized germ cells. These are, for the most part, zygotes that would result in a significantly abnormal infant.

Generalized malnutrition, caloric restriction and protein deficiency in the mother during pregnancy lead to severe growth retardation, thyroid deficiencies and delay in the maturation of the central nervous system in the fetus that are not reversible with feeding or any level of care after delivery. Deficiencies of vitamin A and folic acid produce growth retardation, abnormalties and fetal death.

There are 600 agents that are known to produce fetal abnormalties in laboratory animals, but only 20 that are known to produce defects in humans. Some of these substances and the associated sequelae are:

Anti-convulsants, especially phenytoin, trimethadione and paramethadione, are associated with the production of cleft palate, cardiac abnormalities, cranio-facial abnormalties, immature development of nails, fingers and toes, chromosomal aberrations, defects in the internal organs and mental deficiencies
Phenothiazines can produce an abnormal development of the eye (retinopathy)
Tetracyclines taken during the middle to the end of pregnancy produce a permanent staining of the teeth, defective enamel with caries and retarded bone growth; they are suspected of causing congenital cataracts
Streptomycin, gentamycin, kanamycin damage hearing and the labyrinth
Sulfonamides near delivery can produce severe jaundice
Propranolol can produce a slow heart rate and hypoglycemia in the fetus
Cortisone in high doses causes abnormalities such as cleft palate
I-131, used to treat maternal goitre, destroys the fetal thyroid gland
Triiodothyronine, propylthiouracil and methimazole cause goitre in the fetus
Salicylates such as aspirin in the latter stage of pregnancy can damage the brain of the fetus (kernicterus)
Nonsteroidal antiinflammatory drugs such as ibuprofen in the last three months of pregnancy (known to stimulate closure of ductus arteriosus, other cardiovascular effects unknown)
Maternal viral infections such as rubella (German measles) in the first three months; in 1964, 20,000 infants died or were permanently disabled due to intrauterine rubella infections

Lead is one of the most serious exposures during pregnancy, and it is common. For sources of lead around the house see Hazards of Childhood and Adolescence, chapter IV. Some of the occupational exposures to lead include auto workers and body shops, service stations, lead battery manufacturing and reprocessing, manufacture of ink, paints and pigments, electronics (soldering), and gray iron foundries. One need not be "on the line" to suffer lead toxicity—working in the atmosphere is sufficient. In any of these settings, no eating, drinking nor smoking should take place. Lead is carried from the hands to the mouth during all of these activities.

During pregnancy the only safe course is to take no drugs, including alcohol and nicotine.

Good, professional prenatal management should be instituted early in pregnancy, not merely after the third month. The first three months are the most critical as far as development of the infant is concerned, and this period is frequently neglected. Very often women wait to be certain that a pregnancy exists before scheduling a visit with the physician. All too often a couple view the need for professional guidance as involving only the actual delivery of the infant. Pregnancy and the growth of the fetus are viewed as a natural process that will proceed without any assistance or interference. This benign neglect frequently results in children with congenital malformations. Aside from abstaining from drugs, good nutrition is essential. This can be provided by 1500 calories daily where weight is a problem. Nutrition must be attended to early in pregnancy, preferably starting with day one. Ground lost in the early months is very difficult to regain, especially as pregnancy progresses.

The hemoglobin level always drops about one gram in the last three months due to dilution of the blood by the fetal circulation. There is a serious risk of complications at delivery when hemoglobin levels fall to eleven grams or below. Overeating and eating junk food can be just as harmful as undernutrition. Total weight gain during pregnancy should be between eighteen and twenty-two pounds. Excessive weight gain runs the risk of toxemia of pregnancy with its threat to both the mother and the fetus.

Exercise takes on added urgency during pregnancy. Proper and adequate excercise facilitates good circulation and reduces the risk of phlebitis, and keeps the heart and lungs "tuned up."


## NURSING

In general, antibiotics, antihistamines, alkaloids, isoniazid and chlorpromazine that are taken by the mother are delivered to the infant in a higher concentration than is present in her tissues. Barbiturates, sulfonamides, diuretics and penicillin are delivered in the milk at an equal concentration. Nursing is generally not permitted when the mother is taking atropine, oral anticoagulants (coumarin and phenindione), antithyroid drugs, anticancer drugs, laxatives, iodides, mercurials, narcotics, radioactive drugs, bromides (sleeping and nerve medications, most available without prescription), ergot (for migraine headaches), tetracyclines and metronidazole (for trichomonas).


## INHERITED RISK FACTORS

G6PD (glucose-6-phosphate dehydrogenase)

Deficiency of this enzyme is a genetically transmitted metabolic disorder. It is X-linked (transmitted on the X chromosome), fully expressed in males and homozygous females, and variably expressed in heterozygous females. Ten to fifteen percent of American black males and one to two percent of American black females have this disorder. It is also seen in people from the Mediterranean basin, such as Italians, Greeks, Arabs and Sephardic Jews at a lower frequency than that seen in blacks. Hemolysis of the older red blood cells in the circulation, sometimes with a profound hemolytic anemia, occurs after exposure to certain drugs or other substances that cause oxidation of the hemoglobin and red blood cell membrane. More than forty substances are capable of provoking this response, including aspirin, sulfanilamides, nitrofurans, phenacetin, naphthalene, chloramphenicol, antimalarial drugs such as primaquine, some forms of vitamin K and fava beans.

Hemolytic anemia may also be precipitated in these individuals by acute viral and bacterial infections and by diabetic acidosis. Characteristic Heinz bodies may be seen in a blood smear early, but these are removed by the spleen, and a specific enzyme assay is the best test. Recovery occurs after removal from the offending agent.


## SICKLE CELL ANEMIA

This disorder is a chronic hemolytic anemia which occurs almost exclusively in blacks. Homozygous individuals have sickle cell disease (about 0.3 percent of blacks in the United States). Hemoglobin levels in these individuals usually run about 8 grams compared to a normal of 14 to 15 grams. Heterozygous individuals demonstrate the sickling trait but no anemia (8 to 13 percent of blacks in the United States). The frequency of the inherited gene is greatest in regions with a high prevalence of malaria, such as central Africa. About 30 percent of the population of Nigeria have inherited the trait. The inheritance of this form of hemoglobin provides some protection against one of the forms of malaria (falciparum). The individuals with this gene thus tended to survive onslaughts of malaria more successfully than those without the disease. This is a vivid example of the principle of the survival of the fittest.

Acute hemolytic episodes, which are variable in their occurrence, may be accompanied by thrombosis, infarction and pain. Episodes of severe abdominal pain with vomiting may mimic an acute abdominal problem such as appendicitis. There is no treatment for this disorder, and many patients die during childhood of pulmonary emboli, renal failure, intercurrent infections or thrombosis of an artery to a vital structure.

## ALPHA-1-ANTITRYPSIN DEFICIENCY

Homozygous expression of this disorder is rare. About 10 to 15 percent of the population demonstrate a heterozygous deficiency, which results in a mild impairment of the ability to inactivate proteolytic enzymes in the lung. Proteolytic enzymes are released in the lung by the alveolar macrophage as a defense against bacteria and other foreign substances. Normally these enzymes are inactivated by alpha-1-antitrypsin before the enzyme damages the lung tissue. Deficiency of this substance permits accumulation of the enzyme with resultant damage to the lung tissue.

These individuals may develop emphysema by middle age, even in the absence of exposure to dust and other substances that might damage the lung. The disease progresses even more rapidly and to a more severe stage in the presence of exposure to dusts and all of the substances that tend to affect the airways adversely. The emphysema progresses to chronic obstructive lung disease, which is a major cause of disability and death. Chronic obstructive lung disease is second only to heart disease as a cause of death in the United States. It is found in 15 percent of older men and 10 percent of women. The mortality rate from this affliction has been doubling every five years.

Measurement of the level of this substance is easily done by a blood test, and this should be done in any individual with an unusual degree of problem with bronchitis. It should be done early in such cases, and should be determined in anyone with a family history of bronchitis, emphysema or chronic obstructive lung disease.

## MALIGNANT HYPERTHERMIA

This is a genetic, inherited disorder marked by the onset of an acute, life-threatening hyperthermia following the administration of any of the commonly used inhalation anesthetics. It is discussed in chapter XI, Hazards of Temperature Extremes.

# VI

# Hazards of Food and Water

## ADDITIVES

At the turn of the century there were no laws governing the adulteration of food by chemicals and preservatives. Additives which were commonly used included boric acid (which is very toxic to the liver), salicylic acid and formaldehyde. While these agents were effective in prolonging the shelf life of food, they lacked similar benefits with regard to the health of humans.

The Food and Drug Act that was passed in 1906 resulted from the efforts of a chemist, Dr. Harvey W. Wiley. Several additions and amendments have been tacked on over the years, but many of these later efforts have been marked by the confusion and inconsistencies typical of legislative bodies. Some of the confusion results from the phraseology, such as a sentence composed of one hundred thirty-five words in the Federal Food, Drug and Cosmetic Act of 1976. Much confusion also results from the scattering of regulations among various sections of the law and among various bureaucracies.

The Environmental Protection Agency, for instance, has waged a relentless campaign to remove lead from our gasoline and from shotgun shells. One would assume that at least as much concern would be expressed for the lead that leaches into our soup from the soldered seams of the cans. The corrosion that is seen at this seam on the inside of the can is not comforting. Fortunately some of the food industry is moving to eliminate this threat.

Some companies have been using extruded cans for several years. These cans can be recognized by the absence of a seam along the length of the can and at the bottom. The only seam is where the lid is joined to the body of the can. The bottom of the can is slightly rounded at the bottom margin, and is continuous with the side. More recently many companies have switched to a welded seam in the can, which also eliminates the contamination of the food with lead. Some of these cans are marked as welded, but even when not marked the seam can be readily identified, especially when compared with the soldered seam of the soup can. The welded seam has been ground on the outside of the can and presents an even, ground appearance.

The soldered seam, on the other hand, is an irregular, crimped seam. If you look carefully you can see the small beads of solder. You can also scrape some of the soft solder off with a knife. There has been no excuse for using soldered cans for the past several years, since the technology to eliminate this risk has been available. Lead from soldered seams is a particular risk in highly acid foods such as tomatoes and many soups.

Another source of lead in food comes from improperly glazed dishes, cups and pitchers. The hazard results when the temperature during firing is not high enough to properly seal the lead in the glaze and the lead in some pigments. Highly acid foods and beverages then leach some of the lead out of the glaze. Tomato containing foods and orange and other fruit juices are particularly active in this respect. Decals on the inside of cocktail glasses have also been a source of lead contamination of drinks.

Most of the incriminated lead containing dinnerware has been imported. The Food and Drug Administration has issued twelve recalls of imported dinnerware since 1982. These materials came from Italy, Spain, the Netherlands, Hungary, Mexico, Taiwan and Thailand. One of the most recent recalls by the FDA was in July of 1987, and involved an expensive line of dinnerware from Palermo, Italy. The FDA invoked more stringent standards in 1971, but domestic dinnerware manufactured prior to that continues to be a source of lead poisoning. Even dinnerware and coffee mugs that are properly fired and safe at purchase can be rendered hazardous by washing in the dishwasher. The glaze is eroded by the strong cleaners in automatic dishwasher detergents, releasing the lead in the pigments beneath. Moonshine whiskey continues to be an occasional source of lead intoxication, being leached out of the soldered joints of the still.

In the summer of 1987 lead poisoning in six adults and one child, all relatives in a family in New York, was reported to the Centers for Disease Control. The source of the lead was a homemade beverage that was stored in a ceramic bean jug that had been brought back from Mexico. Numerous cases of lead poisoning traced to imported ceramic ware have been reported. These cases are especially serious when they involve children since they can result in permanent brain damage. In 1988 the Food and Drug Administration signed an agreement with the People's Republic of China that will safeguard against unsafe ceramic ware being imported from that source. Japan had already instituted such safety precautions. Items that are brought back by individuals from vacations or business trips are not monitored and continue to be a risk.

Mexico is the most common source of unsafe ceramic ware because much of these products are made in small operations rather than factories. They also are frequently not imported in large shipments that can be monitored, but are brought back by tourists or relatives of residents in the United States. Any suspect ceramic ware can be tested for lead by most local laboratories. A qualitative test is simple and inexpensive. If you have difficulty in finding a laboratory that will do this test for you, contact the local health department for assistance.

Even low levels of lead present a serious threat to children. Lead produces mental retardation in infants and infertility in women. Any quantity of lead that is consumed by a pregnant woman presents a threat of damage to the developing fetus. It affects the brain less in the adult, but may result in personality changes. Lead produces serious damage to the kidneys. The decline in the fertility and vitality of the Romans has been attributed to the lead in their pewter dishes and drinking utensils. Contemporary pewter should have no lead, being composed of tin, copper and antimony. It has been discovered recently that harmful effects to the various organs of the body can occur at levels below what has been considered acceptable in the past. This will require some reassessment of test results.

Federal authorities have expressed considerable concern recently over the discovery that lead has been found to be leached out of soldered joints into the water supply. This has occurred in areas where the acidity of the water is unusually high. Soft water supplies erode soldered joints to a lessor degree, and this is not a problem in most homes. The lead consumed from this source is much less than that consumed from foods. If you are concerned about the lead content of the household drinking water it can be readily measured. If any question exists regarding this threat, do not use hot water for cooking and drinking. As an added precaution, run the cold water for a short period each morning to flush out the lines as a simple precautionary measure.

Federal agencies have mandated that ordinary solder be replaced with so-called tin solder, or lead-free solder, in the plumbing of all new construction. The solder widely available and used up to the present is a mixture of tin and lead, usually in a 50–50 proportion. A eutectic mixture of tin and lead (the mixture that melts at the lowest temperature) is 63 percent tin and 37 percent lead. This proportion flows best, provides the strongest joint and seals most efficiently. Any significant deviation from this formula results in very difficult soldering and very poor results, as many of us discovered during and after World War II, when tin was in short supply. Solders introduced to meet the new federal demand are composed either of 95 percent tin and 5 percent antimony, or a mixture of zinc, silver and antimony in the tin base. They cost about twice as much as the conventional solder. It remains to be seen how satisfactory and durable the new solder will be (See Soldering, chapter III).

Over 2500 substances are added to food to render it more tasty, more creamy, smoother, or a more appealing color. Many of these substances are not harmful (ascorbic acid, calcium gluconate, lecithin, carnauba wax), some are known to carry a risk, and others are yet to be categorized. Coloring agents are used for the sole purpose of rendering the product more pleasing to the eye; they serve no other purpose. With the exception of caramel, all of the widely used food coloring agents are synthetic substances, so-called coal tar dyes for the most part. Butter yellow, which was found to be highly toxic and to cause cancer in the liver and urinary bladder, was removed from the market place in 1919, after years of acceptance and use. In 1960 FD&C orange number 1 and number 2 were removed from the market for their toxicity to internal organs, and red number 1 for causing liver cancer. Yellow numbers 1, 2, 3 and 4 all were removed as a result of intestinal lesions and heart damage in humans. Red number 4 and citrus red number 2 were markedly restricted in what they could be used for. FD&C violet number 1 was banned in 1973.

Ironically the FDA banned the use of red number 2 (amaranth) in 1976 as a result of great pressure from the press and the Congress. This pressure was generated as a result of misinformation and a botched experiment. Red number 40, a substance about which we know much less to this day, was substituted. Extensive retesting of all currently approved food colors is underway, and nearing completion. This is an effort by the FDA to establish the safety of all approved colors, and to eliminate provisional approval status.

By 1973 allergists were reporting a growing number of hypersensitivity reactions among patients, especially asthmatics, resulting from food dyes such as red number 3 and yellow number 5 (tartrazine). Similar reactions to preservatives such as sodium benzoate were also recorded. More recently sulfites (sodium sulfite, sodium and potassium bisulfite, sodium metabisulfite) have been identified as having caused severe reactions, including life threatening reactions, in many asthmatics and sensitive individuals. The sulfites were widely used in salads and wine and on fresh fruits and shellfish to maintain freshness. Approximately 11,000 drugs contain sulfites as preservatives.

The Food and Drug Administration banned the use of sulfites in fresh fruits and vegetables effective in August, 1986. This restriction applies to salad bars also. Sulfites may still be present in many foods served in restaurants, such as seafood, sauces, soups, coleslaw and sauerkraut. Individuals who are sensitive to sulfites must exercise the same precautions as those who are allergic to seafood. Sulfites are much more pervasive than seafoods, however. As of January 1, 1987 all packaged foods containing 10 parts per million or more of sulfites must be so labeled.

Sodium nitrate and sodium nitrite have been widely used as preservatives for a long time. They have been very effective in preventing the production of botulism toxin in foods such as sausage and lunch meats. These additives are also being phased out because of concern over their role in the production of nitrosamines in the stomach. Nitrosamines are among the most dangerous cancer causing agents yet discovered. Most of our knowledge about them has been collected only since about 1960. They have the distinction of being one of the few substances that have caused cancer in every species of animal studied. In the past it has been very difficult to produce cancer of the stomach in experimental animals. This cancer can be readily induced in the stomach of the rhesus monkey with nitrosamines, however.

Several different nitrosamine compounds have been identified, and they each seem to be organ specific. One causes liver cancer, another lung cancer, another cancer of the urinary bladder. In addition to being formed by chemical action in the stomach, they are produced when cooking meats, especially in grilling. Several different nitrosamines are found in tobacco. There is strong suspicion that the nitrosamines in tobacco play a role in the production of cancer, especially cancer of the mouth caused by smokeless tobacco. Potassium nitrate (saltpeter) has also recently been discontinued as a food additive.

Monosodium glutamate (MSG) is a common food additive, seen chiefly in meats and meat dishes, and it has become well known for the "Chinese Restaurant Syndrome" that it precipitates in some people. This consists of a burning sensation throughout the body, headache and chest pain. It appears to be dose related, and varies considerably among individuals.

Brominated vegetable oil was widely used in soft drinks to prevent deterioration of flavor until about 1981. Concern over its potential to cause cancer prompted its discontinuance. Brominated compounds in general are suspect in the production of cancer.

Several nonintentional additives find their way into our food indirectly. One of the most common, and one of great concern, is antibiotics. Cattle are frequently administered antibiotics to treat various illnesses. Both beef cattle and poultry are raised on feed that almost always contains antibiotics. Commercial growers have learned that better production of meat is thus achieved, and fewer episodes of illness encountered. The problem is that these antibiotics are retained and are present in the meat when it is consumed. This can be a problem for those individuals who are allergic to them. Of even greater concern is the problem of resistant strains of bacteria emerging as a result of this common practice. We cannot develop new antibiotics fast enough to keep ahead of the emerging resistant strains. The cultivation of resistant strains in growing our beef leaves us defenseless when these strains cause disease in humans.

Other substances are also commonly fed to cattle, pigs and poultry to stimulate greater growth. One of the best known is estrogen, which increases growth in poultry. This has been discontinued after the extensive publicity about the cancer risks of this practice. Other growth promoting substances continue to be used, however, with no assurance of their safety. All of these substances undergo enzymatic transformation in the animal that may render them even more hazardous to humans upon consumption.

Other potentially harmful nonintentional additives include:

Animal and insect feces and parts
Microorganisms (bacteria, fungi)
Parasitic organisms
Toxic metals and their compounds
Glass
Toxic chemicals such as solvents

Decaffeinated coffee continues to be a source of undesirable food additives in our diet. For many years trichloroethylene was used for removing the caffeine, until someone observed that this was also the substance used in dry cleaning our clothes. It had also been universally used in industry for degreasing metal parts until concern over liver toxicity prompted the substitution of trichloroethane, a substance with no less risk. Methylene chloride (dichloromethane) has been used for some time now to remove caffeine from coffee. While it has some less toxicity in the liver, recent revelations of its cancer causing potential have raised fresh concerns. The only safe process for decaffeinating coffee currently known is the so called "water process." This seems to be used only in Europe. Coffee shops carry several blends and types of coffee that have been decaffeinated by this safe process.

The discovery of aflatoxin in grain and milk samples in eight states in 1988 caused alarm because it had not previously surfaced in this food source. The contaminated corn had been fed to dairy cattle, and, as with most substances, it was passed on to the milk. Aflatoxin, which is one of the most potent cancer causing agents known, is produced by a fungus that usually grows when storage conditions are less than ideal. It has been found frequently in peanuts that are not stored properly, and has thus shown up in peanut butter for a long time. Peanuts are a staple in the diet of some African tribes, and a high incidence of cancer of the liver in these people has been attributed to aflatoxin.

## PESTICIDE RESIDUE

All fruits and vegetables grown commercially are subjected to repeated applications of pesticides. This greatly increases the yield (and thus reduces our cost) and enhances the quality of the food. Strict regulations exist governing what products may be used on food and how close to harvesting time they may be applied. These regulations are not always adhered to, as witnessed by the poisoning of over one thousand people when aldicarb (Temik) was illegally applied to melons (see Pesticides, chapter I). Some residual pesticide is likely to remain on any fruit or vegetable. Concern has been expressed over the possibility of some quantity being incorporated into the fruit itself. Such residue levels are controlled under Section 408 of the Food, Drug and Cosmetic Act. Most of what reaches our tables is not inspected nor measured, and it is only prudent to wash thoroughly all such products before consumption. Washing does not remove pesticides or other chemicals that are absorbed or incorporated into the fruit or vegetable, however. It is of some comfort to note that in the few instances where these foods have been tested, residues have been few and of low concentration.

# FOOD POISONING

So-called food poisoning can be caused by either eating a toxin that has been produced in a food or by an infection resulting from eating food or water that has been contaminated by microorganisms. Many thousands of cases are reported in the United States each year, and many thousand more are suffered or treated and not reported. The number of such cases has increased dramatically during the past decade. This may be due partly to the increase in the practice of eating away from home, and partly to the increase in travel. Too many people die from such diseases, and many people who are afflicted wonder if they are going to expire because of the severity of the symptoms and the suffering.

Virtually every case of food poisoning could have been prevented very simply by adequate cooking and by proper storage and handling of food. The latter includes the simple measures of hand washing and the wearing of latex or vinyl disposable gloves by food handlers. We have become very complacent in the United States because of the extremely high level of sanitation and refrigeration that we have achieved.

The practice of permitting meat products, particularly an item as bulky as a turkey, to cool slowly at room temperature prior to refrigeration provides the opportunity for organisms such as salmonella to reproduce. Under the same conditions, Clostridia bacteria produce spores, which are very difficult to destroy. Destruction of these spores requires a temperature of 248 degrees Fahrenheit for thirty minutes, and thus can be accomplished only in a pressure cooker. Foods that are canned without the destruction of these bacteria present the potential for the production of botulism toxin. Staphylococcus organisms in these circumstances produce a potent toxin in the food, on the spot. This toxin is not destroyed by brief rewarming. Eating the food results in a severe illness two to four hours later.

Contrary to what we have been led to believe, all such foods should be placed in the refrigerator or freezer and cooled as rapidly as possible, as soon as possible. Refrigerator temperatures must be no higher than 40 degrees Fahrenheit, preferably lower. The temperature in the freezer must be 0 degrees Fahrenheit or below. There is no way to be assured that adequate temperatures have been maintained without an accurate thermometer. Every homeowner should keep a thermometer in both the refrigerator and the freezer.

Meats are the most critical foods with regard to refrigeration, both because of the presence of harmful bacteria that may multiply, and because of the tendency for this food to deteriorate at temperatures above 0 degrees Fahrenheit. Fresh meat should be kept in the refrigerator no longer than two to three days before use. Ground meat should be used within twenty-four hours. It should be kept in mind that ground meat is a particularly good growth medium for bacteria. It should be handled as little as possible. Use of disposable gloves in handling this food minimizes bacterial contamination. Meat left sitting at 45 degrees or above may be unfit for consumption after as little as two to three hours.

Even at temperatures below 0 degrees Fahrenheit meat cannot be kept indefinitely. Flavor will deteriorate before spoilage occurs at these low temperatures. Adherence to the following tables assures retention of flavor and absence of microbial growth, if the freezer temperature is kept at 0 degrees Fahrenheit or below:

| | |
|---|---|
| most beef (except ground) | 6–12 months |
| poultry, including turkey | 6 months |
| ground meat, minimal handling | 3–4months |
| pork | 3–6 months |
| ham | 2 months |
| lamb and veal | 6–8 months |
| fish | 6–8 months |
| shrimp | 3 months |
| vegetables | 8–12 months |

After meat is removed from the freezer, it should not be left sitting at room temperature to thaw. If the size is reasonable, it can be thawed in the microwave oven prior to cooking. A large item such as a turkey should be thawed in the refrigerator over a period of twenty-four to forty-eight hours. In cooking, it is especially imperative after thawing frozen meats to be certain that the center of the meat reaches an adequate temperature for a sufficient period of time to assure destruction of disease causing organisms such as salmonella. The center of the meat must reach a temperature of at least 170 degrees Fahrenheit in order to accomplish this. A thermometer in the center of the meat is the best way to assure this.

Brief rewarming of foods is not sufficient to destroy some toxins produced by the bacteria in these foods. Some toxins are not destroyed by boiling (212 degrees Fahrenheit) for one hour. The toxin that is produced by staphylococcus bacteria can withstand this temperature for 20 minutes without losing its toxicity, and it is not inactivated by normal canning methods. The toxin of botulism, on the other hand, is destroyed by heating to 212 degrees Fahrenheit for 20 minutes. Keep in mind that this temperature is achieved by boiling only at sea level. Elevations of 700 to 800 feet, commonly seen in most of the midwestern states, do not make a significant difference. If you are backpacking in the Rockies at an elevation of 9,000 feet, however, you cannot achieve this high a temperature. A longer time will be required, therefore, in order to accomplish this same destruction of toxins or spores.

When more than one person who ate from a common source, or who ate the same food, become ill at about the same time, we can be reasonably certain that we are dealing with food poisoning. For instance when 57 percent of the 343 passengers on board a jet liner became ill, the illness was traced to a toxin produced in the food by a contaminating staphylococcus. The source of the staphylococcus was an infection on the finger of one of the food handlers who prepared the food.


## STAPHYLOCOCCUS

This is the most common food POISONING seen in the United States. The illness is caused by a toxin that is produced in food by staphylococcal organisms, usually when the food sits at room temperature. Refrigeration markedly reduces the production of this toxin. This toxin is heat stable and it is not destroyed by heating at 212 degrees Fahrenheit for 20 minutes. It is not uncommon for an outbreak to occur as a result of contamination of food by pus from an infected wound or pustule on the hands of a food preparer. Common foods involved in staphylococcus food poisoning are potato salad, cream pastries, meat dishes, especially ham, turkey and chicken, or any dish containing meat or egg products. These foods **SHOULD NOT** be left sitting at room temperature for any length of time. Food handlers should wear disposable latex or vinyl gloves when preparing these foods for the general public. This includes catering for any occasion and when preparing food for lunch counters, vending machines and the airlines.

Since this illness is caused by ingestion of a toxin that has already been produced, the onset of illness is much more rapid. Symptoms normally occur about two to six hours after eating the contaminated food. Characteristically, three-quarters of all of the people who eat the tainted food will experience symptoms. These include intense vomiting, lasting up to twenty-four hours. Antibiotics are of no value, since this is not an infection. Intravenous fluid and electrolyte therapy are required in severe cases, usually in about one-fourth of the victims. The organism is usually not recovered in the stool. The suspected food should be examined by health authorities, who have the expertise and technology to detect the presence of toxins.

Examination of food for bacteria or toxins should always be conducted when a food-borne illness is suspected. This is particularly important when several individuals who have eaten the same food become ill. In an outbreak at a country club in 1986 where over 800 people were served, one-third of them developed staphylococcal food poisoning. About one-third of those who became ill required emergency medical treatment. Staphylococcus was found in the nasal passages of two of the food handlers and in the stool of two. Staphylococcus was found in the turkey, which had been allowed to cool at room temperature for three hours. The Centers for Disease Control reported that the most likely source of the contamination of the food in this example was hands. Proper hand washing and the wearing of gloves for food preparation would have prevented the illness in these people.

## SALMONELLA (other than typhoid)

This species of bacteria is responsible for the most common food-borne infections in the United States. About 50,000 cases are reported to the Centers for Disease Control each year, a number which, as stated above, has been increasing. Many cases go unreported. The majority of cases result from the consumption of foods of animal origin, especially eggs and poultry. This is partially because these foods are commonly contaminated by salmonella in their natural form or in processing, and partially because these foods are good culture media for salmonella when inoculated by the hands of a carrier. Potato salad again is a common source of infection. Raw milk is also a source of infection. Unpasteurized milk carries many health risks, but it remains popular in isolated regions of the United States.

Salmonella organisms are found in virtually every animal species, and are found in all of the animals in the food chain of humans. There has been much publicity recently over the "discovery" that a large percentage (40 percent or higher) of chickens and turkeys are contaminated with salmonella organisms. This is partially due to feeding habits of these birds, which includes ingestion of each other's excrement. Rupture of the intestines or other careless handling techniques during processing spreads the organisms to the meat. This is a fact that has been well-known for the past forty years. It must be assumed that all meat from poultry contains salmonella, and appropriate precautions should be taken.

Since eggs are delivered through a common alimentary port, their shells are also commonly contaminated with salmonella. It is of interest that eggs contain a natural coating that inhibits the penetration of the egg by bacteria. This coating is readily removed by washing or by excess handling, permitting penetration of the shell by the salmonella. The organism then multiplies within the egg, particularly when stored at warm temperatures.

Outbreaks of infection from foods prepared from eggs, such as ice cream, omelets and scrambled eggs, have been reported with increased frequency. Investigation indicates that some of these outbreaks occur because the salmonella has invaded the egg. Failure to maintain cold storage during shipment permits the organism to multiply in the egg. Thorough cooking as well as proper handling can prevent these cases of food poisoning. Products such as eggnog should be pasteurized. Consumption of any product that incorporates raw eggs carries a distinct risk of serious and unpleasant illness.

Outbreaks of salmonella food poisoning involving as many as one hundred people have also resulted from consuming unshelled steamed shrimp in a restaurant. The simple expedient of having food handlers wear disposable plastic gloves while preparing such foods could prevent much suffering. Frequent hand washing, especially after handling poultry products, including eggs, would also prevent inoculating other foods with this organism. Faucet and refrigerator handles and counter tops that have been contaminated by poultry products should be thoroughly cleansed before handling other food products or utensils.

Poultry products must be kept properly refrigerated at all times. If a large mass of meat such as a turkey is placed in the refrigerator when it is hot, the center can remain warm enough for twenty-four hours to permit salmonella to multiply. In one elementary school 350 children and staff became ill with salmonella food poisoning after eating turkey salad. The Centers for Disease Control reported that the turkey had been deboned then stored in the refrigerator overnight in an eight-inch deep pan. The temperature inside any mass of meat this large can stay warm enough to allow bacterial growth. In order to assure that the center of the meat will be chilled promptly, turkey and ham should not exceed four inches in depth when placed in the refrigerator warm. The temperature in the refrigerator should be below 40 degrees Fahrenheit, and a thermometer should be kept in the refrigerator to monitor this.

Salmonella organisms reproduce in the intestinal tract of humans, establishing an infection that results in the gradual onset of fever and diarrhea about ten to thirty-six hours after the food has been eaten. Stool cultures demonstrate the organism. Antibiotics prolong the course of the disease and increase the risk of recurrence. Resistance has developed to most of the commonly used antibiotics. A new class of antibiotics recently introduced (quinolones) is effective against salmonella as well as many of the other organisms that cause diarrhea in man. If past experience is any indication, this breakthrough may not benefit us forever, since the development of resistance usually occurs. This is one of many diseases that is better and more easily prevented than treated.

## LISTERIA

Infections caused by this genus of bacteria have not been reported previously as a result of eating meat. A case that resulted from eating frankfurters that contained the organism was reported to the Centers for Disease Control in December 1988. Listeriosis mainly afflicts newborn infants, individuals past forty and those whose immune system has been compromised by diseases such as cirrhosis, lymphomas, other cancers and AIDS. It remains to be seen whether or not this case represents another instance where we are challenged by organisms that have not previously troubled us much.

## CLOSTRIDIUM PERFRINGENS

This is a bacterium which is widely distributed in feces, soil, air and water. It is the third most common cause of food poisoning in the United States. Outbreaks generally result from eating poultry, other meat, or meat products that have been partially cooked, but not long enough to kill all of the organisms. The meat is then allowed to cool at room temperature during which time the organisms multiply and produce a powerful enterotoxin. The meat is then refrigerated. Upon rewarming, the organisms and their toxin are not destroyed. These organisms also produce additional toxin in the intestinal tract after being ingested. Diarrhea with marked abdominal cramping and pain are experienced after a relatively short period, six to twelve hours. This is another unpleasant illness that illustrates the risks of allowing cooked meats to cool slowly at room temperature prior to refrigeration. The bacteria in such meats multiply and come back to haunt us.

## SHIGELLA

This is another group of bacteria that produce an infection in the intestine of humans resulting in diarrhea, often bloody. An abrupt onset of severe abdominal cramping with pronounced straining is common. Since this is an infection in the body, headache, fever, chills and aching are normally experienced. These symptoms are seen twenty-four to seventy-two hours after ingestion of the organisms. Antibiotics are helpful, but resistance to most of these has developed. The new class of antibiotics mentioned previously (quinolones) have proven effective against shigella in laboratory tests, but are not as yet (July 1989) approved for this use. Such approval should be forthcoming shortly. Drugs to relieve the cramps prolong the clinical course of the disease.

Approximately 24,000 cases of shigella infection are reported to the Centers for Disease Control each year. About 15 percent of the cases of diarrhea acquired by travelers in Mexico are caused by these organisms. Of fifteen cases of shigella infection among visitors to Cancun, Mexico during an eight-month period in 1988, eight were found to be resistant to the antibiotics commonly used for this disease. The practice of taking these medications prophylactically when traveling contributes to the development of resistance, and thus renders them less useful. For this reason most medical authorities now advise against this practice, recommending greater attention to avoidance of food and drink known to present a risk of acquiring these organisms, and to personal hygiene such as hand washing. Specific antibiotic treatment should be reserved for proven infections. Stool culture in these infections will reveal the causative agent and also determine what medications are effective.

## AMEBIASIS

Entamoeba histolytica is a protozoan that produces diarrheal disease in over 5,000 individuals in the United States each year. It

86

is spread from feces to mouth through poor sanitary practices (lack of hand washing), and by contamination of food and water. Fruits and vegetables, including salads, are commonly contaminated by carriers. The infection may be mild or may be marked by a pronounced diarrhea, cramping and flatulence. Abscesses in the liver and infection in the gallbladder are not uncommon. A subacute appendicitis may result, in which case surgery should be deferred until treatment has been instituted and the infection subsides. Stool examination may require special techniques which can be applied by any competent licensed laboratory. Treatment is available, but antibiotics are not helpful.

## BOTULISM

Perhaps the best known of all of the food poisonings, botulism results from a very potent toxin produced by the bacterium clostridium botulinum. Poisoning in adults results from consuming food in which the toxin has been produced after packaging, usually in a sealed container or in frozen fish. The toxin is readily destroyed by cooking the food for thirty minutes at 176 degrees Fahrenheit or by boiling for ten minutes. Regardless of this any food exhibiting evidence of spoilage should not be consumed. Any canned food that appears to be swollen from the internal production of gas should be discarded. Contaminated foods may appear and taste normal. Needless to say, any suspected food should **NOT** be taste tested. This is the most potent poison known to mankind. You must also take precautions to avoid contaminating your hands with any suspected food, particularly if any cuts or abrasions are present.

In contrast to the toxin produced by the clostridium organisms, their spores, which are widespread in nature, can survive boiling water for several hours. These spores can produce toxin even under refrigeration, and this has been seen in frozen fish many times. The spores are destroyed in a pressure canner after thirty minutes at fifteen pounds of pressure, or after twenty minutes at twenty pounds of pressure (278 Fahrenheit). This is the only system that should be utilized in home canning, particularly of low acid foods such as fruits, vegetables, meats, fish, peppers and mushrooms. Home canned foods account for most of the cases of botulism in the United States, since there is minimal chance that the spores will survive commercial canning processes.

The number of cases of botulism that result from eating in restaurants has been increasing however (forty-two percent of reported cases between 1976 and 1984). These cases frequently result from home-canned low acid foods such as peppers and mushrooms that have been acquired by the restaurant from an individual. Illness and even deaths have resulted in recent years from type E botulism as a result of eating ribyetz or kapchunka, which is ungutted whole whitefish. Smoked freshwater fish such as gelfite has also been associated with type E botulism. The organism is known to survive in the gut of these fish, and the consumption of smoked or salted uncooked fish carries this risk. The fish tastes and smells normal.

Of the 123 cases of botulism reported in 1984, 99 cases occurred in infants. This occurs most frequently among infants two to three months old. Unlike the adult cases, those among infants result from the production of toxin in the stomach of the child by the organism after it is swallowed. This occurs by virtue of the fact that the immature digestive system is unable to inhibit the activity of the organism. Honey used in preparing formula has been responsible for numerous cases, and this should never be fed to a child of less than one year of age. Other sources identified have been contamination of food by soil or vacuum cleaner dust. Careful cleaning of the breast should always precede breast feeding of infants in order to minimize the risk of this disease.

Botulism carries a high mortality if not properly treated. Hospitalization is essential, and reduces mortality to below ten percent. Vomiting and neurological symptoms such as blurred or double vision, dry mouth and sagging of the eyelids appear twelve to thirty-six hours after ingesting the contaminated food. Weakness of the muscles of the arms and legs then sets in. Diarrhea is rare with this disease because of the paralytic effect of the toxin on the nerves that mediate the intestinal activity. The poison is a potent toxin to the nervous system and paralysis of respiration is life threatening.


## VIBRIO PARAHAEMOLYTICUS

This organism causes a bacterial diarrhea and is acquired from seafood, particularly shrimp and crab. The practice of eating these foods with only brief cooking increases the risk. Frequently outbreaks have occurred as a result of contamination of cooked shellfish in a kitchen by shellfish that has not yet been cooked. Several outbreaks have occurred on cruise ships. An inspection of cruise ships in early 1989 revealed that half failed to meet acceptable sanitary and food handling standards. Cruise ships are not subject to the inspection and regulation by local health departments that apply to restaurants, and have thus delivered a higher incidence of food-borne illnesses. The incidence of this disease is much higher in Japan due to the common practice of eating uncooked seafood.

The disease is ushered in by acute diarrhea and moderately severe abdominal cramping, about six to forty-eight hours after eating the infected food. Vomiting is seen in approximately one-third of the victims. The organism grows both in the seafood and in the human gut and produces a toxin in both sites. No deaths have occurred in the United States as a result of this infection.

Several cases of the more serious Vibrio cholerae resulting from eating oysters harvested off the coast of Louisiana were reported in 1988. This disease, which is endemic in Asia, the Middle East and Africa, is very uncommon in the United States. This has been accomplished by high public health standards for water supplies and sanitation disposal.


## RED TIDE

During the months of May to October, conditions are favorable for the reproduction of certain dinoflagellates that are part of the marine phytoplankton in the coastal waters of the United States. When the organisms reproduce in great numbers they turn the water a reddish color as they reside suspended near the surface, thus the name "red tide." They produce a very potent nerve toxin, and when bivalve mollusks such as clams, oysters, scallops and mussels feed on them, the shellfish accumulate and concentrate the nerve toxin.

When humans consume the contaminated shellfish they may experience numbness of the face, arms and legs with muscular weakness, diarrhea, nausea and vomiting. These symptoms may begin in as brief an interval as thirty minutes. In severe cases of this "paralytic shellfish poisoning" paralysis, respiratory arrest and death may occur. This latter sequela is more comon in the Pacific Northwest and New England coastal waters than in the Gulf Coast. In some of these areas a quarantine against harvesting shellfish is placed in effect during the months when this activity is common. Gathering shellfish during these periods of quarantine is likely to result in great suffering or worse. Not all toxic shellfish originate from "red tide" areas, and not all such reddish areas contain toxic dinoflagellates. It is essential for residents of these areas to heed the posted warnings of health authorities, regardless of personal observations.


## SCOMBROID FISH POISONING

This poisoning results from eating improperly handled dark-meated fish including tuna, albacore, bonito, bluefish, mackeral and mahi mahi. When these fish are not refrigerated or placed on ice immediately and continuously after being caught, bacteria in the fish convert the amino acid histidine to histamine. Since histamine taken by mouth is metabolized in the intestine it is normally not toxic even in large doses. Other elements produced by the bacteria in the fish thus are necessary to produce the toxicity. Researchers have postulated that other toxins are produced that either inhibit the metabolism of the histamine, or otherwise enhance its absorption. These elements have not been identified as yet.

In any event, cooking does not destroy the toxins. The only means of preventing the disease is by prompt and continuous icing or refrigeration of all dark meated fish. No change in appearance, smell or taste can be relied upon. The history of the handling of imported fish of this class cannot be readily obtained, thus consumption carries an obvious risk. One must rely upon the integrity of the supplier.

The onset of illness occurs from one to several hours after consumption of the fish. Symptoms include nausea, abdominal cramping, diarrhea, sweating, redness of the face and burning of the mouth and throat. More severe allergic-like symptoms typical of excessive histamine levels may occur. Prompt medical attention is urgent.


## CIGUATERA FISH POISONING

This is distinct from scromboid poisoning. It has afflicted large numbers of diners in restaurants in Florida, Puerto Rico, Cuba and the Virgin Islands. The illness results from a toxin, or more likely a mixture of toxins, produced by a single-celled plant similar to the one that produces the red tides. This plant and its toxin, however, do not float near the surface and cannot be observed. Fish consume the plant as they feed on algae attached to coral. These fish are then consumed by larger fish such as barracuda and yellowfin grouper, resulting in a high concentration of the toxin in these species. As with scombroid poisoning, this toxin also is not destroyed by cooking.

In excess of 400 different species of fish have been reported to cause ciguatera poisoning, including barracudas, groupers, jacks parrotfish, sea basses, snappers, surgeonfish, wrasses and eels. The toxin occurs only in warm waters and only in certain regions. These regions cannot be predicted, however, and it cannot be safely ascertained where any given fish have been feeding. This is particularly true of the high risk barracuda, yellowfin grouper and hogfish. It is unsafe to eat any of the native fish caught in the waters around the Virgin Islands. Virtually every resident who has done so has experienced this disease. Some aggressive restaurateurs in Florida have been known to sell barracuda as red snapper, which presents the potential for a very unpleasant surprise besides the price.

Symptoms include abdominal cramping, nausea, vomiting and diarrhea that may persist from eight to eighteen hours. Headache, face pain and muscle pain are also experienced. Numbness and tingling may persist for months. There is no specific treatment available.

## VIRUS

Diarrhea resulting from viral enteritis is attributable to two categories for the most part. **Rotavirus** includes a group of agents that causes disease worldwide, mainly in infants and young children. It is frequently seen in adults, however, especially family members of younger children who have the disease. It is also seen in older people and in immunodeficient individuals (such as in AIDS patients). This disease, which occurs mainly during the winter months in the United States, is the chief cause of diarrhea that results in severe dehydration and hospitalization in children. It can be fatal in young children if adequate fluids and electrolytes are not administered. Administration of oral rehydration solutions, such as the World Health Organization's solution, is usually adequate in all but the severely ill. There is no specific treatment for the virus.

The rotavirus replicates only in the small intestine, where it causes significant damage to the lining by destroying the cells there. This results in impairment of the normal absorption of nutrients, which accounts for the diarrhea and dehydration. Large numbers of the virus are shed in the stool, and the disease is spread from hands to mouth by virtue of this. Adequate hand washing after visiting the bathroom or changing diapers could prevent virtually all of these cases. The failure of this most basic personal hygiene measure accounts for the spread of this virus as a food borne disease. Contamination of drinking water by improper handling or treatment of sewage is another common soure of infection.


NORWALK AGENT

This is the other category of viruses causing diarrheal disease, and this includes a variety of related viruses, most of which have not been fully defined. The Snow Mountain agent and the Marin Agent are two examples of viruses in this group that have been recognized to cause disease. These agents are about one-half the size of the rotaviruses, and they cannot be grown in cell cultures nor in laboratory animals. They are also shed in the stool but in much smaller quantities than is the rotavirus. As a consequence, our knowledge of this group is extremely limited and incomplete.

In contrast to the rotaviruses, the Norwalk Agent causes diarrheal disease all year long, not seasonally. There is serological evidence of a previous infection in 60 to 70 percent of adults worldwide. The Norwalk Agent accounts for about one-third of all of the epidemics of acute gastroenteritis in the United States. Many of these have been related to food items such as oysters, salads and ice in beverages. Outbreaks on cruise ships, in nursing homes, summer camps and schools have been traced to contamination of the water supply. Spread of this disease is also by fecal contamination of water or of food by improperly washed hands.

The Norwalk Agent group cause a less serious illness in infants than does the rotavirus group. Malabsorption also occurs in this disease, but is less severe. This virus also replicates only in the small intestine (jejunem), but no one has been able to demonstrate the precise cells where this takes place. The vomiting and diarrhea begin approximately twenty-four to seventy-two hours after consumption of the contaminated food or water. This persists for about twenty-four to forty-eight hours. There is no specific treatment, no test to demonstrate the disease, and no immunity following infection. For this latter reason, a vaccine is unlikely.

In the fall of 1987, following a college football game in Pennsylvania, 158 students were treated at the health center for nausea, vomiting, diarrhea, fever, chills, headache and aching. Fifty-five members of the team later developed the same complaints after exposure to ice from the same source. These symptoms began about thirty-six hours after the game. A virus of the Norwalk group was identified as the cause of illness. Two days later an outbreak of acute diarrheal disease struck a group of 750 people attending a fund-raising event in Delaware.

In both outbreaks the disease was traced to drinks that contained contaminated ice that had been purchased from the same manufacturer in Pennsylvania. The source of water for the manufacturer of this ice was wells that had been flooded two weeks previously by a stream following heavy rains. Several residents along the stream who draw their water from wells also developed the disease. The ice had been sold in Pennsylvania, Delaware and New Jersey. A total of 5,000 people became ill as a result of this distribution of ice. Disinfection of the wells ended the outbreak. (Case report from the Centers for Disease Control.)


## SUSHI

Unlike the seafood illnesses produced by heat stable toxins, all of the parasitic infestations from fish can be prevented readily by adequate cooking.


## ANASAKIASIS

This is a parasitic infestation caused by the ingestion of a small white worm, 1 millimeter in diameter and 1.5 to 2.5 centimeters in length. It is found in haddock, mackeral, cod, pike, herring, bonita, salmon, squid, Alaskan pollack and Pacific red snapper. It occurs only in fish that share waters with dolphins, whales, seals, porpoises and other large sea mammals. It is common in Japan and some parts of Europe, but has been reported with increasing frequency in the United States with the rising popularity of sushi.

After ingestion, the worms burrow into the lining of the stomach and small intestine where they produce tumorlike granulomas. They may penetrate the intestinal wall and invade other organs. The typical case produces fever, vomiting and abdominal pain and tenderness. Peritonitis and intestinal obstruction can occur. Diagnosis is difficult unless the worm is seen in vomitus, since no test exists to detect it. The admonition to examine the sushi visually to manually remove the worms, then chew well to destroy the remaining parasites is appropriate if one is adventuresome. Otherwise, cooking is advisable. Consumption of uncooked seafood carries a significant risk of contracting this and a number of other diseases. No treatment is available to eradicate the worm, as is true of many parasites.

## DIPHYLLOBOTHRIUM LATUM

The fish tapeworm is acquired by eating inadequately cooked freshwater fish. Salmon has been incriminated in the Northwest. The organism is present in fish in the United States in Florida, the Great Lakes region and along the Pacific Coast. The increased contamination of bodies of water by sewage has increased the incidence of the disease. The recent popularity of sushi has also resulted in an increase in the number of cases reported. Symptoms are mild in most cases, consisting of mild abdominal discomfort. Treatment is available although it entails some risk.

## ENTEROTOXIGENIC E. COLI

This bacterium is the most common cause of traveler's diarrhea, accounting for between 50 and 75 percent of the cases. It is rarely acquired in the United States, although outbreaks among newborns in nurseries in the U.S. have occurred, with disastrous results. E. coli grows normally in the intestinal tract of humans, but these pathogenic strains produce a toxin that results in diarrhea and vomiting about twenty-four to seventy-two hours after eating. Agents to relieve the abdominal cramping are useful. Little is known or understood about the production of toxins by some strains of this common intestinal organism in humans, and why the problem is rampant in some countries.

## TRAVELER'S DIARRHEA

Virtually all cases of traveler's diarrhea are caused by consumption of food or water, including ice, contaminated by feces. The hands are frequently the transportation agent. Obviously all of these cases could be prevented. Hand washing would eliminate much of the problem, particularly in the case of those waiters who serve your soup with their thumb in the bowl. Especially risky foods are raw vegetables and raw or inadequately cooked meat and seafood. Salads, ice in beverages, milk and desserts should be avoided when traveling to areas of risk. Foods that are served hot are safer than those served cold. Avoid buffet food that is served at room temperature. Food from street vendors has been responsible for many outbreaks. Carbonated bottled beverages are generally considered safe. Purified bottled water is available in most areas, and this should be the sole source of water for consumption, face washing, brushing teeth and for enemas and douches. For the latter, packaged preparations carried from home are much safer.

Enterotoxigenic E. Coli account for somewhere between 50 and 75 percent of the cases of traveler's diarrhea. Shigella organisms account for approximately fifteen percent of the cases from Mexico. Various viruses, amoeba and Giardia together are responsible for fewer than 10 percent of cases. Most cases of simple traveler's diarrhea can be resolved in a reasonable period of time without serious consequences. Amebiasis, shigellosis, salmonellosis and hepatitis are far more serious illnesses, however. The prevention of these diseases assigns great urgency to strict adherence to frequent handwashing and other hygienic measures outlined above.

Much advice has been dispensed about what drugs the traveler should take with him to deal with this vexing and common problem. It has been common practice for physicians to prescribe trimethoprim/sulfamethoxisole (Bactrim or Septra) or doxycycline (Vibramycin) for their patients to take prophylactically when traveling outside of the United States. Unfortunately, antibiotics worsen some types of diarrheal diseases. This practice has also led to the bacteria developing a resistance to these drugs, so that they become useless when the treatment of infection is needed. Another problem with such prophylactic use is the development of sensitivities to the drugs by the traveler. This has been a particular problem with sulfa preparations. The most common reaction is skin rash, but nausea may also develop. Doxycycline (Vibramycin) also produces a photosensitivity that makes the traveler much more susceptible to sunburn.

As of early 1989, the consensus among medical experts is that antibiotics should not be taken prophylactically when traveling; rather they should be reserved to treat any infection that might occur. This was the recommendation of the National Institute of Health Consensus Conference on Travelers' Diarrhea in 1985, and it has gained general approval in the medical world since. Drugs to relieve the painful cramping also may worsen some infections. The new group of antibiotics mentioned previously (quinolones) appears to be effective against all of the organisms that commonly cause traveler's diarrhea. If this proves to be the case, this is a much welcome addition to a long-time plague to travelers. They should be reserved for proven cases of infections, however. Otherwise they will become as useless as some of the previously effective agents have. Pepto-Bismol in a dose of two tablespoonsful four times daily gives relief and does not interfere with recovery from any of the diseases. In recent studies it has been shown to be more effective than antibiotics in eliminating Campylobacter infections. Several studies and clinical trials of this subject are currently underway.

In any case of prolonged vomiting or diarrhea, replacement of fluids and electrolytes (sodium, chloride and potassium) is essential. This may be done by mouth if vomiting does not preclude this approach. These solutions are sold in drugstores, or they may be mixed much more economically by following the World Health Organization formula. This latter formula has saved thousands of lives in developing nations.

In any instance where vomiting or diarrhea persist for longer than twenty-four hours, or in the event of a high fever or bloody stool, medical attention should be sought. This is a difficult problem when outside of the United States. Directories of physicians outside of the United States are available from travel agencies and health authorities. The traveler also can seek assistance at the U.S. Consulate. Local health departments have personnel who have current information on travel conditions throughout the world. It is advisable to consult with these authorities, either directly or through your physician, regarding conditions at your travel destination. They can advise you as to what immunizations and other prophylactic measures are recommended. Make these contacts at least three months prior to departure in order to allow adequate time to complete all necessary measures.

The enormous growth of the restaurant and fast food industry in the United States over the past two decades is abundantly in evidence as you drive through the streets of your hometown. This growth stems in large measure from the affluence that has been achieved by the middle- and working-class of our society. Many families who never ate in a restaurant a generation ago now eat out on a regular basis. A considerable proportion of this increased expenditure at food establishments is contributed by teenagers, who also enjoy a level of wealth unimaginable a generation ago.

That we do not suffer the level of food-related diseases experienced by some other societies is a testimonial to the public health laws and endeavors of the state and local governments. These have evolved over the past fifty years to the present commendable levels. In spite of this, many thousands of food-borne illnesses are reported each year. A study of the many outbreaks clearly illustrates the need for greater efforts in public education regarding these risks, and how to avoid them. Such education should be instilled at home, but certainly this subject deserves attention in the public schools equal to that for sex education and the hazards of AIDS.

Even the most intense public educational effort will fail, however, if a strong sense of responsibility is not instilled at home. No level of effort by the school system or the government can compensate for the shortcomings of parenthood that neglects its obligations. As representative from the Centers for Disease Control recently remarked, "How do you arrest people for not washing their hands?" It should not be necessary to even pose the question.


## WATER

Prior to 1900 typhoid epidemics were a commonplace annual occurrence in virtually every city in the United States. Cholera epidemics imported from Asia repeatedly struck both the United States and England. These two water-borne diseases accounted for many deaths and much suffering. These epidemics resulted from the contamination of food and drinking water by the excrement of infected individuals. The incidence and severity of such epidemics became more intense as the population density increased following industrialization of the United States. It was deduced by a few perceptive individuals of the time that contaminated hands from handling the sick or their bedclothing transmitted the disease to otherwise healthy individuals. This was graphically demonstrated by John Snow in the now classic case of the Broad Street pump in London. He had the pump handle removed, and the cholera epidemic promptly subsided.

By 1870 several states in the United States had established boards of health to deal with sanitation and the control of filth. These efforts resulted in a pronounced decrease in the incidence of typhoid, cholera and dysentery by the early 1900s. Today every major city, county and state have well organized and effective health departments. The result is a level of sanitation and safety of food and drinking water that is unmatched in the world. We have taken this for granted and have been little aware of the efforts to extend these practices to the many regions of the world where thousands die annually from their absence.

We cannot continue to be complacent, however, for once again population density and industrial development are threatening our environment and food and water supply. With the growing move to rural areas more and more people are relying upon wells and septic systems. Approximately half of the households in North America are served by these systems. The installation of these facilities is supervised and controlled by the local health departments. With increasing frequency the underground aquifers from which wells draw their water are discovered to be contaminated by chemical and industrial waste, however. Seepage from landfills has accounted for some of this contamination.

Such seepage more readily contaminates the aquifers in some geologic strata than in others. Sand and limestone in some areas permit seepage of wastes from dumps and septic systems into the underground water supplies. Some wells in these areas are grossly contaminated and unsafe. Many older homes have septic systems on small lots, and wells that are forty to sixty feet deep on the same lot. Wells in such circumstances are very likely to be unsafe.

Dumping of wastes into streams and other bodies of water is another source of contamination of our water, and this practice threatens even municipal water supplies. The standard treatment techniques of filtration, aeration and chlorination do not remove toxic chemicals. They also are not always effective against some viruses and the cysts of giardia and amoeba. The great increases in the recreational use of bodies of water from which municipalities draw their water, coupled with the increased incidence of diseases such as giardia, add to the urgency of this problem.


## GIARDIA LAMBLIA

This is a protozoan which establishes itself in the small intestine of humans and other animals where it persists and reproduces. In excess of 26,000 cases of acute diarrheal disease caused by this organism are reported in the United States each year. Formerly it occurred mainly in the developing countries, where wells are consistently and chronically contaminated. It is now the most common cause of outbreaks of water-borne diarrheal disease in the United

States. It occurs most commonly in the Rocky Mountain states and more frequently in visitors there. Drinking from mountain streams assumed to be pristine, but in reality contaminated by excrement from beavers and perhaps other animals, accounts for many of these cases. Pockets of communities have emerged elsewhere in the United States where wells have become contaminated with this organism, most likely by animals.

Giardia forms cysts in the small intestine which are then passed in the stool, thereby infecting others when food or water are contaminated. These cysts may survive in water for months and are not destroyed by chlorination. Boiling the water effectively destroys the cysts. Since they are fairly large (on the order of ten microns) they are removed by the filters sold for backpacking. Cases of Giardia induced diarrhea have resulted in individuals who used these filters, however, possibly due to faulty handling of the filter or contamination of the filtered water. Outbreaks of the disease have also occurred in day-care centers and nurseries. Simple handwashing after handling diapers and the use of disposable gloves is effective in preventing transmission in these circumstances. These practices also help guard against the acquisition and transmission of hepatitis which is a significant risk in day-care centers.

The water supply in Leningrad is heavily contaminated with Giardia, and over fifty percent of visitors to that city have suffered the disease. The incubation period is ten to twenty days, so the onset of symptoms frequently occurs after one returns home, fortunately. This onset is marked by a profound watery diarrhea, with as many as forty to fifty stools per day. Bloating, abdominal pain and cramping that may be severe accompany the diarrhea. These symptoms may persist for weeks or even months if untreated. Effective treatment is available.

Diagnosis of Giardia is difficult. Cysts are found in the stool in less than half of the victims. Repeated laboratory examination at intervals of five to seven days for several weeks may demonstrate the organism. After the acute phase, however, the cysts are seen infrequently. Duodenal aspiration or biopsy will usually help to establish the diagnosis. This is an unpleasant procedure, however, and is not as readily accomplished as a stool examination. The infection can also be acquired by eating food that has been contaminated by a carrier who has neglected hand washing. Individuals who have previously had a gastrectomy, or who are on acid inhibiting medication for an ulcer are at a particularly high risk of contracting the disease upon exposure to the Giardia cysts. This organism is shed in the feces of pets, which may be an additional source of infection in the home and among children playing on the ground or in sandboxes (see Hazards of Pets, chapter IX).

## CAMPYLOBACTER JEJUNI

Prior to 1972 this organism was not associated with intestinal infections, but by 1979 it had become second only to Giardia as a cause of water-borne diarrheal disease in the United States. The diarrhea, which begins two to ten days after exposure, may be pronounced. It is accompanied by a fever, and bloody stools may be present, especially in children. It is found in contaminated milk and water. This is yet another disease acquired by drinking raw milk. Since 1983 several instances of Campylobacter illness among school children visiting dairies and consuming raw milk products have been reported in California, Michigan, Minnesota, Pennsylvania, Vermont, and British Columbia.

Campylobacter jejuni is present in the intestine of domestic and wild animals and poultry. Excrement from these sources contaminates streams and water supplies. Contamination of food by excrement from pets in the home is a potential source of infection. The organism reproduces in the human small intestine, and has recently been associated with duodenal ulcers, where it is suspected of playing a role. Pepto-Bismol has proven more effective than antibiotics in eradicating the organism in ulcer patients in some studies. More recent studies utilized a combination of Pepto-Bismol and an appropriate antibiotic. This combination proved very effective in eradicating Campylobacter jejuni and in preventing a recurrence of the ulcer.

## TYPHOID

Only about 400 cases of typhoid fever are reported each year in the United States currently, thanks to the public health measures described previously. About half of these cases are acquired outside the U.S. It continues to kill many people worldwide, however. This occurs chiefly in underdeveloped countries and in nations where water and sanitary systems are of inferior quality. The only source of Salmonella typhi, the causative organism, is human beings. It is theoretically possible, therefore, to eliminate it, as we have smallpox. The organism is dispersed in large quantities in the feces of infected people. Infection of others occurs only by fecal contamination of water supplies or of food, either by flies or by contaminated hands. The latter could be prevented if hands were washed appropriately with soap and warm water, and if latex or vinyl disposable gloves were worn at all times when preparing and handling food for public consumption.

Typhoid fever, which has killed thousands of troops during wars, and tens of thousands of civilians throughout history, is a systemic infection spreading through the blood stream to every organ in the body. It has a particular predilection for the gallbladder, and multiplies there in great numbers. It may remain there in the carrier state. Antibiotic therapy cures most cases, but the response is not as rapid and dramatic as with most bacterial infections. Every effort should be made to eradicate the organism, especially in chronic carriers. Immunization is available for travelers to areas where a risk exists, but its protection is not absolute. Typhoid can still be contracted if a heavy exposure occurs.

## NITRATES

These substances, which are found naturally in well water in some areas, are a hazard chiefly to infants under three months of age. The nitrates, when transformed to nitrites in the stomach by bacterial activity, convert hemoglobin to methemoglobin, which cannot carry oxygen. Thousands of cases have been reported, and about eight percent of infants die. Agricultural runoff of fertilizers can deposit these substances into drinking water supplies in some areas. The local health department can inform you as to whether or not nitrates are a problem in your area. The use of bottled water in preparing formula is mandatory in those regions where it is present in drinking water in significant amounts. These areas include southern California, Illinois and other scattered areas. The integrity of the source of bottled water should be determined, for purchasing water in a sealed container is no guarantee of its purity.

## DBCP

Dibromochloropropane has similarly contaminated wells in southern California's Kern County. This chemical was used extensively to control root worms in commercial agriculture until it was discovered in 1978 that it caused sterility among male workers in the fields. This sterility is caused by a direct toxic effect on the germ cells and is accompanied by a reduction of the number of Sertoli cells in the testicle. This reduction is sometimes profound and the sterility has been permanent in some workers, both in agriculture and in the manufacture of this chemical.

More recently it has been observed that there is a tenfold increase in the incidence of childhood cancer and leukemia in areas where this chemical is found. These toxic and carcinogenic risks were noted by researchers, who warned of its dangers, long before it was widely used in agriculture. Brominated compounds in general are viewed with suspicion. Ethylene dibromide which is also used as a fumigant, and TRIS, which was widely used as a flame retardant on children's pajamas, share these toxic and carcinogenic risks with DBCP. Since testing began in 1979, forty percent of the wells in the San Joaquin Valley have been found to be contaminated with DBCP.

## THM

Trihalomethanes are a group of chemicals that includes chloroform and trichloroethylene, and have been found to be contaminating public drinking water supplies. These substances are formed in municipal water supplies by chemical action between the chlorine used to treat the water, and organic matter occurring naturally in the water as a result of the decay of plant and animal material. Trihalomethanes are known to cause cancer, and the unanswered question is whether the concentration in drinking water is sufficient to cause concern. These chemicals have also contaminated wells and public drinking supplies as a result of being leached out of dumps and landfills, and by direct industrial pollution of water supplies.

## MERCURY

Both metallic mercury and its various compounds discarded into bodies of water have been the cause of many tragedies. It has been common practice to dump inorganic mercury waste products into bodies of water because it was felt that these compounds were nontoxic. They are absorbed only in very small amounts, and thus pose little threat in themselves. Recent studies have discovered, however, that these inorganic compounds are bioaccumulated by plankton and algae present in the silt of rivers, streams and lakes, as well as by fish. They indeed are converted to organic mercury compounds such as methyl and dimethyl mercury by these microorganisms, and perhaps by the fish. Previously it was believed that all organic mercurials were man-made. These recent findings pose serious questions that will require careful assessment. They have added to the concern about the risks of consuming fish taken from bodies of water that contain other chemicals that accumulate in the fish, such as PCBs.

One of these organic compounds, methyl mercury, is particularly toxic, as was tragically demonstrated at Minamata Bay in Japan in 1953. Hundreds of men, women and children, who lived off the fish from the bay, developed severe nervous system disorders that included inability to walk, deafness and visual defects. The death rate reached forty percent. A factory manufacturing vinyl chloride had been dumping methyl mercury, a waste product, into the bay, and this practice continued for a long period of time. This tragedy resulted not from bioconversion, but from the direct dumping of large quantities of very toxic methyl mercury into streams that emptied into Minamata Bay.

Similar poisonings of large numbers of people by these organic mercury compounds have resulted from eating seed grain treated with the chemical, and from eating birds that had eaten seed grain. The largest recorded epidemic occurred in Iraq in the winter of 1971–72, resulting in the admission of over 6,000 victims to hospitals, and over 500 deaths. Eating bread containing wheat that had been imported as seed grain, coated with methyl mercury as a fungicide, was responsible for this disaster. The mercury compounds used in agriculture, which include phenylmercuric salts used as fungicides and herbicides, are also washed into lakes and streams, where they are taken up by the resident fish. Recommendations for restricting the consumption of fish taken from these bodies of water, which include the Great Lakes, have been published.

## PCB (polychlorinated biphenyls)

These substances have also been found in hazardous quantities in fish in the Great Lakes. They have been found in particularly high concentrations in fish that have been taken from the Hudson River and Lake Ontario, and several other rivers and streams throughout the United States. These substances serve as fire retardants and are widely used in industry in electrical transformers and capacitors. They also are used in the manufacture of paper and waxes, in many plastic products such as telephones, and a multitude of other items. They are extremely persistent in the environment, enduring even longer than the pesticides that have evoked such great concern. The toxic ramifications of the PCBs in man and animal include suppression of the immune system, adverse effects on liver enzymes and tumor production. The fact that they are stored and accumulated in the body fat depots is of particular concern.

## SEWAGE

Residential septic systems were discussed in chapter II. They are the rule in rural homes, in contrast to the widespread use of privies as late as the 1940s. These private systems are effective and safe when design standards are adhered to and if proper maintenance is not neglected. It is ironic that the major threat to public health today comes from municipal sewage systems. Many municipalities foolishly constructed combined storm and sanitary sewer systems years ago, and this has come back to haunt them. During periods of heavy rain, the sewage treatment plants are inundated, and raw sewage pours directly into the rivers, streams and oceans. These cities now face the necessity of digging up streets and neighborhoods, at enormous expense, to install systems that should have been put in place fifty years ago. A few cities in the United States had the foresight to install dual, separate systems initially.

Even more disgraceful is the practice of dumping raw sewage directly into the ocean, as many cities along the eastern seaboard have been doing for the past fifty years. This practice has contaminated all of the shellfish from these regions with the Hepatitis A virus, introducing a major public health threat. In a vain effort to mitigate the hazards presented by this shortsightedness, sewage pipes have been extended ever further seaward, to no avail. Bathing in these waters carries a significant risk, but eating shellfish from them entails an even greater one. These sad facts may help to explain why Hepatitis A, which in the past occurred as an epidemic approximately every seven to eight years, is now with us year round, every year.

Sodium in drinking water supplies should be of concern to anyone who has high blood pressure, or a significant family history of high blood pressure. It is known that a high salt intake early in life has an adverse effect on blood pressure later in life. It was only after years of effort that salt was finally removed from baby foods (it was put there for the benefit of the mother's taste, not the infant's). Many municipal water supplies are relatively high in sodium content. The highest concentration, however, is in drinking supplies drawn through a water softener. This water should not be used for drinking or for cooking where a no-added-salt diet is desired. A separate tap that bypasses the water softener should be installed at the sink whenever a water softener is installed.

# VII

# Hazards of Recreation

## ACCIDENTS

By far the greatest hazard of recreational activities is accident and personal injury. The leading causes of accidental death in the United States, in descending order, are motor vehicle accidents, falls, drownings, and fires and burns. Over 45,000 people are killed each year in motor vehicle accidents. Falls account for 12,000 deaths, half of which occur at home. More than 5,000 people die by drowning, about 700 at home. Fire kills slightly under 5,000 people each year, the majority of which occur at home.

These are the statistics. They tell nothing of the emotional trauma of those who are touched by these deaths. They also do not assay the financial hardship of those who are left behind. They tell nothing of the cost to society, financial or otherwise. Most of these deaths need never happen. While death is inevitable for everyone, untimely death invariably leaves a deep scar and levies a heavy burden.

Many recreational activities naturally carry an element of risk. Skydiving, for instance, carries a risk of parachute failure, which is not preventable in many instances. Many drownings, on the other hand, could be prevented if proper floatation devices were used religiously, and if greater swimming proficiency were acquired. The one hundred or so people who are killed by lightning each year might not be victims if they avoided seeking refuge under trees during a thunderstorm. Smoking in bed probably cannot be classified as a recreational activity, but many people die in fires as a result of this foolishness each year.

# HEARING

Damage to hearing is related to both the loudness of the sound and to the length of exposure. High-pitched sounds are much more damaging than low-pitched tones. Hearing loss, therefore, is most frequently seen in the frequencies of 2,000 hertz (cycles per second) and above. Exposure to jet engine noise and rock music have resulted in loss of hearing in the high frequency range in many individuals. A single exposure may result in fatigue of the inner ear and a loss that may be temporary. Hearing may recover after a period of freedom from exposure to that noise source. If that sound is repeated, and if it is frequent enough, the hearing loss may become permanent due to the destruction of the cells in the inner ear. These cells are never repaired nor replaced. Such a hearing loss may result from repeated exposure over a long period of time, or it may result from a brief exposure to very loud noise.

Noise-induced hearing loss normally begins at 4,000 hertz and spreads to the frequencies above and below this. Audiograms of workers exposed to noise typically demonstrate a significant hearing loss between the 3,000 and 6,000 hertz range. The human ear is much less sensitive to low-pitched sounds than high-frequency sounds. The loss is invariably insidious, with the individual unaware that any change has taken place. Frequently the first evidence of hearing loss is the inability to understand what has been said, even though the statement had been heard. This deficit in "discrimination" occurs because the hearing loss at the higher frequencies results in parts of words, usually the consonant sounds, not being heard.

In a recent routine health screen of 123 employees of a small company, over 70 percent of the employees demonstrated a significant hearing loss, chiefly in the high-frequency range. Most of these were individuals in their forties, and the majority were not job related. Virtually none of these employees was aware of any hearing loss. A sampling of dentists in the Seattle area in 1987 revealed that 77 percent in the 40-to-50 age group had a moderate to severe hearing loss as a result of exposure to the high speed drill.

Exposure to noise on the job and the resultant hearing loss is the most common occupational risk in the United States today. About eighty million dollars is paid each year in workers compensation claims for loss of hearing. This is a greater sum than is paid for any other occupational disease. These facts introduce a compelling financial incentive to take measures to reduce this morbidity.

107

Governmental agencies charged with this responsibility have been aware of the problem for many years. Technology sophisticated enough to measure noise levels and the related hearing loss was not available until well after World War II. Standards were set and more precise controls outlined with the passage of the Occupational Safety and Health Act in 1970. The history of these efforts and their current status are discussed in chapter VIII.

Significantly, much of the hearing loss in our society today results not from the job. While we have made much progress toward protecting the hearing at work, the loss of hearing at play has increased. The level of noise that we are exposed to in our everyday lives away from the work place is not at all appreciated. Some of these noise levels, measured in decibels, are listed in the table below. (The decibel is a logarithmic expression of sound pressure levels. Each ten decibel increase represents a doubling of the sound pressure level at the ear.) Any exposure at 100 decibels or above entails a high risk of a hearing loss.

| | |
|---|---|
| Conversation | 65 |
| Lawn mower | 93 |
| Diesel garden tractor | 83–95 |
| Chain saw | 105 |
| Grinding | 115 |
| Rock and roll band | 110–130 |
| Shooting a .44 magnum | 140 |
| Jet plane taking off | 145 |
|     at 50 feet | 130 |
| Thunderclap, overhead | 120 |
| Pain threshold | 100 |

Headphones with portable music sources are particularly insidious, for they deliver loud music directly to the ear, at a very high level in some instances. The lack of any apparent immediate adverse effect prompts individuals to discount any hazard. As discussed above, hearing loss is insidious, is not readily apparent, and is progressive over time. Ringing in the ears after such a noise exposure is a warning of the danger.

Noise levels below 80 decibels do not induce a hearing loss. Sustained noise levels of 85 decibels present a definite risk of hearing loss. Hearing protection should always be worn during activities that expose individuals to a noise level over 85 decibels for any period of time. This covers all shooting activities, and should include many other activities, obvious from the table above, where protection is never utilized. The human ear should never be exposed to a level in excess of 140 decibels. Hearing protection is available in the form of earplugs and earmuffs, with the latter giving greater protection. These are available at any gun dealer and at most sporting goods sections of department stores where guns and hunting supplies are sold.

Hunting and shooting are two of the most common causes of a hearing loss. This loss is easily prevented by wearing protection. I have seen an eardrum ruptured and virtually destroyed as a result of permitting a shooting partner to rest a .357 magnum on the victim's shoulder and fire it. The damage required reconstructive surgery. Damage to the inner and middle ear from such abuse may not be reparable.

Some hearing loss with age is inevitable. This involves the higher frequencies more than the lower ones, and results in difficulty understanding conversation in a noisy room, or with background noise such as a television set. There is no cure for any hearing loss, and no absolute prevention for the loss that occurs with age. The latter can be developed sooner and made more severe, however, by unnecessary noise exposure. Hearing loss that results from noise exposure outside of the workplace has received very little attention, and the general public is not aware of the danger. Ringing in the ears after a noise exposure such as shooting is a warning that hearing protection should have been utilized. Continual ringing in the ears, while frequently caused by drugs such as aspirin and certain antibiotics, may also be evidence of a noise induced hearing loss. Assessment of noise exposure, both at work and at play, should be undertaken when this is noticed.

Noise has been defined as any undesirable sound. In this vein, beauty is in the eye of the beholder. What is music to one ear is noise to another. The disturbing effects of noise depends upon both the frequency and intensity. As stated above, the human ear is more sensitive to high-pitched sounds. Aside from damage to the hearing apparatus, loud noise can produce physical and psychological stress. Some studies have indicated that noise increases the pulse rate, elevates the blood pressure, causes constriction of the arteries and tensing of the skeletal muscles. Individuals chronically exposed complain of nervousness, sleeplessness and fatigue. The adverse effects of excessive noise have been appreciated virtually from the beginning of civilization as evidenced by the many laws that have been passed over the decades in an effort to control it.

These symptoms that result from excessive noise exposure are most frequently produced in the home by music of one form or another. Dogs barking are also a frequent contributor, and this is particularly offensive during the night. Sounds produced in the course of normal activity and play by children and teenagers can at times contribute to stress. All of these sources of noise, while usually well tolerated by the young individual with normal hearing, are not always well tolerated by individuals with a hearing loss, especially age-induced hearing loss. This is not merely a reduction in the hearing level, but a distortion of hearing that makes comprehension of speech more difficult. Age-induced hearing loss (presbycusis) makes it much more difficult to listen to two conversations at the same time. With this condition, attempting to carry on a conversation with background music or with the television set on is difficult and frequently stressful. This is what accounts for the demands of the middle-aged parent to turn down the television or music box when the telephone rings.

In the home, it is not practical to walk around all day wearing hearing protection. Much can be done, however, to control the sound level. Sound absorbing materials such as draperies can be used throughout the house. In new construction, sealing of all cracks reduces noise from the outside. Dual pane windows not only conserve energy but reduce the noise levels transmitted from the outside. Insulation that is installed for energy conservation provides similar benefits in noise reduction. In apartments or duplexes, many measures can be taken to prevent noise transmission between units, such as staggering the studding in the walls between units. This architectural design does much to dampen noise transmission and should be used universally.

Builders are familiar with other sound insulating techniques that should be utilized when planning new construction or remodeling. In existing homes, noise can be isolated to a single room, to a degree, by installing sound absorbing tile or other material in that room. Acoustic tile on the ceiling, for instance, reduces noise transmission from the room where it is applied. In the extreme, the wall can be lined with acoustic tile or cork. The efficiency of sound absorption of various materials can be obtained from building supply dealers. Typically, these materials absorb seventy percent or more of the sound that strikes them.

Most people appreciate the fact that placing distance between them and the source of noise renders it more tolerable. For each doubling of the distance, sound is decreased by six decibels. Most homes do not provide enough space to utilize this principle to render noise acceptable, however.

# ULTRAVIOLET RAYS—SUN

One of the most serious hazards of recreation is excessive exposure to the sun. The major complications of long term exposure to ultraviolet radiation are premature aging of the skin with irreversible loss of the normal elasticity; skin cancers, which include squamous cell carcinoma and its precursor, actinic keratosis; and malignant melanoma which is the most lethal of all cancers. Such lesion are seen more frequently in sportsmen, farmers, ranchers, sailors and sun worshippers. All of these events occur more commonly in individuals who demonstrate poor tanning, that is, those who have a fair complexion, light hair and light colored eyes. People of Celtic heritage have an ethnic predisposition to skin cancer for unknown reasons.

It is known that a single severe sunburn early in life, prior to age twenty years, predisposes to skin cancer later in life. Ultraviolet radiation from the sun produces cellular damage, with alteration in the DNA, proteins, lipids and other cellular components of the skin. It is theorized that this damage is responsible for the development of skin cancer subsequently.

For a child born in the United States in the 1930s, the risk of developing one of the skin cancers during his lifetime was one in 1500. That risk has increased fifteenfold for children born today. The risk now is one in one hundred. Between 80,000 and 100,000 individuals develop squamous cell carcinoma of the skin each year, 1900 deaths occurring in 1985. Malignant melanoma develops in 23,000 Americans each year, with 5,600 deaths recorded in 1986. Melanoma accounts for 74 percent of all the deaths from skin cancer. The risk of contracting this lethal disease has increased 1,000 percent in the past fifty years. One severe sunburn in the first ten to twenty years of life triples the risk of developing malignant melanoma later in life.

The dramatic increase in the standard of living in the United States during the past forty-five years has given us much more time for recreation. It has also given us the discretionary income to utilize that recreational time in ways that were not available to us in the past. This has resulted in dramatic increase in activities such as golfing, boating, water skiing and visits to the beaches. It has become a national pastime to jet off to the beaches of southern climates where the sun is in abundance during the winter season. All of these activities have greatly increased our sun exposure. On those days when the sun does not cooperate in our efforts to cultivate the

111

tan that everyone worships, we can skip down to the neighborhood tanning parlor.

This entire spectrum of increased exposure to ultraviolet rays has produced a dramatic increase in the incidence of associated skin diseases. These include actinic keratosis, elastosis (loss of elasticity), premature aging of the skin and of course the skin cancers. The tanning parlor will assure you that their UV-A radiation does not burn and damage the skin. These UV-A rays do penetrate the skin deeply, however, where they damage the collagen and elastic tissues as well as the blood vessels. These changes account for the premature aging of the skin manifested by wrinkles, dilated blood vessels in the skin and permanent redness. UV-A has also been found to increase damage done by UV-B, particularly the damage that leads to skin cancer. Most of the tanning devices that produce UV-A also produce some UV-B, although efforts are being made to develop units that deliver pure UV-A. Approximately 700 burn injuries occur in tanning parlors each year.

It is ironic that the incidence of skin cancer that results from excessive exposure to the sun has increased so dramatically during an era when very effective sunscreens have been available. Use of a sunscreen with a sun protective factor (SPF) of fifteen enables us to remain exposed to the sun all day with no apparent effect on the skin, so long as the screen is renewed to compensate for loss by perspiration, swimming, and wiping with towels. The sunscreen preparations that contain para-aminobenzoic acid (PABA) and its esters provide protection against UV-B but not UV-A. The products that contain benzophenones provide protection against UV-A but not UV-B. Products that contain opaque shields such as titanium oxide provide protection against both UV-A and UV-B. This is what skiers, mountain climbers, pilots and people who live at 10,000 feet should use. They are not as cosmetically appealing as the "invisible" screens, however. It is also important to note that SPF ratings apply only to UV-B. No rating scheme has been devised for UV-A.

Repeated applications do not extend the protection beyond the factor listed on the label. In other words three or four applications of a product labeled fifteen still protects for a period fifteen times as long as would be the case with no protection. From a practical standpoint, nothing is gained from protection extending beyond a true fifteen, since that would extend protection into the darkness. Even preparations that are promoted as waterproof need to be reapplied after swimming. Sunscreens should be applied about an hour prior to sun exposure in order to permit penetration into the skin for maximum effectiveness.

While most sunbathing is done at beaches that are close to sea level, skiers need to be reminded that the closer one gets to the sun the stronger the effects. At 5,000 feet the intensity of the sun is 20 percent greater than it is at sea level. Much skiing takes place at altitudes of 8,000 to 10,000 feet. The time period that the skier can be exposed to the sun is thus shortened significantly. Attention to protection of exposed skin becomes much more urgent at these altitudes. The risk of ultraviolet burns of the surface of the eye, keratoconjunctivitis, is also greater at higher altitudes, especially when snow is reflecting the sun.

Evidence has evolved recently that ultraviolet radiation also plays a roll in the development of cataracts. Plastic (acrylic) and glass conventional lenses screen most ultraviolet radiation. Contact lenses may screen 30 to 80 percent, depending on the type. This has offered a market for the promotion of both conventional and contact lenses that protect from ultraviolet radiation. The consumer has no way to measure the effectiveness of any of these products. You must rely upon the professional advice of your optometrist or ophthalmologist.

It is also important to keep in mind that most of the commonly marketed sunscreens do not protect against photosensitivity reactions that are invoked by certain medications. These include certain antibiotics, tranquilizers, diuretics and oral diabetic medication. Not all medications in any of these groups cause this reaction. Phenothiazines can provoke such a reaction if accidentally applied to the skin, and this problem has been seen in nurses and pharmacists. A similar phototoxic reaction can occur after ingesting furocoumarins that are found in parsley, celery, and limes. This reaction can occur after simply rubbing these substances on the skin. This has been observed in individuals handling produce in grocery stores, and in workers harvesting celery with pink rot disease.

Photoallergic reactions can be provoked by the antibacterial agents incorporated into common household hand soaps, one being tribromosalicylanalide. Hexachlorophene also carries this risk. Sunscreens that contain 6-methylcoumarin can even cause a reaction. Some individuals develop a sensitivity to some of the chemical constituents in the sunscreen products. If this occurs, switching to a different preparation with different ingredients may resolve the problem.

Photosensitivity reactions are provoked by the UV-A fraction of the sun, against which the commonly used sunscreens do not protect, as mentioned above. As a result they can be provoked by sun irradiation though a window or an automobile glass. Although UV-B is blocked by glass, UV-A is not. UV-A, even though it is a less potent cause of sunburn, is no less potent in causing skin damage including aging and cancer. UV-A radiation reaches the earth's surface fairly constantly throughout the day, whereas very little UV-B does so before 10:00 A.M. and after 3:00 P.M. It is thus possible to experience exposure to UV-A for twice the period each day as for UV-B. This exposure is not noticed because less erythema is produced.

Snow and white sand reflect UV radiation very effectively, and a burn can result even in the protection of an umbrella or other source of shade. A thin cloud cover also permits 50 percent or more of the UV radiation to penetrate. The security felt under these circumstances is frequently unwarranted.

Total avoidance of the sun is mandatory with some acquired and familial diseases. Lupus is perhaps the most common example. If a sunscreen is to be relied on it should be one of the so called broad spectrum products that contains protection for both UV-A and UV-B. The opaque screens such as titanium oxide offer better protection. The use of these products cannot offer total protection. Avoidance of sun exposure to the fullest extent possible is still the wisest course of action with these diseases. The herpes virus is also frequently activated by sun exposure due to the immunosuppressant action of UV-B. This is mediated through several mechanisms including suppression of lymphocytes.

## TEMPERATURE DISORDERS

Many recreational activities expose the individual to excesses of heat or cold that threaten serious consequences. These disorders are covered in chapter XI and that information should be reviewed before undertaking recreational activities in extremes of heat or cold. Familiarization with these disorders of heat and cold exposure will permit individuals to avoid some serious and painful consequences. Some activities, such as strenuous running, especially in hot weather, have resulted in publications of descriptions of special disorders that are merely variations of previously recognized heat stress diseases.

## ALTITUDE SICKNESS (MOUNTAIN SICKNESS)

This results when people travel from the altitude of the cities of the midwest (700 to 800 feet) to an altitude of over 8,000 feet in a short period of time. This classically happens when skiers travel by jet to one of the popular resorts in the Rockies. In the milder form the only symptoms are headache, nausea, loss of appetite, weakness, shortness of breath with exertion and a general feeling of sickness. The symptoms are provoked by a sudden drop in the oxygen available to the blood. This stimulates increased activity in the lungs which alters the acid/base balance in the body. Breathing is diminished during sleep, aggravating the oxygen deprivation.

In a sudden ascent to 12,000 feet over 50 percent of the people will experience headache, about 10 percent will suffer severe headache and nausea and vomiting. If the individual attempts any physical exertion, such as skiing, on the day of arrival, hospitalization may well result. At 17,000 feet the air entering the lungs provides only half of the oxygen that it does at sea level. The reduced atmospheric pressure compounds this deficiency by decreasing the force that drives oxygen from the lungs into the bloodstream.

In the severe form of the disease fluid accumulation in the lungs occurs. Bleeding into the lungs also occurs in some instances. A similar condition in the brain sometimes accompanies the pulmonary edema. Even the administration of pure oxygen at high altitudes does not rectify the crisis. The reduced atmospheric pressure does not permit the adequate transport of oxygen from the lungs into the blood. Fatalities occur every year at resorts that are located at altitudes above 8,000 feet. Sleeping below 8,000 feet avoids these deaths. The only certain prevention is to spend a minimum of two days at an altitude of about 7,000 feet before attempting skiing at 11,000 feet. If staying at an altitude of 11,000 feet is better to drive in, where some acclimatization is made automatically by the trip, than to fly in where no adjustment period is provided. No amount of cardiovascular or muscular conditioning prior to the trip helps with this problem. Living and sleeping in an altitude chamber for three or four days prior to the trip would provide the necessary transition, if you have one accessible.

# BITES AND STINGS

## INSECTS

For most people a sting by a bee, wasp or hornet is a painful experience. For the many people who have become hypersensitized it may be fatal. Three times as many people die each year as a result of bee stings as from snake bites. Death results from anaphylaxis (shock) due to an allergic reaction. Sensitive individuals should carry a kit that contains epinephine that is marketed for this purpose. These individuals should consult with their family physician regarding the use of the kit, and other recommended procedures. The stinger should be gently teased out by scraping rather than by pulling, to avoid injecting additional venom into the skin. Perfumes and bright colors attract bees, and should be avoided when in bee territory. Desensitization is available and is effective.

The fire ant, which was imported from South America, is now established in thirteen southern states. It has for the most part displaced all other ants in these regions, and presents a serious problem for humans. Its bite may result in a severe allergic reaction and death. The bite may result in a severe vesiculation of the skin with necrosis (decay). Infection is common following these bites. The risk is all the more serious since many ants may attack an individual at the same time.

Bites of ticks, chiggers, mosquitos and deerfly may result in disease in addition to the local discomfort. These diseases, including Lyme disease, are discussed in detail in chapter IX. These risks can be minimized by wearing appropriate clothing and insect repellents such as diethyl-meta-toluamide (DEET) when in the field or woods. The pant legs should be tucked into the tops of boots or socks. Hunting or boot socks serve this purpose well. If this does not fit your dress style, some alternate system to prevent ticks from crawling up your pants leg should be devised (perhaps leggings).

The body should be inspected daily, more frequently with extended exposure, for the presence of ticks. These should be removed by careful traction, taking care not to leave the head. If the head remains lodged in the skin, it should be surgically excised, for it can continue to migrate deeper into the tissues. Care should be taken not to compress the body of the tick to avoid injecting disease producing organisms that may be harbored there. The hot cigarette technique for persuading the tick to dislodge has been abandoned, for it causes the tick to regurgitate, thus injecting more of its toxic and infectious materials.

## INSECT REPELLENTS

These substances are one of the most valuable discoveries of our era. During my younger years we applied citronella liberally, burned rubber tires or anything else that would produce smoke and noxious fumes, but still were eaten alive by mosquitos. Diethyl-meta-toluamide (DEET), which is the only truly effective repellent, is remarkable in its effectiveness. Products that contain 25 to 50 percent of DEET are more effective and last longer than the less concentrated preparations. These stronger products are also more effective against the black fly, which is the ultimate challenge.

Products that contain 98 percent are now available, but are not normally needed, and they increase the risk of sensitivity and toxic reactions. Diethyl-meta-toluamide is absorbed through the skin, however, and has been reported to have produced toxic reactions in the nervous system of children. Some children have died, usually after excessive use. It is safer to avoid skin contact in children, especially in the very young. It has also been reported to have produced skin rashes in some individuals. This has usually occurred after heavy applications.

In using the more concentrated preparations these adverse re-actions become more probable. A new long acting DEET preparation that contains 35 percent DEET along with a polymer that inhibits both evaporation and skin absorption will be marketed in 1990. This should do much to reduce both the sensitivity problem and the nervous system reactions. A new product designed to repel ticks has been marketed under the name of Permanone Tick Repellent. This product contains the pesticide permethrin, a synthetic pyre-thoid (see Pesticides, chapter I), and is for application to the clothing, not the skin. Field trials by the Air Force and others have demon-strated that when both DEET and permethrin were used on clothing, protection was virtually 100 percent. This dual application to the clothing will be very useful in the battle against Lyme disease, and indeed all of the tick-borne diseases.

In view of the prolific use and abuse of this substance over a period of many years, it is remarkable that so few problems have surfaced. We should, however, exercise much greater caution in applying this chemical to the skin. It is safer to apply it to clothing, where it also lasts much longer. Perspiration shortens the period of effectiveness. Wearing of long-sleeved shirts and pants, and spraying the repellent on them, provides more safety and better protection. These are mandatory protection against ticks. The pump spray bottles are safer and more economical than the aerosol cans.

In using the aerosols keep in mind that they are flammable, and should not be used in the presence of a lighted cigarette or open flames. They should never be sprayed into the face; rather the repellent should be sprayed onto the hands, then applied to the face and ears, avoiding the eyes and mouth. A recent study has discovered that DEET works by interfering with the receptor cells in the mosquito that respond to the lactic acid that is excreted through our skin. This opens the way for development of additional substances to thwart this mechanism.

## COLORADO TICK FEVER

This is a viral disease that replicates in ticks and is not transmitted from animals. It has been identified in Colorado, Idaho, Nevada, Wyoming, Montana, Utah, Oregon, Washington and California. It has been misdiagnosed as Rocky Mountain Spotted Fever, partially because it outnumbers that disease by twenty to one in Colorado. It occurs mainly in May and June (March through September for the full season). About one week after the bite of a tick the victim experiences fever of 102–104 degrees Fahrenheit, chills, severe aching and headache. There is rarely a rash. The symptoms last from one to three weeks, depending upon age. There is no effective treatment, and recovery is almost universal.

## ROCKY MOUNTAIN SPOTTED FEVER

This disease is caused by a rickettsia that is transmitted to humans by the bite of a tick. It was so named because it was first detected in the Rocky Mountain states, but few cases are seen in that region today. In 1986, 755 cases were reported to the Centers for Disease Control. The largest number of cases occur in North Carolina (129 in 1986). Other states recording significant numbers of cases include Texas, Oklahoma, Arkansas, Kansas, Mississippi, Alabama, Georgia, South Carolina, Virginia, Kentucky, Tennessee, West Virginia, Ohio, Pennsylvania and New York. In 1987 four cases occurred among residents of New York City, none of whom had been outside of the city for the previous three weeks. There appear to be ticks in residence in the parks of the city. This development, along with the discovery of ticks that cause Lyme disease on lawns of suburban homes, forces us to alter our previous concept of tick-borne disease as a risk only in the woods or fields.

Ticks are the natural reservoir for Rocky Mountain Spotted Fever. They live off of the blood of small animals such as ground squirrels and rodents. Adult ticks can survive for two years without feeding. The female tick transmits the rickettsia to subsequent generations of ticks through the eggs that it lays. Ninety-five percent of the cases each year are reported between April 1 and September 30, the period when ticks are active, and when people are in tick country. The disease may be seen throughout the year in the south.

The onset of symptoms occurs above seven days after the tick bite. Typical is a fever of 103 to 104 degrees Fahrenheit, chills, muscular pain, and a pronounced headache. A rash appears on the fourth day of illness in over 80 percent of the cases. It appears first on the wrists, ankles, palms, soles and forearms, then spreads to the rest of the body. Only about 65 percent of the victims can recall a tick bite. When a tick bite is recalled, typically it occurred within the preceding two weeks. Untreated cases may progress to pneumonia and circulatory failure with brain and heart damage. Encephalitis may develop. Early treatment with antibiotics has significantly reduced the mortality, which was formerly about 20 percent, much higher in patients past fifty. There are no significant sequelae if early treatment is instituted.

There is no vaccine for this disease, prevention is the best control. This is accomplished by wearing proper clothing and by application of an effective insect repellent. The diagnosis is not considered in some cases, primarily due to the absence of a rash. A significant percentage of cases (about 20 percent) never develop the rash.

As with all tick-borne diseases, a careful search of the exposed portions of the body for ticks every two hours should be routine whenever in the woods or brush where ticks are present. Any ticks that are found should be removed carefully by steady, gentle traction with tweezers. If the head is left behind, it must be removed surgically as mentioned above to prevent migration deeper in the skin. The bare fingers should not be used. Protective clothing should be worn, with bands around the ankles. Insect repellent (DEET) is effective and should be used. The new permethrin clothing spray mentioned above, Permanone Tick Repellent, should also be used with DEET. This provides virtually 100 percent protection against ticks. These measures should bring about a reduction in the incidence of this as well as Lyme disease, and indeed all tick-borne illnesses.

DDT and dieldrin were effective in controlling tick populations in wooden and brushy areas around rural homes, but are no longer available. Diazinon is currently marketed for this use, and some of the other organophosphates should be effective. Chlorpyrifos (Dursban) for instance is effective against ticks, and it can be applied as a spray in areas of known tick habitation. This is particularly important for those homes that are in regions where Lyme disease, babesiosis, Rocky Mountain Spotted Fever and tick paralysis are reported (see chapter IX). With the widespread cultivation of litigation as an income-producing industry, and with the current hysteria regarding pesticides, it becomes more and more difficult to obtain effective agents to control the disease vectors that kill and maim humans. It is even more difficult to get objective information on this subject.


## PLAGUE

The dread "Black Death" of the Middle Ages lives on in the United States today, albeit at a much lower incidence. The advent of effective antibiotics that control the disease in most cases, lessens our risk. The most important factor in the reduction of the incidence of this serious disease has been the control of rat and other rodent populations that have been the resevoir for the bacterium that causes it. The major population of that resevoir in the United States currently is the ground squirrels that abound in the southwestern portion of the country. This is a particular problem in and around Los Angeles because of the great increase in the population there, and the building of homes in the countryside among the ground squirrels.

Plague is transmitted from the rodents to humans by the bite of the rat flea, which transmits the bacterium. Even with prompt treatment the mortality rate is about 10 percent. This is a disease to avoid. During recreational activities in southern California and Arizona appropriate precautions should be taken. Pants legs should be tucked into boots or socks, and insect repellents should be applied. If pets such as dogs or cats accompany the outing, they should be dusted with Sevin before returning to the living quarters. For further information on plague, see chapter IX.

## MURINE TYPHUS

This is another disease that is transmitted by fleas from rats and mice to humans. It is caused by a rickettsia that infects virually all rats and mice at some time during their existence. It has been reported in virtually every state but it is more common in seaports and near food storage facilities. Murine typhus is prevalent in the southeastern states and along the Gulf Coast. The incidence in the United States has been greatly reduced by taking measures to deny access to grain and food storage by rodents. Although this form of typhus produces a pronounced illness, it is treatable with antibiotics and has a low mortality rate. Recreational trips to the regions of greatest incidence, or in areas where rats and mice are in evidence, should prompt the same preventative measures as described above for plague. Pets will be a major factor in bringing this disease home (see chapter IX).

## MOSQUITOES

Throughout the history of mankind these insects have delivered more death and disease than any other insect. Diseases transmitted by mosquitoes have killed more of the earth's human inhabitants than all of the wars throughout history combined. In the United States they are responsible for the transmission of the four types of encephalitis, California, eastern equine, western equine and St. Louis. In California an Aedes species has transmitted malaria from a returned soldier to campers at a Girl Scout camp. Several cases of dengue fever have been transmitted by Aedes aegyptii in the Rio Grande valley of Texas since 1980. The recent introduction of the Asian tiger mosquito, Aedes albopictus, into Texas through a shipment of used tires from Asia has raised the specter of far more widespread outbreaks, not only of dengue fever, but of other viral diseases not yet seen in the United States. For a more detailed discussion of these diseases, see chapter IX.

It will become ever more urgent to take every precaution to avoid attacks from mosquitoes during our recreational activities. Fortunately we have a very effective repellent in diethyl-meta-toluamide (DEET). As discussed previously, it is widely marketed by several different manufacturers in varying concentrations. The products with the higher concentrations of 25 to 50 percent have the longest duration of action. In order to avoid possible sensitization to these products, it is best to avoid any unnecessary skin contact, applying the repellent to clothing instead wherever possible. When the new formulation of 35 percent with the added polymer becomes available, it should be a substantial improvement.

None of the electronic devices are effective in controlling mosquitoes. The zappers that destroy larger insects are not effective against mosquitoes. When camping, netting on tents is essential. To control a tent full of insects that gain entry as a result of repeated passage by children, spraying the tent with pyrethoid aerosol 30 minutes before bedtime is effective. Exit the tent after spraying to avoid inhaling the aerosol.

## EHRLICHIOSIS

This is another serious disease transmitted by ticks to humans. It was first reported in 1986 and many cases were misdiagnosed as Rocky Mountain Spotted Fever. It is caused by a rickettsia that is transmitted from dogs to humans by ticks. A total of 46 cases have been identified from eleven different states, mostly in the southeast and south central U.S. Early diagnosis and treatment is essential. A blood test is available from the Centers for Disease Control. This provides an added incentive for travelers to these regions to exercise precautions against ticks.

## SAND FLIES

Also called biting midges, these are related to mosquitoes and other blood-sucking flies. They are about one to four millimeters in length, about the same size as the dog flea. Their attacks are rapid and aggressive. Severe itching may follow, and the treatment is antihistamines by mouth and topical cortisone cream to the bites. **DO NOT** apply cortisone products to the face. Sand flies do not transmit disease to humans in most regions of the United States. They are common vectors of some significant parasitic infestations in Africa and the Mediterranean region. They inoculate a protozoan into the skin of humans in Central and South America, Mexico and south central Texas. This parasite is transmitted from dogs and rodents to humans by the fly. It also transmits sandfly fever, a viral disease, in Africa, the Mediterranean region and Panama.

## BLACK FLIES

These are small (about five millimeters in length) highly aggressive biting flies that attack throughout the day and in the open. They are encountered in huge numbers during the late spring and early summer in northern climates, such as Canada, where they extract a heavy penalty for a day of fishing. They have invaded Michigan in lesser numbers. In Africa, South America and Mexico these flies transmit the parasitic worm, Onchocerca, to humans causing "river blindness" and filariasis. In the United States they do not transmit disease.

## CHIGGERS

These are the larval form of the harvest mite, which feeds on vegetation, not man. The mite lays its eggs in fields where larva hatch, then climbs vegetation to lie in wait for a victim. A change in the carbon dioxide level of the air signals them to drop onto passing animals including humans. The larva then attaches to the skin, usually the ankle or higher, and ascends until it encounters tight clothing such as the belt. It then penetrates the skin and secretes a tissue digestant. It feeds for three or four days before dropping off. The itching and inflammation may persist for weeks. Any organisms that are found still feeding can be removed by a physician.

Antihistamine tablets and topical cortisone cream can be used to relieve the itching, which may be intense. Infection may result from scratching. Bites by chiggers can be prevented by taking the same precautions as for ticks, wearing pants legs tucked into boots or socks, tight clothing and application of an effective insect repellent, which means diethyl-meta-toluamide (DEET).

## SPIDER BITES

Black widow spiders, Latrodectus mactans, are found in virtually all areas of the United States. In the fifties and sixties several bites on the scrotum were reported each year, acquired while visiting outside privies. Progress in the installation of indoor plumbing seems to have reduced this risk. The bite is followed by severe muscle cramping, and abdominal cramping may mimic an acute abdomen, such as appendicitis. These bites are more serious in children, where convulsions may be seen, and in people over sixty years of age.

The brown recluse or violin spider, Loxosceles reclusa, was introduced into the southern United States in 1964. It is seen now chiefly in the central and midwestern states. It produces a potent toxin that may result in extensive tissue destruction. Excision of the bite early, if identified, is advocated by some, but this practice is controversial. It is important to identify the spider, since bites by other, less toxic spiders may mimic the bite of the brown recluse. Fatalities are rare, even in children. The chief harm from these arachnids is the necrosis and loss of tissue that may require surgical repair.

## SCORPION BITES

The only species of scorpions in the United States that present a threat to humans are found in Texas, New Mexico, Arizona and southern California. The sting is followed by considerable pain and discomfort. There is generally no threat to life, however, except in young children, the aged and the debilitated. The sting, which is inflicted by the tail, may be accompanied by a burning and swelling. In some species the burning sensation is followed by a numbness and tingling sensation. The entire arm or leg may become numb, and nausea and vomiting may ensue. Hyperactivity may be followed by coma, convulsions and death. The venom produced by scorpions is more toxic than that of snakes, but only a small amount is injected. No tissue destruction is seen. Antivenom is available and should be used if symptoms are pronounced.

Scorpions are nocturnal creatures and seek refuge in shoes, clothing and bedding. The sting results from an accidental encounter. Precautions should include shaking out shoes and clothing in the morning before donning them. The same precautions should be taken before using towels and washcloths.

# RABIES

This is a viral disease that is 100 percent fatal without treatment, and people continue to die from it in cases where there is no known exposure. A high level of awareness must be maintained during all recreational activities where exposure to wild animals, either by humans or by pets, is a possibility. Virtually all dogs are immunized, and thus are unlikely to bring rabies home to you. This is not true of cats, however. Cats are by nature a hunter, an animal of prey, and as such they are much more likely than dogs to encounter wild animals with rabies. The number of cases of rabies in cats now outnumbers that in dogs. It does not take a lot of imagination to see the risk from this source even at home, much less on outings.

Rabies is commonly found in skunks, raccoon, bats and fox. It has been found in bats in every state except for Hawaii. If your recreational activities include cave exploration, a risk of rabies exposure exists. Rabies is rampant in the skunks in central California where they roam in great numbers. Rabies was found in the skunks living under a school and in proximity to where the children played in the Bay area in 1978. Raccoons are common in many communities in the United States, living among the human residents. The potential for contracting rabies lies not only in being bitten by a rabid animal, but by coming in contact with it otherwise, either alive or dead. Rabies can be contracted through a scratch or abrasion on the skin while handling an animal with the disease, or by inhaling the virus. These means of transmission should be kept in mind. A nationwide effort to vaccinate cats must be undertaken, and it must succeed. We have been fortunate thus far.

Rabies is widespread among the wild dogs of Africa, and is common in India, the Philippines and South East Asia. If you are planning a trip to these areas and plan to be in the field, out of contact with modern medical care, please review the section on rabies in chapter IX and consult your physician about your needs.

# AQUATIC

Jellyfish stings produce pain and burning, swelling and redness at the site of contact. The victim may experience muscle cramps, nausea, vomiting and pulmonary edema. Some victims have died within a few minutes, although most survive, fortunately. Drowning is a significant risk following these encounters. In those who survive, all of the symptoms except for the local pain, swelling and redness dissipate within several hours.

The Portuguese Man-of-War, which is found in the coastal waters of the Gulf of Mexico, is somewhat less toxic than the jellyfish. The treatment for stings of both is immediate washing in salt water to dilute and remove as much venom as possible. **DO NOT RUB** the sting area, as this will inject additional venom from the tentacles left behind. These tentacles with their venom should be inactivated by sprinkling baking soda over the area for jellyfish and vinegar or isopropyl alcohol for the Portuguese Man-of-War. The remaining tentacles should then be gently scraped off, taking care not to force further venom into the skin. This task is best accomplished by a physician experienced in the procedure. Rinsing in freshwater, using ammonia and rubbing with sand all tend to result in the deposition of additional venom into the skin.

The stingray is the most common toxic fish sting in the United States, living mostly along the California Coast. Severeal hundred stings are reported each year. These encounters occur primarily in shallow water. The habit of the fish of remaining buried in the sand increases the possibility of an accidental encounter with humans. Many stings on the hand occur among fishermen during attempts to dislodge fishhooks from stingrays when they are caught accidentally. The wound is caused by the tail of the fish which is composed of a bony spine with a skinlike covering. The tail is lashed into the victim, sometimes penetrating an inch or more. Venom is deposited into the wound, and portions of the bony spine may break off in the wound. The skinlike sheath is usually deposited in the wound even when none of the bony spine is left behind. It is indeed ironic that these "friendly little animals" that are petted by many people in the tank at the Epcot Center so commonly inflict so severe an injury on humans.

Severe pain and whiteness are the immediate findings. This is followed by redness and swelling of the area of the wound. Systemic symptoms of muscle cramps, weakness, excessive salivation, heart rhythm irregularities, seizures and death can occur but are uncommon. Treatment is to apply a constricting band, taking all of the precautions to avoid the damage of prolonged tourniquet applications, and irrigating with saltwater to remove as much of the sheath as is feasible. The wound should then be immersed in water as hot as can be tolerated without inflicting a burn, for up to one hour. The venom is readily inactivated by heat. The wound frequently requires surgical debridement and suturing.

Several fish contain venom that can be deposited in the skin of humans by a fin or spine. These include catfish, dogfish, bullhead shark and lionfish. The latter species contains the most venomous fish in the world, the stonefish. There is an immediate severe pain at the site, followed by swelling. This is followed by necrosis and extensive tissue destruction, especially with the catfish and the lionfish. Muscle weakness, heart irregularities, hypotension, seizures and paralysis may follow. Treatment again is to immerse in hot water for one hour until the symptoms subside, to inactivate the venom. Infection commonly follows with these stings, and appropriate treatment should be instituted if this occurs. The indicated tetanus prophylaxis should always be administered with these wounds. This requires an assessment and judgement by a physician.

## SNAKEBITE

The majority of poisonous snakes in the United States are pit vipers, various species of rattlesnakes, copperheads and cottonmouths. Coral snakes are found in Texas, Arkansas, Florida, Georgia, Alabama, Louisiana, Mississippi, and North and South Carolina. Approximately 7,000 people are bitten by snakes each year but only about a dozen fatalities are recorded, mostly in children.

The impact of an attack by a snake can be minimized by wearing long trousers and boots whenever afield in snake habitat. Avoiding such well known risks as stepping over a log or sticking one's hand into likely snake retreats also lowers the odds. Children should not be allowed out into the woods in snake country barefoot and in shorts.

The amount of venom deposited in human tissues after a snake strike varies considerably. No poisoning occurs in about twenty to thirty percent of strikes by pit vipers. A physician experienced in treating such bites can anticipate the degree of envenomation by the appearance of and reaction at the wound. There is no universal agreement upon what constitutes the best treatment, and any consensus that does exist changes from time to time. There is agreement, however, that the victim should seek medical help as soon as possible after being bitten. Appropriate, specific antivenom is available through medical facilities, but must be administered within four to six hours. It is derived from horse serum, and its administration carries a significant risk of reaction, shock and death unless appropriate precautions are taken.

There is no disagreement upon the need to keep the victim quiet, avoiding panic. The bitten extremity should be splinted and kept in the horizontal position. Activity speeds the spread of the venom through the general circulation. Tourniquets are discouraged because their effectiveness has been called into question, and because of their potential for causing gangrene. The effectiveness of incisions over the points of venom deposition is also currently questioned, partially because the venom is usually injected deeper than most people are willing to cut. Making such incisions also runs the risk of damage to underlying nerves and blood vessels. If done at all, it must be done immediately to be effective. This measure is of no value in coral snake bite. Application of cold increases the extent of tissue destruction in snake bites, and such destruction may be considerable anyway.

Identification of the snake is important to subsequent treatment. Saving the snake, preferably inactivated, is more reliable than one's memory under such circumstances. All snake bites must be treated as puncture wounds. Appropriate tetanus prophylaxis is imperative. Bacterial infections are also common, and should be prevented or treated if they ensue.

## POISON IVY

Exposure of the skin to an oily substance produced by certain varieties of ivy, oak and sumac produces a characteristic reaction in some people. It represents a sensitization to the chemical, and this sensitization may occur at any time in life. The absence of a reaction to contact with these plants is no assurance that sensitization will not develop at a later date. It is important to keep in mind also that these reactions may occur in the winter as a result of wearing a sweater that had previously come in contact with the plant. It can be similarly acquired from a dog's coat after it has been out frolicking in the woods and brought back the oil with it. Contact is also made not infrequently from firewood that has vines adhered to it.

The reaction is heralded by itching, redness and a typical fluid filled vesicle. One can frequently see the linear distribution where the vine made contact with the skin. Reactions on the face and eyes can be the result of direct contact, or can be the result of the substance being carried to that location by the hands after they have come in contact with the plant. The fluid from the vesicles cannot spread the involvement. Thorough washing of any contaminated portion of the body with an effective soap will remove the oil, and this should be done as soon as possible after exposure. This will not guarantee against an eruption but it does diminish the risk. All contaminated clothing should also be thoroughly laundered or dry cleaned.

Small, localized areas of eruption may be treated successfully with cortisone creams. It will be necessary to apply these more frequently than the four times daily that is recommended, usually at least six to eight times daily. These applications must also be replenished any time that the area is washed, or after perspiration has washed the cream off. These preparation should **NOT** be used on the face, especially in children. Itching is relieved to some extent by antihistamines such as chlorpheniramine, if the drowsiness can be tolerated. Scratching must be resisted to avoid the possibility of a secondary skin infection. More extensive or stubborn reactions will require injections of cortisone preparations. For those individuals working in areas where these botanicals are found, desensitization injections are available. Hunters who spend much time afield sometimes elect this approach.

## FUNGAL INFECTIONS

These conditions are seen much more frequently in the summer, and in warm climates, since the organisms grow much more readily in warm, moist conditions. For the same reason they occur more frequently in areas of the body where skin folds are found, such as the groin, between the toes, the anal folds and underneath the breasts. These organisms are frequently shared at swimming pools and in public showers. Simple household bleach (sodium hypochorite) is very effective in destroying the fungi in these locations.

Athlete's foot is caused by a variety of strains of fungi and is seen most frequently between the toes. A rash on top of the toes and feet in the absence of involvement between the toes is most likely a sensitization reaction to the dyes or tanning agents in shoes, and not a fungus. Athlete's foot can be avoided by wearing slippers in public bathing facilities and by drying the feet well. A hair dryer is useful for this purpose. Changing socks daily also helps. Shoes with the uppers made of leather or nylon mesh are generally favored by foot and sport specialists.

If a chronic or recurrent problem exists, one may have to wear cotton socks, avoiding all synthetics such as orlon, dacron and nylon. Cotton is not always easy to find. In addition to the measures to dry the feet mentioned above, it may be useful to powder the feet prior to putting the socks on. Talc may be used, but Tinactin is more effective, since it destroys fungi. Micatin (miconazole) is even more effective, but it is more expensive. It is also helpful to leave the feet bare at home whenever possible, wearing sandals, **NOT** walking barefoot through the house to share the disease. When a full-blown eruption develops, with inflammation and cracking between the toes, nothing is more effective than the above measures. The Micatin powder should be applied four times daily, rather than just twice daily.

Jock itch is a fungal infection in the folds of the groin, appearing as a reddened area that may become extensive. It also may be caused by a variety of fungal organisms. The treatment is the same as outlined above for athlete's foot.

Itching and inflammation of the vulva is more commonly due to monilia (yeast) but can be caused by a distressing multitude of microorganisms. These may occur singly, but more commonly they are found in combinations of two or more different varieties. Successful treatment requires identification of the organism, since the treatment varies with each different class. The marketing of agents such as miconazole that have a much broader spectrum has simplified the management of this problem.

In the event of repeated or stubborn fungal infections anywhere on the body, either the proclivity toward or overt diabetes should be considered. Overt disease can usually be discovered by a well-timed blood test. Incipient disease may require a more complex glucose tolerance test.

## SWIMMING

This recreational activity is excellent exercise, beneficial for high blood pressure, the heart, lungs and general circulation. It carries virtually no risk, outside of drowning, but ear infections are a frequent problem. In public pools, the bacterial count is generally well controlled. An otitis media can occur in this setting, however, because it commonly is not an infection at the onset. Individuals prone to develop this problem can minimize it by the same precautions taken when flying. Taking a decongestant tablet such as phenylephrine and chlorpheniramine, and spraying the nose with one quarter percent phenylephrine solution before swimming will lessen the risk.

Swimming in lakes and ponds results in actual bacterial infections of the ear canal, and these require aggressive treatment. This is a common problem, due to the universal contamination of the lakes commonly used for recreation, including water skiing. Infections of the skin due to a variety of organisms occur in addition to the ear infections. The most troublesome infections of the skin and ear are those due to Pseudomonas bacteria. These are resistant to virtually every antibiotic that has been developed. An increasing number of these recreational waters are being contaminated by Giardia and we are seeing cases of diarrhea as a result.

Infections of the eyes (conjunctivitis) occur in the same settings for the same reasons. The most recent eye infection to evolve is that caused by Acanthamoeba. This serious infection does not respond to any of the conventional treatments and may result in a corneal transplant or loss of an eye. It is a particular danger for contact lens wearers. Contact lenses should never be worn when swimming; this practice carries a risk of a serious eye infection. Farm ponds carry some additional risks that are discussed in Zoonoses, chapter IX. Recreation in any of these bodies of water carries a significant health risk.

## METAL TOXICITY

The most common metal toxicity encountered in recreation is that of lead. Even at low levels lead causes damage to the brain, the kidneys and to other organs of the body. Young children in the household are particularly susceptible (see Hazards of Childhood, chapter IV).

Lead is much less frequently encountered from auto exhaust today, and plans have been put in place to eliminate it from gasoline completely. Until this has been accomplished one should avoid inhaling exhaust from automobiles, tractors, power mowers and gasoline engines in general. These vehicles and appliances should not be run inside a closed structure such as the garage or yard barn. Keep in mind the risks other than lead that are entailed by exposures to engine exhausts. These include carbon monoxide and oxides of nitrogen that cause pulmonary fibrosis. (See Diesel Exhausts in chapter VIII and Hazards of Air, chapter X, for a discussion of these problems.)

Another recreational source of lead exposure is associated with casting of bullets or toys. Whenever lead is melted, high concentrations of lead fume accumulate in the local atmosphere. In addition, the dross (lead oxide) that forms on the molten lead results in dust contaminating the floor and surroundings. The formation of this dross can be greatly reduced by adding about 200 grains of pure tin to every 10 pounds of lead. If pure tin is not available, twice that amount of a 50–50 solder will accomplish the same goal. This does not affect the hardness of the bullets and it improves the flow of the lead in the mold.

Lead may enter the body either by inhalation, through the skin or by ingestion. These projects are frequently carried out in a basement or garage workshop, without any ventilation. Even with an efficient exhaust fan, with adequate ventilation flow, high levels of lead and lead oxide form over the work. The average dust mask does not protect against this exposure. The 3-M Company markets a "Sanding Respirator" that is a more sophisticated dust mask. It provides better protection than the common dust mask, but the weak point is still the seal around the edge. Any leakage here permits the entry of hazardous particles into the lungs. These operations, therefore, call for great caution and care. The dross should be disposed of carefully in a closed container such as a plastic trash bag, and the work area should be vacuumed carefully. A central vacuum system is preferable for this job.

Ordinary solder contains 50–60 percent tin and 40–50 percent lead. A eutectic mixture, that which melts at the lowest temperature, is 63 percent tin and 37 percent lead. For the soldering normally done around the home, there should be no significant lead exposure. If an individual has a large wiring project that requires use of a molten pot of solder, or a similarly large plumbing project requiring a molten pot, he should avoid inhaling the fumes, and provide adequate ventilation. For soldering residential plumbing, federal regulations, prompted by the concern for lead leaching into the water supply, now require the use of a nonlead solder.

One such product on the market is composed of 95 percent tin and 5 percent antimony. Another product contains zinc, silver and antimony in addition to the tin base. The latter product is advertised to flow better, a major problem with any solder that deviates far from the common 50–50 tin–lead mixture. A eutectic mixture melts at 183 degrees Celsius, the tin-silver at 245 degrees Celsius and the tin, silver and antimony at 240 degrees Celsius. Significantly higher temperatures are required for the new solders, a factor that complicates many of the common soldering projects.

Automobile manufacturers have reduced the tin content of the solder that they use in radiators to FIVE PERCENT, believe it or not. This cost cutting measure not only guarantees a greater frequency of repairs, and sooner, but also assures a significantly increased lead exposure when repairs are made. If these repairs are undertaken as a weekend mechanic project, care should be taken to provide good ventilation, and to not inhale the fumes. The heating or melting of the solder should not be done in a closed garage or in the basement workshop, unless adequate ventilation is available.

Even more hazardous than lead in bullet casting is cadmium. This metal is not customarily added to lead for such purpose, since antimony provides the desired hardness in bullets. Cadmium is a frequent component of wheel weights, however, and they are sometimes collected for use in casting bullets. They should not be. Inhalation of cadmium fumes can produce a severe emphysema as well as damage to the kidneys. These fumes are severely toxic and should be avoided. Cadmium is also an almost universal component of silver solder, and it has been responsible for many severe lung disabilities in that application. Silver soldering is not a simple, easy technique for the home handyman. For those who do tackle the job, however, this serious risk should be kept foremost in mind. It is mandatory that the fumes not be inhaled. The damage will not be apparent immediately, but when it does appear it cannot be undone.

## MERCURY

This liquid metal and its salts are not as commonly encountered in recreational activities as they are on the job. The compounds are used as fungicides on seed grain, however, and in paints and stains to inhibit mildew formation. The liquid metal has a low vapor pressure and toxic levels accumulate in the atmosphere from an open container. It seeps into concrete floors when spilled, and many laboratories are contaminated through this means. It then vaporizes and produces a hazardous level in the room air where it is inhaled. Great care should be taken at home to avoid spilling this substance on concrete floors or into cracks and crevices where it cannot be cleaned up. If this spillage does occur, the mercury should be cleaned up carefully. If a vacuum cleaner is used the bag should be disposed of carefully. If some residual mercury persists in an inaccessible spot it can be amalgamated with tin metal foil and then vacuumed. A similar product for this use is marketed. There is no practical means to remove metallic mercury from concrete floors after it has permeated them.

There has been much publicity about the health hazard of the mercury in dental fillings. Many people have had their money extracted from their wallets through the misconception that these fillings should be replaced with a safer material. There is no better, nor safer material for dental restorations than the silver-mercury amalgam. It is stable and the mercury bound in this amalgam is not released into the body. This is and has been the firm position of the American Dental Association.

## HOT TUBS

These oversized bathtubs are a recent addition to the recreational field, and some serious skin infections have resulted from communal sharing of them. The most serious of these skin infections has been produced by Pseudomonas bacteria, which have become notorious for being resistant to virtually every antibiotic available. Another serious infection that is acquired in hot tubs is Acanthamoeba eye infections, and this subject is discussed in chapter XII. Contact lenses should never be worn in hot tubs.

These infections are a serious problem that mandates much greater care in maintaining hot tubs. Every person entering the hot tub should bathe carefully before and after the activities. Every human body is host to a multitude of organisms that can cause serious illness. The organisms that seem to cause no harm in one individual can readily cause death in another. Careful cleaning and use of effective chlorine products periodically can minimize this risk. Instructions for the proper care and maintenance of these appliances accompany the purchase, and they should be adhered to strictly.

Alcoholic beverages should not be consumed prior to entering a hot tub. This is particularly imperative if you are entering the hot tub alone and unsupervised. Aside from the effect that these substances have on the temperature sensitivities and the cardiovascular system, people have drowned as a result of mixing these two pleasures. Sensible temperatures should be adopted and adhered to. Many people have suffered serious burns from hot pads because the sensory perception of the skin was dulled after a period of time. Since it no longer felt warm, the tendency was to turn the dial higher. A similar phenomenon occurs in a hot tub. The goal should not be to see how much heat can be tolerated.

# TETANUS

This infection is a risk with many recreational activities. Contrary to popular belief it does not require a rusty nail. Tetanus spores are present in the the soil all around us and on most of the objects that penetrate the skin during recreation activities. Tetanus infection is a risk whenever a thorn from a rose or barberry bush penetrates the skin. Prevention is by far the best approach to this potentially fatal disease. Immunization is readily accomplished by a series of injections. This immunity can be then be maintained by a booster injection every ten years. In the event of an injury a booster may be indicated at that time, depending on the injury and the length of time since the last booster. These are judgments to be made by the family physician.

Tetanus can carry a mortality of fifty percent once contracted, even with the best of medical care. The majority of people who suffer invasion by thorns and splinters do not succumb to tetanus infection. This fact is a graphic demonstration of the effectiveness of the immune and protective systems of the body. With a high mortality rate, however, and with effective immunization readily available at a reasonable cost at any family physician's office, this is a foolish risk to take. Not a single member of the United States armed forces in World War II died from this disease, although it killed many in previous wars. This is a remarkable testimonial to the effectiveness of immunization and to the diligence of the armed forces of the United States in executing immunization programs.

# VIII

# Hazards of the Workplace

The hazards encountered in the work environment are so numerous that a simple discussion of all of them would fill a volume larger than the entirety of this book. These risks have been greatly reduced, both in magnitude and in number, since the passage of the Occupational Safety and Health Act by Congress in 1970. Some serious risks have been eliminated entirely, and progress continues year by year on the remainder. Vocal critics abound who, as with advocates of a pure environment, feel that all risks should be swept aside immediately through the passage of federal laws.

While no one can quarrel with the objective, pragmatism dictates that it will be achieved only after considerable study and thought. Solutions to all of the problems cannot be accomplished overnight. Neither can solutions be effected by the stroke of the pen or a magic wand. Congress certainly has never demonstrated that it possesses a magic wand. Obviously industry and the country cannot be precipitously shutdown. What has been lost sight of in this struggle is that industry exists solely to serve us. It provides us with not only jobs and other resources that we need for every aspect of our lives, but also the commodities that we demand. If it did not produce that we want, it would pass into obliviation.

I know of no one who is ready to return to a horse and buggy or kerosene lamps, or the washboard, or the wood-cooking stove. Those systems were not all that free of pollution, anyway. So it behooves us to accept the fact that the problems of industry today are our problems. We need not commit hara-kiri. Solutions will come from the same fountain that produced the problems.

## INJURIES

The full extent of workplace injuries is not known, primarily because many are not reported and tabulated. Approximately eight percent of workers in the United States in a given year suffer injuries that require treatment. About three million workers each year suffer severe disabling injuries on the job, and about 70,000 of these disabilities are permanent. Over 20,000 amputations occur on the job each year, 93 percent being fingers, usually caught in machinery, belts, saws or other cutting devices. Approximately 10,000 of the on the job injuries are fatal each year. These result from falls, blows, crushing injuries, fires, explosions and electrocutions. Many of these events could be prevented, perhaps even the majority.

## CHEMICALS

While injuries and accidental death account for the majority of job related events, exposure on the job to agents that cause cancer is perhaps the most feared. Many agents are suspect, but enough data has been collected on eighteen categories of substances to merit their being listed by the Occupational Safety and Health Administration (OSHA) as **CANCER SUSPECT AGENTS**. All work areas where exposure to these substances is possible, and the entrance to these areas, must be identified by a sign reading Cancer Suspect Agent. These agents are:

| | |
|---|---|
| 4-Nitrobiphenyl | 3,3-Dichlorobenzidine |
| Alpha-Naphthylamine | Bis-Chloromethyl ether (BCME) |
| Methyl chloromethyl ether | Beta-Naphthylamine |
| Bendizine | N-Nitrosodimethylamine |
| 4-Aminodiphenyl | Vinyl chloride |
| Ethyleneimine | Inorganic arsenic |
| Beta-Propiolactone | 1,3-dibromo-3-chloropropane (DBCP) |
| 2-acetylaminofluorene | Acrylonitrile |
| 4-Dimethylaminoazobenzene | Coke oven emissions |

Aside from cancer, there are literally hundreds of chemicals that cause damage to the liver, kidneys or brain and nervous system. Virtually every job in industry exposes workers to some of these chemicals, or to the physical agents such as dusts, that may cause harm. Harmful effects most often result from breathing the vapors or fumes, or from skin contact with the substance. Most of the toxic chemicals are readily absorbed through the skin and thus are harmful to the internal organs through this route as well as when inhaled.

Some of the toxic chemical exposures on the job result from the manufacture of these chemicals. Thus the vinyl chloride monomer used in the production of polyvinyl chloride induces a rare tumor in the liver in workers exposed to it. This substance is now used only in closed systems in order to eliminate exposure. BCME (bis-chloromethyl ether), used in the manufacture of resins for water filters, carries a similar risk for lung cancer, even among nonsmokers. Inhalation of this substance and skin contact with it must be avoided.

Other chemical exposures in industry result from ancillary processes, and are thus seen outside of plants that manufacture chemicals. The use of chlorinated hydrocarbon solvents for degreasing is a common example, since this process is is used in every plant where machining, stamping, shearing or shaping of metal takes place. Trichloroethane is the substance commonly used today, and it is well absorbed through the skin as well as the lungs. It is very difficult to avoid exposure, and it produces a significant toxicity in the liver as well as the nervous system. Chlorine and ammonia gas may cause severe irritation of the lungs and bronchi. This exposure may be fatal, depending upon the concentration and the duration of exposure. Hydrogen sulfide gas has killed a number of workers in sewers and in sewage treatment facilities.

Many organic solvents such as acetone and ketone can produce muscle weakness, irritability, memory loss, changes in personality, difficulty concentrating and other nervous system disorders. These substances are commonly encountered in glues and adhesives, paints and lacquer, dyes, plastics, printing inks and in degreasing and cleaning operations. Adequate ventilation is essential in minimizing the exposure to these chemical substances. This requires properly engineered booths and ventilation system as mandated by the Occupational Safety and Health Administration. Ordinary respirators provide no protection against vapors. An appropriate charcoal canister filter does offer protection, if it is well fitted and properly maintained. If skin contact is required, special solvent resistant gloves and aprons are necessary. These solvents penetrate most gloves, but materials such as Viton provide some protection. Manufacturing systems that avoid all contact are preferable.

With every toxic substance exposure one must be mindful of the interaction with other agents. It takes much less alcohol to damage the liver, for example, after that organ has been exposed to trichloroethane and similar agents. Exposure to asbestos increases an individual's risk of developing lung cancer by a factor of 6 to 8, but if that person smokes cigarettes, the risk is increased to at least 80 times the normal. Similarly, a welder who smokes cigarettes carries a much greater risk of developing lung disease than does a welder who does not smoke.

## LEAD

Lead is commonly encountered in jobs in industry. It carries a very high risk to the developing fetus, resulting in mental retardation among other effects. It is well absorbed from the stomach, so any dust that is inhaled and swallowed, or accidentally introduced into the mouth through smoking or eating, produces a risk. As a consequence, any woman who might become pregnant should have no exposure to lead. This often poses a dilemma for both management and the worker. It places an unfair burden on women, but perhaps the burden to the developing fetus is greater.

Some areas of employment where lead exposure is encountered are:

Auto manufacture
Battery makers: lead-acid storage batteries
Brass foundries
Ceramic and pottery makers, dinnerware
Chemical manufacturer, various
Glass workers
Insecticide manufacture
Lead shields for x-ray and other radiation devices
Lubricant manufacture
Match manufacture
Paint and enamel manufacture
Petroleum refining
Painters
Plumbers
Solderers

## CUTTING OILS

Insoluble cutting oils (neat oil) have long been known to produce acne, inflammation of hair follicles and cancer of the scrotum. The exact mechanism or culprit is not known, but cancer of the scrotum in young chimney sweeps, resulting from the tars collected during their work, was reported by Sir Percival Potts in 1775. Butlin reported similar cancers in England as a result of exposure to pitch, tar and mineral oil in 1892. More recently it has been found that nitrosamines, among the most potent carcinogenic agents known, are formed in soluble cutting oils. This reaction between nitrites and amines may result from the bacteria that are known to reproduce in these oils. Eczematous skin reactions are also much more frequent with soluble oils due to the additives such as ethylenediamine. Workers exposed to these agents can lessen their risk by changing clothes daily, laundering these clothes well, and by showering well daily after work. Wearing of an impervious apron offers some additional protection.

## HYDROQUINONE

Loss of the pigmentation of the skin can result from contact with hydroquinone and related compounds. This phenomenon was first reported forty years ago in workers wearing rubber gloves. It continues to be a risk in rubber workers today as well as in those who come in contact with printing inks, lubricating and cutting oils, germicides and photochemicals. The loss of pigmentation is permanent, and there is no cure for it. This presents a serious problem with sun exposure, both because of the risk of sunburn and of the development of skin cancers.

## CHLORACNE

This is a very resistant form of acne. It results from exposure to chlorinated hydrocarbons such as PCB (polychlorinated biphenyls) and PBB (polybrominated biphenyls) that are used as a fire retardant in the manufacture of paper, plastics and electrical and electronic components. They also are present in biphenyls that are used in herbicides. Most of the substances are now processed in closed systems to avoid contact. Contact still occurs due to trace contaminants and in handling cables where lubricants contain chlornaphthalene and biphenyls. Chloracne associated with TCDD (dioxin) is discussed in detail in chapter I.

Under federal and state right to know laws, workers must be apprised of potentially harmful chemical and physical agents to which they are exposed. Labels must be on the containers, and the hazards must be listed. It is very foolish for a worker to not acquaint himself with these substances and their risks. Some management individuals have little concern for the health of their workers. Some workers, on the other hand, insist upon exposing themselves in spite of the best efforts of management. Both positions are to be condemned. Gambling should be reserved for the casinos, and it should never involve health.

## PESTICIDES AND HERBICIDES

The hazards related to exposures to pesticides, herbicides and fungicides are covered in detail in chapter I, and this should be reviewed for the occupational consequences. Occupational exposures to these agents occurs in their manufacture, in farming, among ground keepers, commercial growers and harvesters and during aerial application (including the pilots, mixers, loaders and flagmen).

## MERCURY

The toxic consequences of exposures to mercury compounds are described in chapter VII. Suffice it to say that individuals working where mercurial fungicides are manufactured, stored or applied to seed grain are at serious risk. Inhalation of dust in such facilities has resulted in death, including two female stenographers who worked in a warehouse where diethylmercury was stored. The serious consequences of exposure to mercury compounds was immortalized in 1865 in *Alice in Wonderland*. The Mad Hatter portrayed the behavioral changes and the tremors that reflect the damage to the nervous system that were characteristic of workers in the felt hat industry of the day. The tremors were assigned the name "The Danbury Shakes," in honor of Danbury, Connecticut. Mercuric nitrate is still used in the felt hat industry today for the same purpose, but with some improvement in controls.

These toxic effects of mercury have been recognized since medieval times. Ellenbog described the effects of lead and mercury fumes in a pamphlet in 1473. Paracelsus and Agricola followed with the publication of their observations in the sixteenth century. Ramazzini published his comprehensive works, *De Morbis Artificum Diatriba*, in A.D. 1700. The observation of the dire consequences of this occupation led to the practice of assigning only slaves and convicts to such labor. Although much of the mercury used industrially in the United States today is imported, it is mined in Alaska, California, Idaho and Nevada. The ore is cinnabar, mercuric sulfide, which is commonly refined by distillation, a process which increases the concentration of mercury vapors in the atmosphere and thus the risk. Precautions must be taken to contain such vapors and to prevent workers from inhaling them.

Mercury has long enjoyed wide use in medicine. Calomel, mercurous chloride, was a favorite diuretic and cathartic until about 1940. It is still used in some skin creams for some mysterious reason. Mercuhydrin was the only potent diuretic available for some forty years, but it has been supplanted by safer and more potent agents. Mercuric chloride and bichloride were used extensively to sterilize instruments and were very effective, and very deadly. Thimerosol, also a mercurial, is still used as a perservative in some medicines and cosmetics, although it is a common cause of sensitization and reaction (see Contact Lenses in chapter XII). Ammoniated mercury ointment is still available and it is used by some for acne and other skin problems. It also causes sensitivity reactions and more serious toxicity when it is absorbed through skin lesions. Better medication is available.

Mercury and its compounds are very widely used in industry. Some examples of applications where it is encountered follow:

Aluminum alloys, some
Barometers
Batteries, dry cells
Catalysts in some chemical processes, as in chlorine manufacture
Dentistry
Dyes
Electronics
Fireworks, pyrotechnics
Fluorescent lamps (activated by mercury vapor)
Fungicides for seed grains
Gold mining
Herbicides
Mercury vapor lamps
Paints and pigments
Percussion caps for explosives
Plastics manufacture
Silent light switches
Tattooing
Thermometers
Thermostats
Ultraviolet lamps
Wood preservatives

# AIR QUALITY

Since about 1979 there has been an increasing number of incidents of complaints of respiratory symptoms such as burning throat, cough, nasal congestion, and burning of the eyes in the workplace. These incidents have invariably occurred in offices, where such complaints have not been common in the past. Numerous investigations have been undertaken to identify the culprit in these mini-epidemics. In most cases, the usual and expected agents have been measured, frequently without success. Particles (dust), carbon monoxide and formaldehyde have been implicated in some cases. Formaldehyde finds it way into the home and office through insulation, urea foam padding in furniture and in adhesives in plywood and particle board. It is an irritant to the eyes and respiratory system and is suspected of causing cancer.

Some of the highest levels of formaldehyde have been found in mobile homes. The levels in these units have exceeded by many fold the level recommended by the American Conference of Governmental Hygienists of one part per million. In new buildings the elution of various gases from the building materials and furnishings has been identified as the source of many complaints. Some of the gases that have been identified are 1,1,1-trichloroethane, toluene, styrene, xylene and benzene. Benzene has been associated with the development of leukemia, and styrene causes concern because of its structural relationship to vinyl chloride, a known carcinogen. These substances are less readily identified and measured than particulates and carbon monoxide. Some of the complaints seem to abate after about six weeks, with virtual disappearance of problems after four to six months. Delay of occupancy in new buildings, with adequate ventilation to air the building out, would appear to be a prudent measure to take to avoid these problems.

In many outbreaks, absence of the usual culprits prompted a search for other irritants. In cases where the complaints included fever, chills, fatigue, chest tightness, cough and wheezing, hypersensitivity pneumonitis was suspected. Many of these outbreaks were traced to the presence of actinomycete or other fungi in the circulated air. It was discovered that these organisms were growing in the moisture or water pools in the air conditioning units or in humidifiers. It was thus that the term "humidifier fever" was coined. Other organisms such as amoeba and bacteria have also been isolated as causes of this syndrome. Persistence of these symptoms over a period of time can produce pulmonary fibrosis with permanent lung disability.

The presence of the Legionella bacteria in air conditioners and humidifiers was first identified after the death of American Legion members attending a convention at a hotel in Philadelphia. Several outbreaks have occurred subsequently, the most recent having occurred in a hotel at the Detroit airport in June 1985, resulting in three deaths.

In sixteen large studies, 281 cases were traced to actinomycete, Bacillus subtilis, Flavobacterium or Cephalosporium. These were found in the humidifier systems, in the ventilation ducts and in air filters. In these cases anywhere from a few to seventy percent of the occupants of a given facility were affected. Through investigation of such outbreaks, it has been established that whenever thirty percent or more of the workers in a facility complain of symptoms that clear up within eight hours after leaving the job (particularly noticeable on weekends), the problem lies with the work environment.

The marked increase in the frequency of complaints of the "sick office syndrome" has been traced to energy saving measures of the past decade. These have resulted in much tighter buildings and in a marked reduction in the circulation of outside air. It has become customary for ninety percent of the indoor air to be recirculated, with only ten percent of fresh air being introduced from outdoors. The result has been the recirculation of air and all of its accumulated contaminants. These include carbon monoxide, carbon dioxide, dust, bacteria, ozone and other vapors from the resin in the toner in photocopiers, formaldehyde and other gasses from building materials, furniture and carpeting, cigarette smoke and detergent residues (sodium lauryl sulfate) from improper carpet cleaning techniques. In submarines such unhealthy accumulations are taken care of by sophisticated filters and air scrubbers. No such precautions are taken in office buildings.

A source of irritant totally overlooked until recently is cigarette smoking. In the past it had not been the practice to measure hydrocarbon levels that result from smoking. When this finally was done, some surprises were in store. In one study the hydrocarbon level of the outside air was measured at 210 micrograms per cubic meter, while the level indoors in the work area, where only 15 percent of outside air was being introduced, was measured at 1627 micrograms. When the system was reset to circulate 100 percent outside air through the work area, the hydrocarbon level fell to 364 micrograms.

This one case graphically demonstrates the simple solution to most cases of "sick office syndrome," that of adequate ventilation. It has been determined that four times as much outside air must be introduced into ventilation systems in offices where smoking takes place as has been the custom. It is recommended that at least twenty cubic feet of outside air per occupant be introduced to accommodate for smoking, rather than the customary five cubic feet. Proper air balance is also essential to bring this benefit to all areas in the work place. This requires a professional assessment and adjustment of heating and cooling ducts. These practices have been resisted because of the increased cost of heating and cooling such outside air brought in. The savings in wages and salaries due to lost work time would go far toward compensating for such increased costs.

Skin rashes and itching have been traced to fiberglass or mineral wool fibers from faulty ventilation systems. The simple solution is to install efficient filters in the ventilation system or outlet ducts. Fibers imbedded in contact lenses are a tip-off to this problem. Fibers are readily detected in particulate sampling, a simple procedure for any competent industrial hygienist. A further clue to the cause of this problem is the clearing of symptoms after showering, and relief from the complaints after a period away from work, as over a weekend or during a vacation.

## ASBESTOS

One of the most serious and most frequently encountered risks in the workplace is that of the mineral fiber asbestos. The seriousness lies in the propensity for this substance to bring about a severe and disabling fibrosis of the lung. In this characteristic it is similar to silica sand. The inhalation of asbestos fibers also carries a significant risk for the development of a cancer. One of the cancers that develops as a result of inhaling asbestos fibers is mesothelioma, a cancer of the lining of the lungs (the pleura). This has been a rare cancer in the past, but it has been increasing in frequency in recent years, reflecting not only the great expansion in the use of asbestos, but the latency period as well.

Mesothelioma does not develop until thirty to thirty-five years after the exposure to asbestos. It does not require prolonged exposure for this cancer to develop, a single exposure may result in cancer thirty years later. This is one of the very few cancers where cigarette smoking plays no role. The incidence is the same regardless of the smoking history. This is a very insidious cancer and there is no cure nor treatment. Very few people survive for two years after it is diagnosed and one-half of them are dead in six months. Crocidolite, which is the type of asbestos mined in South Africa, carries the greatest risk for mesothelioma. Amosite, which has been used in insulation in the United States, also carries a significant risk.

Many of the studies and much of our knowledge of these risks have come from surveys of insulation workers by Selikoff and his coworkers. Chrysotile, which has coiled fibers rather than straight, needlelike fibers, is felt to carry a much lesser risk for the development of mesothelioma. It is the type most widely used, and it is the type of asbestos fibers that was discovered in the water supply of San Francisco and the Bay area in 1978.

The water supply for the Bay area comes from reservoirs in the nearby hills where the rocks contain deposits of chrysotile asbestos. This discovery caused great concern and consternation, but it is generally felt that this presents no significant risk to the residents of the area. This discovery was made at a time when it was discovered that public water supplies throughout the United States contained asbestos fibers that were being leached out of the concrete pipes that carried the water. Asbestos has long been used in concrete to strengthen it, and it has been assumed that the fibers were firmly imbedded in the concrete. The leaching of fibers out of the concrete occurs more readily in areas where the water is acidic.

The concern for asbestos fibers in drinking water lies in the ability of these fibers to migrate to virtually every organ in the body. They have been found in the ovary in association with cancer there. Mesothelioma also occurs in the lining of the abdomen (the peritoneum). It is not known what if any other adverse reactions may be seen. It is not known why or how the asbestos fiber causes cancer. It is not through chemical reaction, as is the case with chemicals that cause cancer. Asbestos in an inert mineral that is virtually indestructible, at any temperature. That property has made it very valuable in a multitude of applications.

Some of the areas where workers are exposed to asbestos fibers are:

Mining, manufacturing, bagging, handling and processing
Plumbers, pipe fitters and insulation workers
Vinyl asbestos floor tiles, manufacturing and sanding
Asbestos papers and felt
Friction materials, brake pads and clutches
Asbestos-cement building materials, water pipes

Lining of furnaces and kilns and insulation of boilers
Spray on materials for sound, fireproofing and insulation
Reinforced plastics
Dry wall construction and spackling
Shipyard workers, maritime crews, U.S. Navy personnel
Stationary power plants
Schools, public buildings

The use of asbestos in dry wall and spackling compounds was banned in 1975. It was routinely incorporated prior to that, so that any remodeling or repair in those homes puts the worker at risk. Workers using these materials prior to 1975 must worry about the long latency period (30 years or more). Many of these workers were young people, many in their first jobs in their late teens or early twenties. Most of them smoked cigarettes. All of these individuals should have regular, careful physical examinations, especially beginning twenty years after their exposure.

The combination of asbestos and cigarettes is about the most potent risk for lung cancers other than mesothelioma that has ever been observed. Workers who are exposed to asbestos get lung cancer (other than mesothelioma) seven to eight times as frequently as those not exposed. For those workers who are exposed to asbestos and who smoke cigarettes, the risk is seventy to eighty times as high as individuals who are not exposed. These cancers are squamous cell or adenocarcinoma. There is a latency period of at least twenty years before these tumors show up. In many cases it is longer. The lung cancers that resulted from asbestos exposure among shipyard workers in World War II (mostly smokers) began showing up in 1978, some thirty years later.

The other serious consequence of inhaling asbestos fibers is asbestosis, a severe and disabling fibrosis of the lungs. It was first reported in 1907. In 1930 Merewether and Price reported that 80 percent of the workers who had spent thirty years or more in a British plant with exposure to asbestos had x-ray evidence of asbestosis. In 1955 Doll reported that the lung cancer risk in asbestos workers with twenty years or more exposure was 10 times as high as the population in general. It is quite apparent that we were aware of the problem and of the risks long before we became concerned enough to take action.

Doll also will be remembered as the researcher who in 1955 reported the high lung cancer risk among smokers. Many, many subsequent studies since have confirmed and reinforced these find-

147

ings. While we may have taken some action, we certainly have not taken the cure.

Asbestosis, unlike mesothelioma, is related to the length and intensity of exposure. The longer and the heavier the exposure, the greater is the chance of developing the disease. All types of asbestos will produce this disease, although not equally so. The disease has developed in wives and children of workers who carried the fibers home on their clothing. It has also been seen in clusters in neighborhoods surrounding a factory. Anyone who has a history of asbestos exposure, especially if it was twenty years ago or longer, should have an examination for this disease at least once yearly. It will be detected by a skilled physician and a stethoscope before it shows up on x-ray.

While asbestos has been removed from dry wall materials, and efforts have been made to substitute fibers such as fiberglass in some materials, it has not been substituted in many applications. The reason for this, very simply, is that there does not exist a satisfactory substitute in most cases. It is a remarkable substance of great and diverse use.

## SILICOSIS

The severe fibrosis in the lung that results from inhaling particles of silica sand, silicon dioxide, has some similarities to asbestosis. Both cause disruption of the cell wall of the macrophages that engulf the foreign particles. This releases enzymes into the lung tissue that results in damage and fibrosis. This process has been demonstrated in silicosis long ago, and only recently in asbestosis. Individuals with silicosis commonly succumb to tuberculosis, and these people should be skin tested for this disease. Individuals who show a positive test should be placed on prophylactic medication.

Silicosis is the oldest, commonest and the most studied of all occupational diseases. The problem was covered in 1546 by Georg Agricola in his De Re Metallica, in which he discussed the need for ventilation in the mines, and the value of human health over financial gain. Bernardino Ramazzini, the Father of Occupational Medicine, published his first edition of De Morbis Artificum Diatriba at the age of 67 in 1700, the same year that he was awarded a chair at the University at Padua. In the first chapter of this work he described the "pneumonokoniosis" of stone masons and miners. He was the first to advocate the inclusion in the patient history of the simple

148

question, "What is your occupation." By the 1830s early death from silicosis was recognized to be associated with the grinding of knives and needles, work in foundries, makers of pottery, mining of virtually all minerals and in stone cutters working on sandstone, but not on limestone (calcium carbonate).

During the depression in the United States, in the 1930s, the Hawk's Nest tunnel was cut through a sandstone mountain at Gauley Bridge, West Virginia, for a hydroelectric power plant. Workers, who came from many different states, worked with no protection and no efforts to control the dust. An appalling 476 of these workers died of acute silicosis, and an additional 1500 contracted the disease by the time the tunnel was completed. Many of the workers were buried in cornfields with no ceremony. Strenuous efforts were made to cover up this atrocity, but a congressional inquiry brought the facts to light and prompted the initiation of measures to control such exposure. If you visit this area for the white water rafting, or skiing, or merely to stop at the turn out to enjoy the view, you may see the plaque commemorating the great engineering feat that was accomplished.

The use of silica sand in sandblasting was banned by law in Great Britain in 1949 and in Europe in 1955, but continues to be used in the United States today. Substitutes such as shot or carborundum are available but are more costly, in monetary terms. The incidence of silicosis as a result of sandblasting has actually been increasing in the United States. Sandstone grinding wheels were gradually replaced by carborundum, alumina or emery starting in 1923. Natural emery may contain small amounts of silica, and the pure aluminum oxide, alumina, is safer. This transformation not only markedly reduced the incidence of silicosis, but also the incidence or crushed chests and skulls from broken wheels.

Sandstone wheels are still used in some areas in Nigeria because they are cheap and locally available, and cases of silicosis still occur in that country as a result. Silica, being the most abundant and widely dispersed mineral on earth, is so widely encountered in occupational, recreational and even household activities, that it is impossible to assemble a complete list without omissions. Some of the more common exposures are listed below:

Mining of coal, gold, silver, tin, lead, copper, nickel, uranium
Quarrying except in pure limestone or marble
Tunneling
Sandblasting
Foundries, making and cleaning molds, grinding castings

Glass manufacture
Pottery, ceramics and china
Kilns, furnaces, boilers (lining and scaling)
Stone masons, monument grinders
Scouring powders, soaps, abrasives
Diatomaceous earth, processing of for filters, soaps, abrasives
Slate, processing for furniture, billiard tables and ornaments
Shipbuilding
Construction
Optical lens grinding
Tire makers, commercial talc lubricant in tire molds
Commercial mica and talc contain both silica and asbestos.

## ACUTE SILICOSIS

The acute form of the disease results from a brief, very heavy exposure, as may occur in sandblasting. The first cases described occurred in workers mixing silica for abrasive soaps in 1929. The exposure that precipitates acute silicosis may vary from a few weeks to a few years. A cough develops, accompanied by fever, shortness of breath and weight loss, all of which are progressive. Death from respiratory failure may occur within two years. There is no treatment and no cure.

## CHRONIC SILICOSIS

The symptoms of chronic silicosis are again cough and shortness of breath, but evidence of the disease usually becomes evident only after fifteen years or more of low-dose exposure. With heavier exposure, the disease may become manifest sooner. It is normally progressive, even if exposure is discontinued, due to the continued presence of silica particles in the lungs and their continued destructive process there. Sandblasting, grinding and packaging of silica and the blending of this product in abrasive soaps carry the highest risks.

There is no cure for the chronic form of silicosis either, and little remedy for the symptoms. The disease slowly progresses to death. If a positive tuberculin test evolves, prophylactic medication should be instituted and continued for life, due to the continued risk of active tuberculosis. Some treatment is available to mitigate the bronchitis and heart complications that accompany the disease. Continuous medical monitoring and care will be required.

Modern technology makes it possible to eliminate most exposures to silica. Substitute materials are available in many cases. Engineering controls could prevent virtually all exposures that result in silicosis. It is very difficult to justify the continued existence of this disease as an occupational hazard today.

## CONTACT LENSES

This innovation in corrective lenses merits special consideration. Individuals who wear soft lenses are aware of the necessity to keep these lenses scrupulously clean, clear of protein and other deposits. Not everyone appreciates the fact that soft lenses, which are thirty-five percent water at minimum, and up to eighty percent in some, absorb and concentrate many chemicals. This precludes wearing these lenses in any atmosphere where these chemicals, such as ammonia and organic solvents for example, are present. Silicone spray will coat the lens and interfere with the normal uptake of water. Hair spray will similarly leave a residue on the lens. Hand creams are frequently found on lenses by the optometrist. Hands should always be washed well with a soap that is free of oils and greases, and rinsed before handling lenses. The problem of fiberglass particles imbedded in lenses was discussed previously. (See chapter XII for a complete discussion of contact lenses.)

## HEARING

Virtually all factory work settings have a high noise level and thus present the threat of a hearing loss. Studies have shown that exposure to noise levels below eighty decibels do not present a risk of a hearing loss (see Hearing in chapter VII for a further discussion of noise and hearing). Studies by the National Institute for Occupational Safety and Health (NIOSH) have indicated that twenty-five percent of individuals age fifty-five years and over who have been exposed to an average of ninety decibels in their employment have developed a significant hearing loss due to occupational noise exposure. Approximately eighty million dollars per year is paid in workers compensation for hearing loss. This is a greater amount than that paid for any other occupational disease.

Everyone working in a noisy environment should have a baseline audiometric test, preferably before starting work. In the event that no pre-employment test has been done, it should be done as soon as possible. A periodic test should then be done to monitor any change. Follow-up tests should be done every one to two years, at least until stability has been established. Hearing loss that results from repeated noise exposure invariably is not recognized until it becomes profound. When a hearing loss is detected, an assessment of noise exposure should be made not only on the job, but at home and at play as well. It does little good to expend great effort to reduce the threat of hearing loss at work if the individual spends all of his time away from the job listening to rock music through headphones at 100 decibels.

The risk of hearing loss on the job has long been appreciated by people concerned with worker protection. The Walsh-Healy Public Contracts Act, passed in 1936, mandated that companies working under contract to the federal government must provide safe and healthful working conditions for employees. The onset of World War II greatly increased the number of such contracts, and thus the scope of the act. The stipulation of precise standards for noise was hindered by the limited availability of technology to measure and assess this risk on the job. Standards to regulate noise exposure on the job were finally adopted in 1969 when the Walsh-Healy Act was revised. The American Conference of Government Industrial Hygienists (ACGIH), which was established in 1938, published recommended limits for noise exposure on the job in 1969. These formed the basis for the standards adopted in the Walsh-Healy Act.

The Occupational Safety and Health Act (Public Law 91-596) was signed into law in December, 1970. The provisions of the Walsh-Healy Act were incorporated into this new law, and the published recommendations of the ACGIH were added. The initial limit for noise exposure on the job was set at 90 decibels for an eight-hour day. The Occupational Safety and Health Administration lowered the action level for permissible noise level on the job from 90 decibels to 85 decibels in 1985. All workers who are exposed to noise levels in excess of 85 decibels must have their hearing assessed and monitored in accordance with specified standards.

Efforts have been made by the National Institute for Occupational Safety and Health since its inception to reduce this occupational noise induced hearing loss. These efforts led to the regulations that were issued by OSHA as outlined above. The noise level permitted, averaged over an eight-hour day, remains at 90 decibels. Workers who are exposed to levels above 85 decibels must be identified, however, and their hearing must be monitored in accordance with OSHA rules. Hearing loss can be substantially reduced by wearing hearing protection in noisy operations. Effective noise levels can be readily reduced by 10 to 15 decibels by wearing efficient, well-fitted ear plugs designed for this purpose.

Absolute noise levels can often be reduced by engineering controls, and this is the preferred approach where it is feasible. Machinery can be installed on mounts that absorb and prevent transmission of sound to the foundation and building, much the same way that motor mounts are used in automobiles. Enclosures constructed of sound absorbing materials can isolate noisy operations from the remainder of the workplace. Machinery itself can be redesigned so that it produces less noise as a by-product of production.

All of these measures are costly and are frequently deferred for this reason, especially in the current era of cost consciousness. The adversary tug of war between labor and management over who is responsible for hearing protection may provide entertainment, but it is small comfort to the worker who has suffered a profound hearing loss. Prudence dictates that the individual accept the responsibility for protecting his hearing. This can be done by wearing personal protective devices in any work environment where the noise level exceeds eighty decibels. Management and labor have the responsibility to work together to reduce the level of noise whenever feasible. The hearing that you save is your own.

The hazards of noise in recreational activities are discussed in chapter VII. A table listing the noise level in decibels of some commonly encountered sources can be found there.

## DIESEL EXHAUST

In August 1988 the National Institute for Occupational Safety and Health (NIOSH) released a Current Intelligence Bulletin in which they recommended that diesel exhaust be classified as a potential occupational carcinogen. This release contained summaries of recent studies regarding the carcinogenic effect of diesel emissions.

Studies of the content of diesel exhaust were conducted as long ago as the 1950s and 1960s, in both the United States and Great Britain. In November 1977 the Environmental Protection Agency (EPA) announced that it was initiating a study of the potential health hazards of diesel exhaust emissions. The explanation for this action was that several of the seven fractions that had been identified in these emissions had been found to be positive in the Ames test, an indirect test for mutagenicity. A study was conducted for the EPA by PEDCO Environmental, Inc., and it was reported to the EPA in March 1978. The findings were in agreement with studies carried out by Daimler-Benz and others, namely that diesel exhaust does contain small amounts of polynuclear aromatic hydrocarbons that are known to cause cancer. This is also true of gasoline fueled engines.

The other substances in diesel exhaust that are of concern are sulfates, nitrogen oxides and ozones. The sulfate emissions are directly related to the quality of the engineering designs of the engine and the quality of the fuel. This is also true of the level of emissions of nitrous oxides. Mercedes Benz recommends fuel with a sulfur content no higher than 0.5 percent. Number 2 diesel fuel marketed in Michigan by both Union Oil and Amoco claim a sulfur content below 0.1 percent. Studies have verified that levels above 0.3 percent are unusual in most areas of the United States. With low-grade fuel, sulfate emissions and the quantity of particulate "soot" are greatly increased. With poor maintenance both these and nitrous oxides are increased. This is very evident when following some of the municipal buses and poorly maintained tractor-trailer rigs.

Occupational exposure to diesel exhausts occurs among those who work in maintenance garages for autos, trucks and buses, in mines, in tunnels, on railroads, on loading docks and on farms. The risk that is outlined by NIOSH is that of lung cancer, which it concludes is associated with inhalation of diesel exhaust on the job. One of the major problems with making such an assessment is the frequency of cigarette smoking, which is the most common cause of lung cancer. It has also been well established that cigarette smoking potentiates the carcinogenic risk of other substances. In addition to the cancer risk, chronic exposure to diesel exhaust, and indeed the exhaust of gasoline engines, carries a risk of the development of pulmonary fibrosis and emphysema. Nitrogen oxides, ozone and many particulates are irritating to the lung, and over a period of time can produce pathologic changes in the lungs. These changes occur more frequently and more rapidly in those who smoke cigarettes. It is imperative that exhaust emissions from any engines be kept to a minimum by proper ventilation and by ducting exhausts directly to the outside whenever possible.

# HEAT STRESS

The human animal possesses a remarkable degree of adaptability to temperature extremes. This ability has its limits, however, and exposure to heat on the job causes much illness and many deaths each year. Most of the fatalities and many of the cases of heat-related illness could be prevented by monitoring the worker and the environmental conditions surrounding him. The application of some well-known principles and procedures would augment any prophylactic program.

Disorders caused by heat are related to the temperature of the air, the humidity of the air, the amount of air movement at the job site, thermal radiation, the level of physical activity required by the job, age, physical condition, drugs, type of clothing worn and body build. These disorders occur much more commonly during periods of prolonged heat, and particularly when the humidity is high. The chief mechanism by which the body dissipates heat is through sweating and the evaporation thereof. This mechanism becomes less efficient during periods of high humidity, because the sweat evaporates from the skin more slowly. Similarly, sweat is evaporated more rapidly when there is an appreciable air movement across the body than when no such movement is present. Short, stocky and obese individuals dissipate heat much less efficiently, both because of the increased body mass and the decreased skin surface area. More heat is produced in the greater body mass, and at the same time relatively less skin surface area is available for sweating and heat dissipation.

Age plays a significant role in the amount of heat stress that an individual can tolerate. This decrement shows up on jobs where there is a heat exposure component at about the age of thirty-five years. After that age the amount of oxygen that is made available to the body is reduced by 25 to 30 percent. This results partially from a decrease in the functional output of the heart and circulatory system, and partially from the reduction in the efficiency of oxygen transport in the lungs. Obviously this deficit, in both of these components, is much more severe in smokers. The greater the age, the more pronounced these physiological deficiencies become. With age the muscles of the heart, as with the muscles of the extremities, weaken and become less efficient.

The circulation similarly becomes less efficient, partially as a result of the weakening of the heart and partially because of arteriosclerosis. The result is that the heat produced in the body as a result of metabolism and muscular activity is not as readily trans-

155

ported to the surface for dissipation. Another factor making older workers more at risk of heat disorders is that there is a delay in the onset of sweating and a reduction in the amount of such activity that is age induced. This results in greater heat retention within the body, and earlier onset of all the heat disorders. The reduction in all of these mechanisms also prolongs the recovery time for heat-related disorders.

During periods of increased heat stress, with the accompanying increased perspiration, there is a significant increase in the amount of salt lost from the body. The resultant dilution of the body fluids results in a false signal from the region of the brain that normally conserves salt. The consequences is that the kidneys excrete additional quantities of salt as well as water. In order to avoid the serious consequences of these heat induced imbalances, it is necessary to increase the salt intake prophylactically. This is best done with meals. Electrolyte solutions can be used during periods of heat exposure if necessary. Tablets should be avoided since they irritate the stomach. The quantity of salt supplementation needed is directly related to the amount of loss and can be calculated. In jobs where a significant loss occurs over an eight-hour day, ten to fifteen grams per day of additional salt are required. A greater quantity is required during periods of acclimatization.

Under normal conditions any excess of salt and water consumed is controlled and eliminated by the kidney. For this to occur, normal conditions of kidney function and normal water intake are required. Kidney function is commonly reduced in diabetes, in high blood pressure and in older individuals. It may also be reduced as a result of other diseases and as a result of exposure to toxic drugs and chemicals. Diuretics, which are commonly taken for high blood pressure, deplete the body of both salt and fluid volume. As a consequence they render the individual more susceptible to heat disorders. Any supplementation of salt requires adequate intake of water at the same time. Prophylactic salt supplementation carries a particular risk for those individuals who have high blood pressure, because salt has a very deleterious effect on blood pressure. In these instances the quantity of salt consumed should be monitored and balanced carefully.

Alcohol consumption renders workers much more susceptible to all of the heat disorders. It suppresses the hormone in the body that regulates salt and water excretion through the kidneys, leading to excessive water loss and dehydration. Excessive alcohol consumption several days before exposure to heat may result in this deleterious effect. Alcohol should be avoided, therefore, by workers who are are exposed to heat stress, especially during periods of prolonged hot weather.

Physical conditioning improves the efficiency of the circulation and of the function of the heart in general, as it does lung function. This improves heat tolerance to a degree, but it does not eliminate the need for acclimatization. Exposure to heat should be undertaken in steps in order to permit time for the increase in capillaries and circulation and the increase in oxygen transport in the lungs that takes place with continued exposure to heat. This acclimatization generally takes about four to seven days. It is somewhat analogous to the acclimatization in oxygen transport through the lungs to the blood that is required for activities at altitudes above 10,000 feet.

Several formulae and criteria have evolved in an effort to predict the levels at which heat stress occurs. These are complex and require trained personnel as well as specialized apparatus. They attempt to factor in the various environmental conditions such as absolute temperature, air movement, wet bulb reading and humidity, as well as physiologic factors. For the individual, the best indication of impending heat stress is the body core temperature (rectal temperature) and the heart rate. The latter varies with age, and a higher rate is acceptable in younger workers than those past forty years. These two measurements give a clear indication when it is time to remove the worker from the hot environment, and to initiate remedial action. They are less helpful in predicting the length of time that a given worker will be able to work in a hot environment.

Some occupations where heat disorders are encountered are:

| | |
|---|---|
| Bakeries | Furnace operators |
| Boiler operators | Glass manufacture and blowing |
| Cannery workers | Iron and steel mills, rolling |
| Chemical plants | Kilns |
| Coke ovens | Metal casting |
| Construction workers | Mining, deep mines |
| Cooks | Outdoor jobs, summer |
| Dry cleaners and press operators | Roofers |
| Factories, especially in hot weather | Ships and shipyard workers |
| Farmers | Smelters |
| Forge hammer operators | Textile industry |
| Foundries | Tire and rubber manufacture |

## HEAT CRAMPS

These are spasms and pain in the muscles of the arms, legs and sometimes of the abdomen after prolonged exposure to heat. The muscles that are in use on the job are particularly affected. These symptoms are caused by an excessive loss of salt with the resultant flow of water into the cells of the muscles. In some cases albumen may show up in the urine. These symptoms may not develop until after the worker is away from the job. The body temperature is usually normal. This condition frequently results from drinking water in response to thirst and fluid loss on the job, without accompanying salt. The water dilutes the fluids in the body, sending a false signal from the pituitary as described above, which reduces the hormone that would normally reduce water and salt loss.

Heat cramps can occur in hot dry climates very unexpectedly, since the profuse sweating evaporates so rapidly that it is not noticed. It can also occur in people at work or at play in cold climates if they are overdressed. Heat related disorders are seldom considered in these settings. Prevention of this painful condition requires supplementation of the appropriate quantities of salt and water when the loss of these substances is excessive.


## HEAT RASH

This is manifested by small raised blisters accompanied by a prickly sensation during exposure to heat. It is caused by a retention of sweat in the sweat glands when the ducts are obstructed by plugs of keratin and cells. The retained sweat bursts through the wall of the sweat glands into the surrounding tissue, and this results in inflammation, and sometimes infection. It occurs primarily after prolonged exposure to heat when the humidity is high. The evaporation of sweat is thus impaired, leaving the skin constantly wet. The inactivation of the sweat glands produces a pronounced reduction in heat tolerance due to the loss of this valuable mechanism for the dissipation of heat. Bathing, skin hygiene and clean clothing are important in preventing skin infections when this condition occurs. Prevention of heat rash is accomplished by limiting exposure under hot, humid conditions, and allowing the skin to dry periodically.


## HEAT SYNCOPE

Fainting with exposure to heat occurs when the worker stands in one place for protracted periods with minimal or no movement.

It results from the pooling of blood in the skin and legs due to dilation of blood vessels. It occurs more readily in the nonacclimatized worker. Treatment is accomplished by removal to a cooler location and having the worker lie down with the head slightly lower than the legs. It can be prevented by acclimatization and by taking brief steps periodically and regularly in order to stimulate the venous return from the legs to the heart.

## HEAT EXHAUSTION

This heat disorder is also called heat prostration, heat collapse, and heat fatigue. It is the mildest form of heat disorder and is the most common. The symptoms produced are not dramatic and are often overlooked. Heat exhaustion occurs primarily in nonacclimatized workers, but it can also occur in sedentary individuals. It is especially common in elderly individuals who are taking diuretics for high blood pressure or heart failure. The imbalances described previously result in a clouding of the mental faculties resulting in less vigilance and in increased risk of injury. An impaired performance results from decreased function of both the nervous system and muscles. Poor job performance and decreased productivity become apparent. As the condition progresses, weakness, dizziness, headache, nausea, vomiting, loss of appetite and faintness appear. These proceed to collapse if the appropriate remedial steps are not taken.

It is important to recognize the threat of this disorder at the earliest possible signs, and to take measures to prevent progression to a more serious stage. These early steps include removal from the hot environment to a cooler one. In the factory the worker should be moved to an air-conditioned location. This would usually be the plant medical facility. Discontinuance of physical activity, removal of heavy clothing and drinking cool fluids will all help to reverse this potentially serious condition. Once the heat exhaustion victim has progressed to the point where assistance is needed, these measures become much more urgent. In addition to removing from the hot environment, the person should be made to lie flat or with the head slightly low.

## HEAT STROKE

This more serious disorder is also called sunstroke, but it is not necessary to be exposed to the sun to fall victim to this disorder. It is a stage beyond heat exhaustion and it is life threatening. Aggressive measures are urgent. In this disorder, the body's temperature regulating mechanism fails. In most cases there is little or no perspiration, the skin is dry, hot and red. The pulse is rapid (160 to 180) and firm. Respirations are rapid and shallow. The blood pressure is usually low. Constriction of the blood vessels prevents the transfer of heat from the body core to the surface. The body core temperature rises rapidly to a level of 105 to 106 degrees Fahrenheit.

If aggressive measures to reduce this are not taken the temperature rise progresses to convulsions and death. Permanent brain damage may occur if the individual survives. Headache, weakness and dizziness are followed by a sudden loss of consciousness. Disorientation may be present and may progress to delirium. Efforts to control the body temperature should be initiated immediately by immersing the victim in cool water or by wrapping him in cool moist blankets or cloth. Immediate hospitalization should be undertaken. The outlook is less favorable for the aged, debilitated and alcoholics than is the case for young individuals in good health.

# IX

# Hazards of Pets and Other Animals

## ZOONOSES:

DISEASES TRANSMITTED FROM ANIMALS TO HUMANS

### TOXOPLASMOSIS

This is one of the most serious of all the zoonoses by virtue of its impact on the unborn child. Infection in the mother during pregnancy may result in spontaneous abortion, stillbirth or premature birth. Infection is transmitted through the placenta to the infant in about one-third of the cases. The mother may have no outward evidence of the disease, symptoms are noticeable in only about 10 to 20 percent of these cases. Blindness and severe mental retardation may result, and since the cause of these misfortunes is obscure, this infection is usually not related to it.

Inflammation of the retina of the eye leading to loss of vision is most often the result of toxoplasmosis acquired from the mother through the placenta prior to birth. Thirty-five percent of the cases in the child and young adult are acquired in this fashion. Strabismus (cross-eyed) may be an early sign of this affliction. Approximately one-fourth of young adults test positive for toxoplasmosis.

Toxoplasmosis is caused by Toxoplasma gondii, a protozoan parasite that invades and multiplies within the cells of various organs in the body. The cat is the only animal in which the disease can reproduce, and it is the only animal that transmits it directly to humans. The oocysts are passed in the feces of the cat, and these are then transmitted to humans through food, hands or inhalation of dust from a litter box. Children frequently acquire the oocysts from playing in a sandbox where cats have deposited feces. The

161

oocysts may also be transmitted to food by insects. The disease may be acquired by eating improperly cooked pork, or even by blood transfusion. The oocysts from cat feces are much more infective, however. The disease is present worldwide except on a few islands in the Pacific where no cats exist.

Symptoms, when they are present, are vague and may mimic mononucleosis. These symptoms may persist or recur for months. Inflammation of the heart or brain carries a significant morbidity and even death. In one case a realtor who cleaned out an old farmhouse developed a severe myocarditis two weeks later and died as a result of toxoplasmosis. Currently approximately one in every one thousand newborn infants is congenitally infected. This is eighteen times the incidence of phenylketonuria and four times the incidence of muscular dystrophy, but thus far this disease has failed to attract the attention of the fund raisers and the politicians.

Where cats are kept indoors, extreme care should be taken in handling litter boxes, and dust levels should be controlled scrupulously. Cats and litter boxes should not exist indoors during pregnancy. Where cats exist outdoors hands should be washed carefully after gardening. Cats should be denied access to sandboxes by covers, and children should be indoctrinated in the art of hand washing. Inhalation of dust carrying the cysts is much more difficult to avoid. Recalling the extent of the spread of pinworm ova by dust in the household, it is easy to appreciate the difficulty of controlling this disease. In the case of pinworms, this means of transmission is so efficient that eighty percent of the members of the household become infested when one child brings it home.


## CAT SCRATCH FEVER

Ninety percent of the cases of this disease follow a scratch by a cat or intimate contact with a cat. This is a self-limiting disease with none of the serious consequences of toxoplasmosis. The causative agent has defied all efforts to identify it. Suspicion has ranged from a virus to chlamydia. Currently an unorthodox small bacterium is suspected, but proof has been elusive. Enlargement of the lymph nodes in the region of the scratch is the most prominent finding. Fever and malaise are usually mild but may persist for two to three weeks. In most cases a small papule that resembles an insect bite is noticed about a week after the scratch. This papule fails to appear in as many as 40 percent of individuals. A skin test is the only available diagnostic test. There is no treatment available, and none is needed. The cat, which carries this unknown agent over the long term, displays no signs of illness.

## RINGWORM

This fungus infection of the skin is caused by a variety of different species and is frequently transmitted to humans from dogs and cats. The infection is seen more frequently in children because of their close contact with animals. The disease may not be readily apparent on the pet. Successful treatment requires attention to the pet as well as to the human. This disease, as with bacterial infections, may also be transmitted to the pet from humans.

The diagnosis should be established by a physician through scrapings from the afflicted area under the microscope or by culture or both. Cure is accomplished by the application of one of the very effective antifungal creams such as Monistat-Derm, Micatin or Tinactin. These may be combined with sulfur, and sometimes salicylic acid, to increase effectiveness. It is a misconception that these infections cannot be cured. Treatment must be persistent, adequate and continued for several weeks. Failure is usually the result of reinfection from the animal or failure to pursue treatment diligently and long enough. Failure to treat the animal will almost certainly result in reinfection of the child.

## BACTERIAL INFECTIONS

Several infections caused by bacteria may be transmitted either from humans to pets or vice versa, as has been seen with impetigo. Dogs and cats have been identified as the reservoir of recurrent streptococcal throat infections in children. It may not be mere coincidence that the upsurge in the number of cases of rheumatic fever in recent years has paralleled the explosion in the dog and cat population. The practice of kissing animals greatly increases the chances of children acquiring streptococcal infections and other diseases from animals.

## CREEPING ERUPTION

This parasitic disease results from hookworm (Ancylostoma braziliense) infestation in the dog or cat. The ova in the feces are deposited in the soil where they hatch. The larva then penetrate the skin when humans sit or lie on the ground. The travels of the larva in the skin produce a winding, erratic trail as well as marked itching. The larva do not reproduce in humans, and they produce no disease in man other than the burrowing in the skin. On rare occasions an intestinal infection is seen in humans.

## ROUNDWORMS

Toxocara are common intestinal infestations of both dogs and cats. Here again the ova in the feces are deposited in the soil. Sand-boxes are a particularly popular site for this sport among cats. After the ova are swallowed by humans, they hatch in the intestine, penetrate the intestinal wall and spread to any portion of the body. They especially invade the liver, lung, eye and nervous system (brain). They may live for many months, producing scarring and sensitization as they migrate. A simple blood count will reveal a marked increase in the percentage of eosinophils (greater than 60 percent). There is no effective treatment.

## TAPEWORM

Dipylidium caninum infests the dog and cat, and may be suspected when the pet is observed dragging his bottom across the floor. It is acquired by humans when they ingest dust or food contaminated by the fecal material of the pet. It has also been acquired by inadvertently swallowing dog or cat fleas, which ingest the eggs of the tapeworm. Once in the human intestine, the eggs hatch and set up housekeeping. Treatment for humans is available. Periodic de-worming of the pets is the most effective control. Humans on occasion may also be afflicted with the rat tapeworm by ingesting rat fleas.

## LEPTOSPIROSIS

This is the most widespread zoonosis in the world, and has been reported in every region of the United States. It is caused by a spirochete, the same type of bacterium that causes syphilis, yaws and Lyme disease. It can be carried by virtually every animal species, including the dog, cat, fox, raccoon, skunk, cow and pig, and is shed in the urine. It is by this mechanism that it contaminates streams and farm ponds. The animals may have no sign of disease and yet may shed the organism in the urine for years. Swimming in contaminated bodies of water or riding motorcycles through contaminated pools of water have accounted for a significant number of cases. It may be acquired through skin abrasions or through the conjunctiva of the eye during these activities. Most cases are acquired by ingestion of food or water contaminated by urine from the cat, dog, mouse, rat, cow or pig.

The severity of the disease varies considerably, depending on the serotype of the leptospira and on the age of the victim. Fatalities may occur in one half of individuals past the age of fifty years. The organism can affect virtually any organ in the body, including the meninges of the brain, the liver and the kidneys. Jaundice indicates a more serious illness.

The most important single prophylactic measure is to avoid swimming in ponds, particularly those shared with cattle or pigs. Precautions are especially urgent during pregnancy.


## TULAREMIA

Also called rabbit fever or deer fly fever, this is a bacterial infection caused by Yersinia tularensis. It is most commonly acquired by humans while handling rabbits, usually in the process of dressing them. Disposable gloves should always be worn when performing this operation, and the hands should be washed carefully afterward. Special precautions should be taken in any circumstance where the rabbit appears ill. Infections have occurred where sick rabbits were assumed to have been poisoned by pesticides. Infection has been acquired by inhalation from poking or stepping on a dead animal. The organism is highly infectious and is easily contracted by airborne aerosols. Rabbits are made ill by and die from this disease.

Indirect transmission from rabbits to humans has resulted from the bite of a pet animal as well as by the bite of the deer fly, tick or even mosquito. Use of an effective insect repellent will discourage insect bites and wearing a hat as well will tend to discourage the deer fly (see Insect Repellents, chapter VII). Cases resulting from insect bites are seen more frequently in the spring and summer, whereas cases resulting from contact with rabbits are seen more frequently during the hunting season. Squirrels, deer and other mammals also serve as a reservoir for the organism. Pneumonia is a serious form of this disease. Mortality is low if adequately treated for a sufficient length of time. Lifelong immunity is usually conferred by this disease. Only 214 cases were reported in 1987, down from the peak of 2,291 cases reported in 1939. Education of the hunting public has had much to do wiith this decline.

## SALMONELLA INFECTIONS

Several species of salmonella cause infections resulting in diarrhea, abdominal cramping and fever (see also Food, chapter VI). These organisms are transmitted by baby chicks, ducks and turtles. Pet turtles produced approximately 14 percent of the estimated two million cases per year of salmonella infection in the early 1970s. A ban on pet turtles went into effect in 1975 and cases reported as a result of handling pet turtles became rare. Outbreaks continue to occur in other countries where such a ban does not exist. Sporadic cases continue to be reported in the United States. In June 1986, a two-year-old and his four-year-old brother developed an acute salmonella infection with fever, abdominal pain and bloody diarrhea after their mother had purchased a turtle that had been sold illegally at a local pet store in Ohio. Turtles carry a very high rate of salmonella contamination. Infections have been spread to humans through handling of the turtles and by emptying the turtle's water into the sink, where dishes were contaminated. No method of controlling this organism in the turtle has been devised, and these animals have no place in the home.

## PSITTACOSIS

This is an infection in birds caused by a bacterium, Chlamydia psittaci. Most cases evolve from parrots or parakeets, but it can be contracted from pigeons or even chickens. It causes a pneumonitis in humans. The incidence has fluctuated considerably since 1930 (170 cases, 33 deaths) in concert with variation in control measures. Routine quarantine and treatment of imported birds has reduced the incidence of the disease in the general public, but the incidence among poultry raisers and processors has been increasing. In 1984, 172 cases were reported to the Centers for Disease Control.

Smuggling of parrots from South America into the United States has reached almost epidemic proportions recently. The birds bring a price of as much $10,000 in the U.S. It is suspected that many cases are simply treated and not reported. Such practice is encouraged by the fact that the disease is readily treatable with antibiotics. Transmission is accomplished by the inhalation of dust contaminated by the excrement, feathers or nasal secretions of an infected bird. Symptoms in the human resemble pneumonia, and may be moderate to severe. Heart involvement occurs on occasion. Treatment should be instituted early in the course of the disease to improve chances of recovery.

## HISTOPLASMOSIS

This fungus disease of the lungs resembles tuberculosis in many ways. It is acquired by inhaling dust contaminated by the droppings of pigeons, starlings, bats and chickens. The organism survives best in moist soil, which may account for its distribution. It is found chiefly in the Ohio and Mississippi River valleys, in a broader range than previously believed. It is found extending into lower to central Michigan, for instance. Infections of groups of people have occurred among children playing under a tree on a school yard in which starlings roosted, while exploring caves where bats resided, after bulldozing of infected areas and after cleaning of dirt-floored chicken coops. It also has been contracted while harvesting firewood from a tree where infected birds roosted.

Most cases involve the lung, and as with tuberculosis, nodules are seen in the lungs on chest X-ray. The disease may spread to the liver and other parts of the body. Death or severe disability can result, but this is uncommon. A distinctive infection in the eye results in a loss of vision to varying degrees. Individuals who wear glasses normally have an eye exam every two years, and this should reveal any involvement. Individuals who have any of the exposures listed above should have a skin test to reveal any past or present infection. Individuals with a positive skin test, and indeed anyone with a significant exposure should have a careful eye exam. Almost all of the chronic progressive lung cases occur in cigarette smokers. Treatment is available for the progressive or disseminated cases, but the drugs are very toxic.

## ANTHRAX

This is a bacterial disease transmitted from animal to humans, but is rare in the United States, due to surveillance measures. Most of the cases that do occur result from handling imported wool, hair, hides or bone meal for fertilizer. Woolsorter's disease is the inhalation form of this disease and is highly fatal, most individuals dying within twenty-four hours in spite of treatment.

## BRUCELLOSIS

Also known as undulant fever, this bacterial infection is transmitted from a wide variety of domestic animals, such as cattle, swine, goats and sheep. Human infection is most commonly acquired from consuming unpasteurized milk and dairy products. It can be acquired through abrasions of the skin when handling animals, however. There is a greater incidence among dairy farmers and cattle breeders. This disease may be seen almost anywhere in the body, commonly in bone (osteomyelitis), the spleen, lung, genitourinary tract and heart. Endocarditis (inflammation of the heart) is the most common cause of death. Treatment is difficult and success limited. About 150 to 200 cases are reported annually, but again many cases go unreported. A vaccine for cattle is available, and where it has been used it has reduced the incidence of the disease significantly. The disease has been eradicated in some countries through strenuous control programs.

## RABIES

This is a viral disease of the central nervous system (brain) that affects all mammals. It is transmitted through the saliva of an infected animal, usually through a bite. It may be acquired through a skin abrasion or by inhaling the virus in droplets. Four cases have resulted from corneal transplant operations where the donor had apparently died of undiagnosed rabies. The required immunization of dogs has greatly reduced the risk from that source. The incidence of laboratory confirmed cases of rabies in dogs has dropped from 7,000 cases in 1947 to 113 cases in 1985. No such success has been achieved in cats, and the number of cases of rabies reported in cats each year now exceeds that reported in dogs. Cats represent the greatest danger among domesticated animals today for the transmission of this deadly disease.

In 1985, the National Association of State Public Health Veterinarians recommended laws requiring the vaccination of all cats. This recommendation has been reinforced periodically since that time, to no avail. Continued removal of all stray dogs and cats is essential in controlling this dread and virtually 100 percent fatal disease. Although there are over one million animal bites in the United States each year, rabies in humans is rare, with three reported cases in 1984.

Many cases continue to occur outside of the United States. Fatalities probably are in excess of one thousand per year. The disease poses a serious threat when traveling to areas such as Africa, where rabies is common among wild dogs. The primary reservoir in animals in the United States is the skunk, raccoon, bat and fox, in order of decreasing frequency. Rabid bats have been reported in every state except for Hawaii and have caused rabies in humans in the United States. The raccoon is a more recent addition to our risk, and is especially important since it increasingly is joining us in neighborhoods.

The ideal procedure following a bite by any animal is the confinement and observation of that animal for ten days. If any illness or abnormal behavior develops in that period of time the brain should be examined by the health department for evidence of rabies. If the animal is alive and well after ten days, the odds are that it does not have rabies. Confining a wild animal, especially one exhibiting abnormal behavior, is very difficult and not without danger. Under these circumstances killing the animal and preserving the head is the next best course. The animal should be handled carefully with surgical gloves. It must also be remembered that rabies can be contracted by inhaling the virus.

In the event of an unprovoked bite by any wild animal, or by any animal exhibiting abnormal behavior, the head of the animal should be preserved (in a freezer in a plastic bag) and the local health department should be called immediately for instructions. Disposable plastic or latex gloves should be worn while handling any such animals. A vaccine derived from human diploid cell is the only vaccine available in the United States currently. It requires five injections, in contrast to the fourteen daily injections previously required, and it provokes fewer reactions. It is highly effective if administered early and if rabies immune serum or globulin is given concomitantly. Rabies, once acquired, is 100 percent fatal. Prevention is the only hope.

Every animal bite should be treated immediately by a physician. In the case of a rabid animal, proper treatment of the wound is an important and integral part of the prophylaxis. Decisions regarding treatment after a bite are complex and require careful professional judgment. There are no second chances with this disease, and it is 100 percent fatal if not successfully prevented.

Pre-exposure prophylaxis for rabies is available to individuals with a high degree of risk, such as veterinarians and laboratory workers. It is more complex than other immunizations such as tetanus, however, and it requires the measuring of antibody titres. This protection is not recommended routinely for travelers to areas where rabies is endemic. If someone is attending business in the remote areas of Africa where no medical facility will be available without many days of travel, prophylactic immunization is probably advisable. Here again this requires experienced professional judgment.


## TRICHINOSIS

This parasitic disease is acquired by eating inadequately cooked meat, virtually always pork, that contains encysted larvae of the roundworm, Trichinella spiralis. A few cases have been reported in recent years from bear meat and wild boar. The pig usually becomes infected from eating raw garbage, although eating infected rats may be a source. The rats feed on raw pork scraps thus helping to maintain the cycle of infection. Laws requiring that garbage fed to pigs be cooked has markedly reduced the incidence of trichinosis in the United States. There has been an increase in the number of cases reported in the Northeastern states in recent years, primarily as a result of noncommercial farmers who are feeding raw garbage.

Once ingested, the encysted larvae are released by the stomach digestion process. Diarrhea, abdominal pain and nausea may be experienced at this time, one to two days after ingestion. The larvae reproduce and are carried through the body by the circulation. They invade and encyst in various muscles, including those of the diaphragm, tongue, eye, arms and legs. This invasion results in severe muscle aching. They may persist in this location in this form for five to ten years. Symptoms of meningitis or encephalitis may appear, in which case the mortality may be 10 percent. If inflammation of the heart (myocarditis) ensues, the mortality may reach 20 percent. A blood count will generally reveal 15 to 50 percent of eosinophils, compared to a normal of up to 4 percent. There is no means of eradicating the larva from the body.

Prevention is accomplished very simply by adequate cooking of meat. Particular care must be exercised when cooking pork in a microwave oven. An adequate internal temperature (170 degrees Fahrenheit), as measured with an accurate thermometer, must be reached to assure inactivation of the larva. All garbage fed to pigs must be cooked. This simple measure has markedly reduced the incidence of this disease in the United States.

## MOSQUITOES

Throughout the history of mankind these insects have delivered more death and disease than any other insect. Diseases transmitted by mosquitoes have killed more people than the combined total of all of the wars in history. In addition to the encephalitis discussed below, an Aedes species has transmitted malaria from a returned soldier to campers at a Girl Scout camp in California. Several cases of dengue fever have been transmitted by Aedes aegyptii in the Rio Grande valley of Texas since 1980. This disease, which can cause hemorrhage and death, has had a sudden resurgence during the past 30 years, for unknown reasons. About 100,000 cases a year occur in the far east. Several large outbreaks have occurred in the Caribbean. An outbreak in Cuba in 1981 involved 350,000 people, with 158 deaths. During an epidemic of dengue fever in Ecuador in early 1988, 420,000 people were infected. This epidemic resulted from a resurgence of the Aedes aegyptii mosquito population.

Ecuador had been declared free of this mosquito in 1958 after a ten-year eradication program to control yellow fever. Spraying with malathion has been resumed since the epidemic. The Pan American Health Organization has reported similar episodes of dengue fever in Brazil, Bolivia and Paraguay in recent years.

The recent introduction of the Asian tiger mosquito, Aedes albopictus, into Texas in 1985 through a shipment of used tires from Asia has raised the specter of far more widespread outbreaks of dengue fever in the United States. It is feared that this mosquito will also introduce other viral diseases that have not yet been seen in the United States. By 1988 Aedes albopictus had been found in 113 counties in 17 states, including Indiana, Illinois, Ohio, Maryland,

Delaware, North Carolina, Tennessee, Kentucky and most of the southern states. This new breed of mosquito is known to transmit dengue and will most likely transmit the LaCrosse virus, which will increase the incidence of encephalitis.

Aedes albopictus is much more aggressive than the other mosquitoes that we have had to deal with. It has already displaced the local species in some areas in the south. It has also demonstrated some resistance to pesticides customarily used against mosquitoes, such as malathion, temephos and bendiocarb. Its hibernation habits make it adaptable to survival as far north as about the Fortieth Parallel, the latitude of Columbus, Ohio. This mosquito transmits viruses to its offspring through the eggs, which survive freezing. This assures the survival and transmission of diseases that would not ordinarily survive the winter season. The only mosquito in the United States previously that was capable of transmitting dengue fever, Aedes aegyptii, cannot survive the winter months in the northern states.

The only effective control measure is to deny the mosquito a breeding pool. Such efforts have been very effective in California but will prove more elusive in other parts of the country. Old tires are a favorite breeding ground for Aedes albopictus. Effective January 1, 1988, the Centers for Disease Control required that all tire casings imported from Asia be certified as clean, dry and free from insects. Fumigation is required as an added precaution, and examination of tire casings since indicates that these efforts have been successful.

It will become ever more urgent to take every precaution to avoid attacks from mosquitoes during recreational activities. Fortunately we have a very effective repellent in diethyl-meta-toluamide (DEET). It is the only effective agent, but it is widely marketed by several different manufacturers. The products with the higher concentrations, 25 to 50 percent, have the longest duration of action. In order to avoid possible sensitization to these products, it is best to avoid any unnecessary skin contact, applying the repellent to clothing instead, wherever possible. None of the electronic devices are effective against mosquitos. The zappers that destroy larger insects permit mosquitos to pass through without making contact. When camping, netting on tents is essential. To control a tent full of insects that gain entry as a result of repeated passage by children, spraying the tent with a pyrethroid aerosol thirty minutes before bedtime is effective. Exit the tent after spraying to avoid inhaling the aerosol.

# ENCEPHALITIS

Four types of encephalitis transmitted to humans by the bite of certain species of mosquitoes occur in various regions of the country. Western equine is seen throughout the United States and carries a mortality of only about 3 percent. Eastern equine is seen along the eastern seaboard, and in western Michigan in recent years. It carries a mortality in excess of 50 percent. Outbreaks in horses precede human cases in both of these types of encephalitis. St. Louis encephalitis has occurred throughout the United States. The California group, which includes the LaCrosse virus, has been widely distributed throughout the U.S. Aedes albopictus is known to be capable of transmitting this form of encephalitis.

Mental retardation, seizure disorder and speech and behavioral problems may persist after recovery from any of these diseases, the pattern varying somewhat according to the type. The disease is seen from spring to fall, when mosquitoes are active. Approximately 100–200 cases per year of these mosquito born encephalitides are reported, but periodically an epidemic is seen. Eight hundred cases of St. Louis encephalitis were reported in the United States in 1975. During the same year 85 cases of eastern equine and 65 cases of California group encephalitis were reported. This was the last large epidemic to date. Control of mosquitoes is highly effective in controlling the incidence of these diseases, as has been demonstrated in California. In that state, the elimination of pools of water in agricultural irrigation systems and the planting of larva eating fish, such as gambusia, in bodies of water where mosquitoes breed have produced significant successes.


# TICKS

Two different groups of these arthropods transmit a variety of diseases to humans. Those that have a hard shell (ixodid ticks) transmit viral encephalitis, tularemia, Colorado tick fever, Q fever, Rocky Mountain spotted fever, babesiosis and Lyme disease in the United States. Twelve different families of hard-shelled ticks exist in Africa, Europe and North, South and Central America. The ticks with a soft shell (argasid ticks) transmit the spirochete, Borrelia, which causes relapsing fever. Soft-shelled ticks are widespread throughout parts of Africa, India and South America, where they commonly attack humans in huts and camps that are universally infested. It has become resistant to DDT in some of these areas, but the pyrethroids and other pesticides such as malathion are still effective. Soft-shelled ticks usually lay about 1000 eggs each, while hard-shelled ticks may lay up to 5000. Some ticks can survive for up to two years without feeding.

A unique product that utilizes a similar principal as the ground squirrel dusting in California is marketed under the name of Damminix. It is a biodegradable tube stuffed with cotton that has been treated with a pesticide. These baited tubes are strategically placed in fields in areas where a disease such as Lyme disease is a threat. The field mice then carry the cotton to incorporate it into their nests, thus killing the Ixodes dammini tick nymphs that feed on the mice. This promises to break the transmission cycle for Lyme disease in those areas where the mouse is the chief host. Ticks belong to the same family as mites (acarina) and are the larger cousin of the clan.

## RELAPSING FEVER

This is an infectious disease caused by a spirochete which is transmitted from ground squirrels or other small rodents through the bite of a soft-shelled tick. It may be transmitted from humans to humans by the human body louse. It is seen in the western mountain states where infected ticks may live for decades. This tick has a particularly long life span. It is a nocturnal biter, and feeds on inhabitants of mountain cabins while they sleep. The tick is a slow feeder, and cannot extract much blood except from a sleeping host. It is thus that visitors to this popular resort area are infected. Cases occur mainly in the spring and summer. Untreated the mortality rate ranges from 30 to 70 percent. With antibiotics the mortality rate is reduced to less than 1 percent.

## LYME DISEASE

This is another spirochetal disease that is transmitted to humans by ticks. The tick vector is of the hard variety (Ixodes dammini) and in the nymph stage is tiny, being only one to two millimeters long, about the size of a pin head. This presents a significant problem when inspecting the body for ticks, for it may give the appearance of a pigmented mole or other skin lesion. Lyme disease was first detected in 1977, but by 1985 it had become the most commonly

174

reported tick-borne illness in the United States. In 1980 when 226 cases were reported from eleven states, it was limited chiefly to the northeastern United States and Wisconsin and Minnesota. Since that time it has spread to an increasing number of states each year, with a marked increase in the total number of cases reported. In 1984 a significant number of cases were reported from each of the six regions of the United States, with a total of 1498 cases reported from twenty states.

By 1988 Lyme disease had been reported in 32 states and on every continent except Antarctica. The tick has also been discovered on lawns of suburban homes, not limited to brushy and wooded areas as previously believed. The mouse and the deer serve as the reservoir for the spirochete. The bacteria are transmitted to the tick when it feeds on the animals, and then from tick to man. Early symptoms may resemble flu or meningitis, and Lyme disease is seldom considered in the diagnosis. The onset of these symptoms after the tick bite may be anywhere from a few days to a month. The tick bite is seldom noticed because of the smallness of the tick. Many cases go undiagnosed and unreported. No laboratory test is available to detect the disease in its early stages.

More than half of the victims do not seek medical help until after the first stage, which can last for several weeks. In the second stage the diagnosis is more obscure, and the heart and nervous system can be affected. Antibiotics are very effective in treating the disease in the first stage, but they are much less effective if not started during this early period. Serious damage to the heart and nervous system as well as a chronic arthritis can result if early treatment is not instituted. Among the nervous system problems are Bell's Palsy, palsy of other central and peripheral nerves, meningitis and encephalitis. Even with treatment some people develop these complications.

Lyme disease shares many of the characteristics of other spirochetal diseases such as syphilis. It is far better to not get the disease at all. Tight clothing with pants legs tucked into boot tops or socks, and insect repellent (DEET) applied prior to exposure are essential when walking in infested areas. The insect repellent must be reapplied at appropriate intervals. Recent studies by the U.S. Air Force and others has found that spraying the clothing with permethrin (Permanone Tick Repellent) in addition to using insect repellent greatly increases the protection against ticks (see Insect Repellents, chapter VII). When inspecting for ticks the size (one millimeter, two millimeters engorged) must be kept in mind.

## BABESIOSIS

This parasite is transmitted to humans by the same tick involved in Lyme disease. The nymphal stage of the tick transmits several different species of a protozoan parasite, Babesia, from a variety of animals. The parasite invades and destroys red blood cells, much as occurs in malaria, and with a similar anemia produced. Over one hundred cases have been reported in the United States, mostly from the New England states and in California. There is no treatment to eradicate the parasite. This disease presents a particular risk to people who have had their spleen removed. The same precautions regarding ticks described above should be observed to prevent babesiosis.

## TICK PARALYSIS

This disease is caused by a neurotoxin that is secreted in the saliva by certain hard ticks while they feed on animals. Dogs, cattle and sheep are affected as well as man. The toxin acts on the cells of the spinal cord to produce a weakness beginning in the legs. This progresses to a paralysis twenty-four to forty-eight hours later, and gradually spreads up the body to involve the trunk, arms, neck, tongue and central nerve centers. Death may ensue if removal of the tick (or ticks) is not accomplished. Tick paralysis is frequently mistaken for polio or one of the other paralytic diseases. The small size of the tick requires very careful scrutiny, including all of the hair and skin fold areas. Removal of the intact tick results in a rapid recovery.

Tick paralysis occurs most commonly in the northwestern United States and in western Canada, where the wood tick, Dermacentor andersoni, is the culprit. The disease has also been reported in the southeastern and Gulf states where the dog tick and a deer tick have been incriminated. People who live in or visit these areas should always take the simple tick precautions of tucking pants legs into boots or socks, and of applying insect repellent, diethyl-meta-toluamide (DEET) to the clothing and bare skin. Also spraying the clothing with the new Permanone Tick Repellent mentioned above gives added protection. Since the tick in this stage is about the size of a pin head, it requires very careful scrutiny for detection. Prevention is far preferable.

# EHRLICHIOSIS

This is another serious disease transmitted by ticks to humans. It was first reported in 1986 and many cases were misdiagnosed as Rocky Mountain Spotted Fever. Eighty percent of the victims did not have a rash, and tests for Rocky Mountain Spotted Fever were negative. It is caused by a rickettsia that is transmitted from dogs to humans by ticks. A total of forty-six cases have been identified from eleven different states, mostly in the southeast and south central U.S. Early diagnosis and treatment is essential. A blood test to establish the diagnosis is available from the Centers for Disease Control. This newly discovered disease provides an added incentive for travelers to these regions to exercise precautions against ticks.


# FLEAS

Various species of fleas attack birds, rats, mice, squirrels, and virtually every wild animal as well as livestock and domestic pets. All of these species will attack humans, given the opportunity. The fleas of wild rodents (rats and ground squirrels) are a serious concern in southern California and in Arizona because they carry the plague bacteria (Yersinia pestis). These fleas can transmit plague to humans when they bite. Careful attention should be given to clothing and to the application of insect repellent (DEET) when involved in recreational or farming activities in these geographic areas. The residential areas of Los Angeles have extended into the hills where ground squirrels abound. This presents a particular risk to everyone living in this area. An innovative program by the health department to control the fleas on these creatures by dusting them through feeding devices has helped to control this disease.

The fleas that most frequently attack humans are the dog and cat flea. They do not establish housekeeping on humans, rather they feed (bloodsucking) and depart. Their saliva produces raised, reddened areas that may itch intensely. These are most commonly seen on the lower legs, which are within reach of this prodigious jumper. If you enter an infested house after the pet has been away for a while, you may readily see these creatures leaping to the attack. Secondary infection of the skin from scratching is occasionally seen. The itching is best controlled by the application of a topical steroid cream such as hydrocortisone. This should not be applied to the face, but flea bites are not customarily seen in that location. In South

America and in Africa, fleas burrow underneath the skin and cause abscesses to form.

Successful eradication of fleas may be a long-term project. It requires treating the pet, the house, the yard and the kennel. The yard, even when fenced, is commonly reinfested by nocturnal visits of other animals. The pet should be bathed and dusted regularly with Sevin (carbyl). This may also be sprayed on the yard. Fleas in some areas have developed a resistance to some insecticides, which may require substitution if reduction in population is not seen. Malathion may be sprayed on the yard as well as dusted in the kennel. Chlorpyrifos (Dursban) is also effective against fleas, and it may be sprayed outdoors. It should not be used indoors on carpets although it is prescribed for this use by some. For use on dogs only it has been marketed recently with a polymer to prolong the release of the pesticide. How much safer this renders the chlorpyrifos remains to be seen. DDT is very effective and safe even for the animal but is not widely available.

All rat runs should be dusted. If you have inherited a population of ground squirrels, you can use the California technique of dusting these animals using tubes lined on either end with a fabric containing malathion or Sevin dust, and a bait in the center. When flea eggs hatch the larva spin a cocoon that may protect it from pesticides. Repeated applications will pick off the survivors. It may well be necessary to continue this battle all summer long. Some years are worse than others.

Eradicating these creatures from the house may be more difficult. They thrive in carpets, as long as they have someone to feed on. The use of an aerosol spray containing pyrethroids and piperonyl butoxide, designed for household use, should produce extinction of fleas within a half hour. The house should be vacated during this period. Thorough vacuuming should then be undertaken to remove as many eggs as possible. The eggs hatch in three days when conditions are favorable but remain dormant in the carpet, dust or the animal nest for months. The stimulus that prompts hatching of the egg is the presence of a suitable host heralded by warmth and vibration. Obviously, retreatment may be required. If this treatment fails, if it is apparent that there is no reduction in the flea population of the living room, a problem exists.

While Sevin and malathion have a low order of toxicity, they are not recommended for general household use. Chlorpyrifos is commonly sold for the control of fleas on pets, and is even prescribed by some as a spray for carpeting. This product is a member of the organophosphate family of pesticides, and is too toxic to be spraying on the carpeting in the house. It is significantly more toxic than Sevin or malathion. It recently has been marketed with a polymer that prolongs its action when applied to dogs. How much safer this renders it is yet to be determined. In households where young children are crawling on the floor, all chemicals should be avoided. (See chapter I for more on pesticides.)

## MURINE TYPHUS (endemic typhus)

This is a rickettsial disease transmitted to humans by the rat flea. This disease infects virtually all rats and mice at some point in their life. Although it does not kill the rodent, the Rickettsia typhi organism remains with them for a long time. The rat flea acquires the organism from this source. It is the nature of all fleas to feed on any available warm host in an emergency, and outbreaks of murine typhus have been reported after campaigns to poison rats. The source of the bubonic plague (Black Death) in the fourteenth century was suspected as a result of the observation that outbreaks were frequently associated with the appearance of dead rats.

Murine typhus has been reported in virtually every state, being much more common in shipping ports, near granaries and food storage areas. It is prevalent in the southeastern United States and along the Gulf Coast. Currently about 60 cases are reported annually, down from the 2,000 to 5,000 cases annually in the 1940s. This dramatic reduction in incidence has resulted from aggressive programs designed to deny rats access to food in storage and in granaries, and by dusting burrows and runs with pesticides to kill the fleas.

This form of typhus, although it is manifested by an acute, pronounced illness, carries a low mortality rate. Deaths occur primarily among the elderly and those with other debilitating illnesses. Shaking chills, headache, temperature of 102 or 103 along with malaise and prostration suggestive of influenza characterize the illness. It can be treated with antibiotics, best results being achieved by instituting therapy early.

## EPIDEMIC TYPHUS

This is a much more severe form of typhus caused by Rickettsia prowazekii. It is transmitted from humans to humans by the body louse. As such it is not commonly a zoonosis, although it can be transmitted from flying squirrels in unusual circumstances. It was prevalent in England and Europe throughout the sixteenth and seventeenth centuries, due to poor hygienic conditions. All of Europe was engulfed in A.D. 1500, when it particularly struck in crowded population centers and among troops. Italy suffered an epidemic in A.D. 1505 and again from 1524 to 1530. Labeled as gaol (jail) fever in England, it killed 510 people at Oxford, being transmitted from person to person from prisoners on trial. In early 1700 it was known as hospital fever in England because of outbreaks of the disease in that setting. In 1784 it was given still another title, factory fever because of the frequent outbreaks there. Finally after about 1800 it began to subside as a result of improvements in hygiene and sanitation.

Epidemic typhus has been common in wartime until World War II. The dusting of entire populations in Europe with DDT powder during invasions by the Allied forces prevented outbreaks of typhus among our troops. This was the first war in history when the armies were not devastated by this scourge. Effective antibiotic treatment is now available, but the disease has been relegated to the back pages in most of the civilized world as a result of increased levels of personal hygiene. It cannot be transmitted without body lice.


## PLAGUE

The most dramatic and far reaching epidemic ever to strike mankind was the "Black Death" or bubonic plague of the fourteenth century. This sweeping disease episode killed half of the population of England and at least one-fourth of the population of all of Europe. The pandemic ravaged the population of Asia and Africa, then spread to the Crimea. From Constantinople it spread to Turkey, Greece and Italy, then north and west until it had engulfed all of Europe and England by A.D. 1350. The death toll was over 60 million people. The disease continued to strike at intervals until the end of the seventeenth century. The Great Plague of London in 1665 killed 69,000 of the population. In Vienna in 1679 it killed 70,000 people; in Prague in 1681, 83,000 died; in Italy in 1630, 500,000 people died as a result of that epidemic of plague. Russia was visited first in this pandemic, in 1601, and 127,000 people died in Moscow.

The devastation of this catastrophic pandemic had profound social, political and religious consequences that changed the world forever. Untreated, the mortality of plague remains close to 100 percent, in spite of the fact that antibiotics are effective. These medications must be instituted early to reduce the mortality to about 10 percent. Unfortunately treatment is often delayed because the diagnosis is not considered. It is always much easier to arrive at a prompt diagnosis in the middle of an epidemic. In modern time, cases of plague arrive erratically and unexpectedly.

Plague is caused by a bacterium, Yersinia pestis, that is transmitted from wild rodents to humans by the bite of the rat flea. In the United States the wild rodents most frequently associated with transmission of the disease are rats and ground squirrels. However, mice, chipmunks and prairie dogs can harbor the disease just as readily. Outbreaks of the disease have increased in frequency over the past twenty-five years in the southwestern United States, due primarily to demographic trends. While cases of plague associated with rats in urban areas, the classic playground for the disease, have become rare, the threat is great in rural and suburban regions. This is especially the case in Los Angeles and Orange County, where the population has spread into the hills surrounding the city, where ground squirrels abound. The plague bacillus and the flea that transmits it are present among the squirrel population in that region.

As with typhus, one of the classic and successful programs to control the disease has been to reduce the flea population by dusting the burrows of the rodent, rat or ground squirrel, with DDT. In California an ingenious device that greatly increases the effectiveness of such control programs was developed. It consists of a length of tubing with a fabric at each end and an attractive bait in the center. The fabric has been dusted with a pesticide. When the ground squirrels take their meal, they dust themselves at the same time, freeing themselves of their fleas. Their gratitude must be overwhelming, particularly considering that the alternative would be to eliminate the squirrel population.

While plague in the cities has been almost eliminated as a result of the control of the rat population, the number of cases acquired from rural and country rodents has been rising. These cases occur most frequently in the spring and summer, and very often among young people who spend more time venturing into the fields. The mortality among these cases is almost twice as high as normal because of the delay in diagnosis. Up to 20 percent of infected individuals develop plague pneumonia, which is almost always fatal unless treated vigorously. Plague pneumonia can readily be transmitted to other humans by droplet infection through a cough or sneeze. Pet cats can catch and return plague infested rodents to the home, or simply bring back the infected fleas. The cat usually dies if it becomes infected. Dogs can similarly bring back the infected fleas, but they often recover if they become diseased.

Plague seems destined to be with us forever. There is an abundant supply of wild rodents that harbor the bacterium. Yersinia pestis also remains viable in the soil, in the burrows of rats and ground squirrels, for prolonged periods. Infected fleas also survive for long periods of time. The disease is well established in Russia, Indochina, India and Africa, as well as in the southwestern United States.

## CHAGAS' DISEASE

This disease is caused by Trypansoma cruzi, another protozoan disease for which we have no effective treatment. The organism is transmitted to humans by the triatomine bug, a member of the reduviid family, and also called the "kissing," "conenose," and in error, the "assassin" bug. The true "assassin" bug is another member of the reduviid family. These insects feed on the blood of vertebrates, chiefly mammals and birds, mainly during the night. One of the most popular hosts is the opossum. They feed on humans wherever they can gain access to the home, and this occurs commonly in communities where housing is primitive. The bites occur around the mouth (thus the name "kissing" bug) and the eyes.

The disease is prevalent in scattered areas of South and Central America and in some areas of Mexico. A few sporadic cases have been reported in Texas and California. The failure of this bug to transmit Chagas' disease as readily in the United States reportedly is due to the habit of the local species of bug of defecating after feeding, rather than during feeding as is the case in South and Central America. The trypanosomes are transmmitted in the feces, not in the saliva, and the disease occurs when the feces contaminates the wound caused by the bite.

Of greater concern than Chagas' disease in the southwestern United States where these bugs are established is the sensitivity that some people develop to the bite. This has resulted in severe anaphylactic reactions, and this trend is expected to expand. While the insect can gain access to any home, this is not common in modern construction, and the insect presents a greater threat when camping in the southwest.

182

## SCABIES

This is not ordinarily a zoonosis, but one form of mange in animals can be transmitted to humans. This is ocassionally seen in veterinarians and pet groomers. The common form of scabies is transmitted from human to human by direct contact or through bedding and clothing (see Scabies, chapter XII).

## RAT BITE FEVER

This is an infection caused by a streptobacillus, the reservoir of which is the nose and mouth of rats. About one-half of wild rats carry the bacterium, and laboratory animals may have a similar incidence; the disease has been contracted from bites in the laboratory. The infection may also be transmitted in contaminated food, and an outbreak in Massachusetts resulting from contamination of milk and ice cream was labeled Haverhill Fever, a dubious distinction for the town of this name. Fever and chills accompany this disease, and a rash is seen in most cases. It is treatable with penicillin.

## Q FEVER

This rickettsial disease is found in cattle, sheep and ticks. Most infections in humans result from inhalation of dust containing the organism; a single inhaled organism is adequate to initiate infection. The organism is extremely resistant, and can survive in dried dust for long periods. Infection may occasionally result from drinking unpasteurized milk. In most instances it produces a mild flulike illness, but it may produce severe illness, with a temperature of 104 degrees Fahrenheit. It may affect the heart, and this sequela may occur many years after recovery. It is often fatal when the heart is involved, particularly in individuals who have previous valvular disease, as occurs as a result of rheumatic fever and congenital heart disease.

## ECHINOCOCCUS

This parasite is uncommon in the United States, being seen mainly among sheep farmers who use dogs. The life cycle of the parasite involves both the dog and the sheep. The eggs are deposited in the stool of the dog. When these ova are ingested by humans through contaminated food or hands, the embryo penetrates the intestinal wall and is carried by the circulation to the brain, liver, lung and kidney. In these locations, cysts are formed that slowly enlarge, producing pressure. The cysts are filled with infectious organisms. About 200 cases are reported in the United States each year, chiefly among Basque sheep farmers in California, the southwestern Indians, and sheep raisers in Utah.

## GIARDIA

This protozoan disease causes intestinal infection in humans (diarrhea) and the organism is shed in the stool of infested pets. It thus can be transmitted to humans by hands or by contaminated food. It is more commonly acquired by drinking contaminated water, either from wells in certain regions of the United States, or from natural bodies of water contaminated by animals, most notably beavers (see Giardia in chapter VI).

# X

# Hazards of the Air that We Breathe

As has been the case on the job (see chapter VIII), air quality at home has become an increasing source of symptoms and complaints. In the extreme, a number of families have been forced to evacuate their homes as a result of excessive levels of formaldehyde. The formaldehyde came from urea foam insulation that was blown into the walls. Similar complaints have come from residents of mobile homes. High levels of formaldehyde in these units were traced to not only urea foam insulation, but to the plywood and particle board components as well. All of these complaints have been magnified in recent years because residences have been sealed more tightly to make them energy efficient. Improvements in insulation materials and techniques have facilitated these efforts and have contributed to the problem. This has resulted in a reduction in the amount of outside air that is circulated through the home. Many substances that have previously produced no symptoms are now increased in concentration to levels that produce discomfort.

Formaldehyde levels that are greatly above the limit of one part per million set by the American Conference of Governmental Industrial Hygienists have been measured in new homes. New materials used in home construction have contributed to the problem. The increased use of particle board, plywood and adhesives adds to the level of formaldehyde and organic solvents in the air. The escape of these gases into the air is not measured by conventional methods. Some of the organic solvents contributed from building materials include 1,1,1-trichloroethane, toluene, styrene, xylene and benzene. The latter has been associated with the development of leukemia and is closely controlled in industrial and laboratory use. The level of these and other gases has been found to be particularly high in mobile homes. This is due to both the greater quantities of materials containing them being used, and to the relatively smaller air volume. These levels gradually subside over a period of six to twelve months.

Carbon monoxide, which kills many people in their homes and apartments every winter, reaches higher levels in a tight home. Most people who are exposed survive, but they suffer vague symptoms, such as headache, that are frequently not related to this potentially lethal gas. Lower levels of carbon monoxide that do not produce symptoms have been suspected of contributing to arteriosclerotic heart disease and angina. These diseases have been noted to occur at a higher than normal rate in cigarette smokers. The level of carboxyhemoglobin (from carbon monoxide) in cigarette smokers is five to fifteen times normal values. Some carbon monoxide is produced in the home from gas cooking stoves. Potentially lethal levels can result from using space heaters, even supposedly safe kerosene heaters. Most serious exposures result from defective or obstructed chimneys, flues or furnaces. A number of deaths have occurred as a result of cooking indoors with charcoal. Charcoal should never be used for cooking or heating in any enclosed space. This is particularly true in homes, mobile homes and recreational vehicles.

Nitrogen oxides are also produced by gas stoves and by kerosene space heaters. These gases are not only a respiratory irritant but they have been incriminated in the production of cancer. Both of these appliances should be vented. An overhead hood vented to the outside is sufficient for the kitchen gas range, if the blower is on during cooking.

Cigarette smoke is the most hazardous indoor air pollution problem that people face. It is the cause of virtually all bronchial carcinoma, the only type of cancer that is on the increase. The only cancer epidemic in the United States today is lung cancer. Cigarette smoking causes 80,000 deaths from lung cancer each year in the U.S. Only about 10 percent of the people with lung cancer live for five years after the diagnosis is made. Only about 15 percent of the cases of lung cancer are due to occupational exposures. The remainder are due to cigarette smoking.

Statistics from the National Cancer Institute show that people who smoke one to nine cigarettes per day have over four times the death rate from lung cancer that is seen in nonsmokers. For those who smoke ten to nineteen cigarettes per day, the rate climbs to about eight times as high. For those who smoke twenty to thirty-nine per day it is about thirteen times, and over forty per day the rate is about seventeen times as high. Fifty times the quantity of tobacco is smoked today as was the case in the early 1900s.

More than four thousand chemical substances have been identified in tobacco smoke, several of which are known carcinogens. The mean particle size of cigarette smoke is 0.2 to 0.5 micrometers, which assures access to the deepest reaches of the lungs. The most potent cancer causing agent in cigarette smoke is benzo-a-pyrene. It is also present in coal tar, in wood smoke and in many other instances of combustion. It is used in the laboratory to produce cancers in animals. Polonium, a breakdown product of radon, is another serious cancer producing substance in cigarettes. Some of the polonium in tobacco originates from the soil where it is grown. Some of it comes from the decay of radioactive lead in the phosphate fertilizer used to grow tobacco. Nitrosamines are also present in tobacco, and their cancer causing propensity was discussed in chapter VI.

Some of the other pollutants in cigarette smoke are irritants and are responsible for the bronchitis and productive cough that is so characteristic of smokers. Acrolein and acetaldehyde, common components of smog, are two such irritants. They produce irritation of the eyes, nose, throat and lungs. Hydrogen cyanide and nitrogen oxides are other irritants. Cadmium is worse than an irritant. It is a potent cause of emphysema, a disease seen commonly in silver solderers who inhale the fume. Cadmium undoubtedly plays a significant role in the production of the chronic lung disease and emphysema that is so common in cigarette smokers.

The carbon monoxide in cigarette smoke has been widely studied. It plays a significant role in the production of arteriosclerotic heart disease. Carbon monoxide attaches to hemoglobin in the blood, producing carboxyhemoglobin. This form of hemoglobin is incapable of carrying oxygen. The desirable level is zero, but levels up to one percent are commonly found in nonsmokers. The level of carboxyhemoglobin in moderate cigarette smokers (one pack per day) is about 5 percent, and it ranges up to 15 percent in heavy smokers. It is not uncommon to see levels of 8 to 10 percent among smokers in clinical practice. In those who already have a compromised circulation to the heart due to arteriosclerosis, this further deprives the heart muscle of oxygen. These individuals have more severe angina than nonsmokers. Repeated studies of large groups of people in several cultures throughout the world have all shown that males who smoke cigarettes have a 70 percent higher death rate than nonsmokers. This mortality is primarily due to coronary heart disease. It is most pronounced in the 45- to 55-year age group.

Adverse effects on the nervous system are also caused by these elevations of carboxyhemoglobin over time.

The effects of nonsmokers inhaling the cigarette smoke from smokers have been the subject of several recent studies. In the work place this exposure has produced irritation of the eyes, nose and throat with coughing and sneezing. The presence of smokers in a room increases the level of particulates that are inhaled into the lungs by three to twelve times. The presence of a smoker in the home increases the level of these respirable particulates to two to three times the normal level. These "passive smokers" demonstrate a carboxyhemoglobin level of over 2 percent. This level is detrimental to health, invoking risks such as coronary heart disease. After two hours in a room with a smoker, the carboxyhemoglobin level in the blood of a nonsmoker was increased from the baseline level of 1 percent to 2.7 percent.

Several studies have suggested that passive smokers suffer an increased risk of lung cancer. Decreased pulmonary function and small airway disease have been measured in passive smokers with chronic exposure. Similar findings have been documented in children whose parents smoke. Sixty percent of the children in the United States today are exposed to cigarette smoke in their homes. These children suffer respiratory illness at a rate 10 to 20 percent higher than children who live in homes free of such pollution. The lung damage in these children persists throughout their life.

Dust in the home also includes fungus (mold) spores, animal dander, pollens and bacteria, all of which many people are allergic to. Even if the cat or dog is not in the house, enough of the dander is blown or tracked in to cause grief. Tree pollens plague many people even during the winter months as a result of wood-burning stoves and fireplaces. Desensitization affords some relief, but this requires an injection every seven to fourteen days.

Adequate filtration of the air by an efficient filter on the central heating/air conditioning unit helps, but does not solve the problem completely. All of these filters have limitations in the materials that they will remove from the air, based upon particle size. The particles of cigarette smoke range up to about one micrometer in diameter. Pollen particles range from 10 to 100 micrometers. Dust particles range from 0.5 to 50 micrometers in diameter. By comparison, the water particles of fog range from 5 to 50 micrometers. One unique type of furnace filter, Space Guard, claims to remove 65 percent of the particles of cigarette smoke and virtually 100 percent of pollen and dust particles. This represents a significant improvement over the simple fiberglass filters commonly attached to furnaces. A high efficiency room filter will clear a 12 by 13 foot room of all cigarette smoke in about three hours.

Adding a room electronic filter, especially in the bedroom makes a significant contribution to cleaning up the air. These units cost in excess of $300, however, and they must be cleaned regularly and at frequent intervals. Not only do they lose their efficiency as they become dirty, but they may actually serve as a source of microorganism and spore propagation. Humidifiers and any unit where water stands, must be cleaned and disinfected with household bleach to destroy bacteria and fungus that tend to collect and multiply there. Many people are allergic to these organisms and may suffer cough, wheezing, stuffy nose and eye complaints. Permanent damage, especially to the lungs, can result from prolonged exposure to these organisms.

The collection of dust can readily be seen on furniture and woodwork, but accumulation in carpeting is hidden from view. Both sources must be cleaned regularly. Furniture polishes are effective for the hard surfaces, but an efficient vacuum cleaner is required for carpeting. This should be a central vacuum system that discharges the exhaust air to the outside. Conventional vacuum cleaners, the type in virtually every home, merely raise the dust from floor level to nose level. Their filters permit significant quantities of the dust particles of the most harmful size to pass through. Installation of a central vacuum system is not a difficult do-it-yourself project.

During the winter months, central heating systems produce a very dry atmosphere. This is irritating to the respiratory membranes and it increases the incidence of cough and respiratory infections. This can and should be remedied by humidification of the air. The most efficient means of doing this is by use of a humidifier on the furnace. These units frequently provide less than the optimal level of humidity, usually due to improper setting or poor maintenance. The elements within these humidifiers that transfer the moisture to the air become caked with minerals and lose their efficiency. Bacterial and fungus growth also need to be cleaned out of humidifiers regularly to avoid dissemination throughout the house.

The area where this humidification is most needed is the bedroom. This is particularly important for young children. An ultrasonic humidifier in the bedroom is very effective in providing the needed humidification during the night. The ultrasonic units also are quiet enought to permit sleep. This simple measure of adding humidity to the air in the bedroom frequently solves a troublesome cough in people with bronchitis, and thus permits sleep. One problem that does arise with the use of these units is that they deposit a light film of minerals on the furniture. This can be avoided by using distilled water, but this requires sizeable quantities, perhaps a gallon or more each night.

Humidification of the air in the home should not be overdone. This is most likely with the use of a portable unit, and in the bathroom. Relative humidities above about 70 percent encourage the growth of mold, especially on windows and in bathrooms. The spores that are released into the air from this growth are disseminated throughout the house. Such growth should be cleaned and treated with a solution of household bleach, which is very effective in killing both bacteria and mold. Permitting stagnant water to stand in any location in the house encourages the growth of bacteria and mold.

In addition to dust, mold spores, dander, pollen and bacteria all cause sensitivity reactions and a cough. Hydrocarbons and particulates from smoking, formaldehyde from urea foam in furniture and adhesives in plywood and particle board, and detergent residue from improper carpet cleaning also add to the irritation of the eyes, nose, throat and lungs. Far more sophisticated air cleaning equipment than exists in the average home would be required to control all of these sources of hazards to health.

Some of the multitude of hazardous chemicals that have been identified in the home are:

Tetrachloroethylene: from dry cleaned clothes
Methylene chloride: paint thinners and strippers
Ammonia: from cleaning agents and oven cleaners
Chlorine: from cleaning agents, laundry bleach, automatic dishwasher detergent and
    toilet bowl cleaners
Hair spray: methylene chloride and other irritants
Para-dichlorobenzene: moth crystals and air freshener (a cancer risk)
1,1,1-trichloroethane: aerosol sprays and solvents
Formaldehyde: furniture stuffing, particle board and plywood (counter tops)
Benzo-a-pyrene, a potent cancer producer: tobacco smoke and wood-burning stoves
Insecticides
Fingernail polish
Cosmetics

The presence of chlorine in the home has been determined to be the cause of premature failure of the combustion chambers in the new gas high-efficiency furnaces. This substance is released into the air from laundry products and automatic dishwasher detergents.

Amana has solved this problem by engineering a process into their furnace that automatically flushes the heat exchanger chamber with water periodically.

All painting projects in the home should be deferred until the weather is warm enough to permit the doors and windows to be opened. The same policy should be adhered to for furniture refinishing. This is not a project for a closed basement workshop. There is a danger of explosion if flammable solvents are used. If nonflammable solvents are used, such as methylene chloride, inhalation of the vapors is hazardous to the liver, kidney and nervous system (brain), and presents a risk of cancer development.

A recent study at the National Aeronautics and Space Administration demonstrated that some common plants, when grown in the home, help to remove some of the chemicals that cause irritation. Philodendron, chrysanthemum, spider plant and aloe vera break down some toxins, such as formaldehyde, in the process of photosynthesis. It is yet to be determined how many plants are required for a given room, and the full extent of substances that these plants are able to devour.

## AIR POLLUTION

There has been an intense and acrimonious debate over air pollution during the past two decades. Much of the propaganda delivered to the general public would have you believe that air pollution and the hazards associated with it are of recent origin. In reality, nothing could be further from the truth. Virtually every home in the United States, as with all of the industrialized world, was heated by coal up until the early 1940s. The emissions from the chimneys of these homes were very obvious after a night of new fallen snow. If you had the misfortune to live anywhere near a factory, the soot from the coal that was burned there darkened the atmosphere even more. Coal-burning locomotives during that era also delivered considerable soot and sulfur dioxide to the air in virtually every city. The outdoor air in the majority of these cities and neighborhoods is much freer of pollution today than it was in the thirties.

Writers documented the pollution of the air by the burning of coal as long ago as the fourth century. The burning of coal by industry and in the home was banned in London in the fourteenth century as a result of the pollution of the air. London has experienced many serious air pollution episodes, by virtue of its propensity for periods of prolonged fog. Most of the components of air pollution become attached to or become a part of the water particles of fog. During a two week period in December 1952, in excess of 3000 deaths resulted from such an episode. The sulfur dioxide level during this fog was raised to nine times the level measured just before this period. Replacement of the limestone figurines on Victoria tower of the House of Parliament in 1948 was necessitated by the corrosion from sulfur dioxide.

One of the earliest well-documented mass poisonings as a result of air pollution occurred in the Meuse Valley in Belgium in 1930. Many people became ill, but the exact number is not recorded. More than sixty people died. The Meuse Valley shares some topographical and climatic characteristics with the Los Angeles basin. Both valleys are surrounded by hills that restrict the movement of air that might serve to cleanse the area. Both have a concentration of industry and vehicles that deliver a heavy burden of pollutants to the local atmosphere.

Another thoroughly documented disaster occurred in 1948 at Donora, Pennsylvania, south of Pittsburgh on the Monongahela River. About 6,000 people were made ill and 20 of them died. Although sulfur dioxide was considered to be one of the chief culprits in this episode, over a dozen other toxic chemicals were identified. These originated in various steel mills, chemical plants, a glass works, a power plant and a railroad. The Pittsburgh area was cleared of much of this smog after natural gas replaced coal and fuel oil in these industries.

Smog is a term that was coined to describe the brownish haze in the Los Angeles area that burns the eyes and throat. The term is a contraction of the two words smoke and fog. Accumulations of pollutants such as sulfur dioxide have historically been associated with the occurrence of protracted periods of fog, for the reason mentioned above. In recent years communities such as Los Angeles and Denver have demonstrated that smog can be cultivated without having fog as a matrix. Smog consists of carbon monoxide, particulates such as soot and dust, ozone, hydrocarbons and oxides of nitrogen (NOx).

Photochemical reactions produce many of the more noxious constituents of smog. These reactions often are produced by the ultraviolet radiation from the sun. This requires a stagnant atmosphere and the reaction is accelerated by increased temperatures. The input materials for these photochemical reactions are oxides of nitrogen, hydrocarbons, water vapor and carbon monoxide. The Los Angeles basin provides all of these elements in abundance. It has gained a reputation as the smog capital of the United States. Other cities vying for this honor are New York City, Houston and Chicago, for all share unacceptable levels of ozone. Even Denver, the mile high city, has grown in population to the point that it suffers from smog. About 100 cities in the U.S. currently violate the 1970 Clean Air Act. Population growth is the underlying cause for most of this problem.

Automobiles have monopolized the attention of the politicians and the extremists as the source of the hydrocarbons, oxides of nitrogen and carbon monoxide that go into the production of smog. This is largely because the automobile is visible everywhere, and has no political clout. Equally to blame, however, are diesel trucks and buses (including smoke-belching city buses), diesel locomotives, farm tractors, industry in its entirety and jet aircraft. Even charcoal lighter fluid and the process of grilling on backyard barbecue grills contribute hydrocarbons to the air. Recent proposals for cleaning up the air include banning the sale of charcoal lighter fluid and the use of grills at home.

These same recommendations also propose to ban the use of gasoline-powered lawn mowers. Substituting electric mowers would not eliminate any of the aggregate air pollution, since the power plant would have to increase production. We are a long way from eliminating the pollutants from power generating plants. It may mean that we would have to return to the hand powered mower to comply with these far out suggestions. New automobiles today emit 90 percent fewer hydrocarbons and 75 percent less carbon monoxide than they did in the 1970s. This has been accomplished at a cost to you of over one thousand dollars for each vehicle. This is not enough for the schemers, however, and they have further plans for your pocketbook.

The irritant substances that are produced by photochemical reactions are aldehydes, nitrates and ozone. The latter has enjoyed the greatest level of attention and measurement. It is generally considered to be the most important constituent of smog in the production of respiratory irritation and subsequent death. Copy machines, negative ion generators, electronic air filters, electric motors and lightening all contribute ozone to the air. Common symptoms produced by smog are burning of the eyes and throat, cough and a heaviness in the chest. People with allergies, asthma and bronchitis are particularly susceptible to the irritant effects of smog. Fatalities during severe episodes invariably include victims who suffer from these maladies.

Nitrogen dioxide is reddish brown in color and this accounts for the color of smog. Several oxides of nitrogen are produced along with the dioxide. For this reason you will see the term NOx to refer to all of these substances. These other nitrogen oxides are colorless. These substances are produced in many industrial processes such as electric welding, except where an inert gas such as argon is used. Gas welding and cutting torches also produce nitrogen dioxide, as does any acid dipping operation such as metal plating. Even gas-cooking stoves and furnaces contribute this substance to the air. Many deaths have occurred from pulmonary edema caused by this gas when it was formed in freshly filled silos. A layer of brownish gas often can be seen in these circumstances. Over 100 deaths were caused by nitrogen dioxide at the Cleveland Clinic in 1929 when a fire ignited cellulose based X-ray film.

Sulfur dioxide is an equally lethal component of smog, when it is present in sufficient concentrations. The deaths that occurred in the air pollution disasters described above were ascribed largely to sulfur dioxide. It was produced by the burning of coal during a period when coal was the only source of cooking and heating in the home and of energy in industry. The main source of sulfur dioxide in ambient air today is the burning of fossil fuels and specific processes in industry, such as smelting of ores. Fossil fuels include not only coal, but gasoline, diesel fuel and home heating oil.

The quantity of sulfur dioxide in vehicle emissions is directly related to the sulfur content of the fuel and to the design of the engine. The amount of sulfur in automotive fuels is generally held below about 0.3 percent out of consideration for its harmful effect on engines. At this level its contribution to pollution is negligible, especially in well-designed engines. Those vehicles that are poorly maintained and those that burn inferior fuel contribute significantly more sulfur dioxides to the atmosphere. These vehicles are frequently identified by the cloud of black smoke that surrounds them.

Sulfur dioxide damages coniferous trees to a far greater extent than it does deciduous trees. This damage around power plants has been mitigated to a large degree by the practice of increasing the height of the stacks to over 800 feet. The discharge from these stacks into the atmosphere is generally three times the height of the stack, so the noxious chemicals are delivered to the air at an altitude of about 2,500 feet. One such chimney in Switzerland was built on a mountain so that the top of the stack was 1,800 feet above the town.

The emissions from the stack would enter the atmosphere at an altitude above 5,000 feet. This neatly solves the local pollution problem, and delivers it to the neighbors. Nuclear power plants would have eliminated all of the pollution problems associated with power generation. This progress was stopped dead in its tracks, however, by the extremists, politicians, special interest groups and by bungling contractors. France generates 75 percent of its power needs by using nuclear power plants.

All of the proposals to resolve the problem of air pollution and smog will prove to be very costly. The burden of this cost will rest upon the consumer and the taxpayer, as is always the case. Many of the proposals are ludicrous, but this is the kind of thinking that goes into most legislation. The basic cause of most air pollution today is the massive increase in population, and the propensity for people to settle in areas that the Indians judged unfit to occupy. I see no simple, quick and easy solution to the problem. It is a problem that should be approached with intelligence and careful study by experts in the various sciences. This is not the manner in which most problems are solved in the United States, however.


## RADON

Concern has been mounting during the past five years over the discovery that homes in certain regions of the United States harbor high levels of radon gas. Many homes have shown levels as high as those shown to cause lung cancer in uranium miners. Homes in Montgomery County, Pennsylvania were among the first discovered to have this problem. The problem was discovered when a worker who lived in one of the homes in this area triggered the radiation detectors as he was going INTO the plant.

It is known that the geologic formation identified as the Reading Prong, which extends from eastern Pennsylvania through northern New Jersey and south central New York, contains deposits of uranium. Homes built over these deposits are at a higher risk of having radon gas accumulate, but there is a considerable variation in concentration among homes in a given region. Even homes built side by side may vary greatly in the concentration of radon gas in the internal air due to construction techniques and the development of cracks in the foundation. Radon gas also enters homes through sump pumps, and sealed covers are now available for these units.

About 70 percent of the homes evaluated in Maine had a significant concentration of radon gas. Similar concentrations were found in homes in Texas (Houston) and Illinois. The Environmental Protection Agency estimates from their surveys that at least seven percent of the homes nationwide exceed its guidelines for maximum exposure, which is four picocuries per liter of air. They contend that houses that exceed this level can be found in almost every state. Even the level of four picocuries is not a desirable level. It carries an increased risk, especially among smokers.

Radon is a gas that evolves as a naturally occurring breakdown product of uranium ore. We have known since about 1950 that it causes lung cancer in miners, and that miners who smoke are at a particularly high risk. The latency period for the development of cancer is approximately twenty years. Data suggests that at least ten years of exposure in the mines is required for lung cancer to develop at a later date. A study conducted in Sweden concluded that women who were exposed to high levels of radon at home had double the risk of lung cancer. It is estimated that radon gas is responsible for 5,000 to 15,000 cases of lung cancer deaths each year in the United States.

As in the case of asbestos exposure, the risk of lung cancer among cigarette smokers is not merely additive, it is increased as a multiple. In other words one plus one does not equal two. With asbestos exposure, for instance, cigarette smoking increases the risk of cancer approximately ten fold over the risk of simple exposure to asbestos. Many individuals who develop lung cancer would not do so if they had been exposed only to asbestos, and not to cigarette smoke additionally.

The risk of lung cancer results primarily from breakdown products of radon gas, chiefly polonium. When these particles are inhaled into the lungs they are deposited there and they produce radiation damage to the nucleus of the cells, which can result in cancer. We do not have enough data nor experience to predict accurately how frequently this will occur in exposed individuals. We do have data for the increased risk of lung cancer in uranium miners. Their exposure levels are ten times as high as that seen in most of the homes that were evaluated, however. One worrisome fact is the great amount of time that is spent in the home compared with that on the job. A National Academy of Science study suggests that spending twelve hours a day in a home with excess radon levels will increase the risk of lung cancer by 50 percent.

Radon gas seeps into the home from the earth beneath and can accumulate to a dangerous level. This seepage can be minimized by appropriate construction techniques. It also has found its way into homes as a result of building materials when radon producing ore was used as aggregate for concrete. Phosphate slag, which emits radon gas as well as other radioactive particles such as polonium, was used in the concrete foundation of homes in southwestern Idaho from 1962 to 1977. Mining of phosphate rock has long been a major industry in Florida. Thousands of homes have been built over the tailings of these mining operations, on reclaimed land. High levels of radon gas have been measured in these homes. Several thousand houses were also built over uranium tailings from mining activities in Grand Junction, Colorado. Other states where a high probability of radon gas exists, besides Pennsylvania, New Jersey and New York are Idaho, Maine, New Hampshire, North Carolina, Wisconsin, Massachusetts, Connecticut, California and Wyoming.

The presence of radon gas can be detected with appropriate measuring devices. Many laboratories and organizations throughout the United States offer radon surveys, primarily through activated charcoal filters, for under $35. The charcoal filter is left in place, usually in the basement, for several weeks. A minimum period is required for an accurate reading, and this time depends upon the type of measuring device. The basement and the house must be kept closed during the measuring period, and winter is the best time to conduct these assessments. The filter is then sent to the laboratory for an estimation of the radon level. If the screening device indicates that a significant radon level exists, a more definitive measurement can then be made at a cost of $50 to $75. State and local health departments can help in locating reliable laboratories that offer this service. As might be expected, some unqualified individuals are attempting to make money from this latest scare.

Screening for radon in the home is certainly advisable in areas where the potential for accumulation exists. Health officials in many states are just now undertaking studies to determine exactly where this risk occurs. The only solution to the problem in a home constructed over such a hazard is special ventilation systems and heat exchangers that conserve up to 80 percent of the heated or cooled indoor air. The cost for these is $1,000 to $2,000. Plugging all cracks in basements, foundations and floors and around all pipes helps to reduce radon infusion and should be the first step. An airtight cover for sump pumps should be installed at the same time. Ventilation systems can then be considered if levels still measure high.

# CHLORDANE

This pesticide has been the mainstay in the control of termites in homes. It has been reported to cause illness when it gained access to homes through cracks in the foundation, or through improper application. It is a very potent and toxic substance. Chlordane is discussed in detail in chapter I, Hazards of Pesticides.

# XI

# Hazards of Temperature Extremes

## HEAT STRESS

Humans, as with other warm-blooded animals, are able to maintain the body temperature within a very narrow range in spite of wide variations in the environment surrounding them. These adaptive mechanisms have limits, however, and failure to recognize this fact and to take appropriate precautions results in many heat-related illnesses and many deaths each year. Most of these cases could be prevented by an awareness of the environmental conditions that lead to heat disorders, and by a recognition of the early warning signs of impending illness.

Factors which determine heat related disorders include the temperature of the air, the humidity of the air, the amount of air movement, thermal radiation, the level of physical activity being expended at the time, age, physical condition, drugs, type of clothing worn and body build. These disorders occur much more commonly during periods of prolonged heat, and particularly when the humidity is high.

The chief mechanism by which the body dissipates heat is through sweating and the evaporation thereof. This mechanism becomes less efficient during periods of high humidity, because the sweat evaporates from the skin more slowly. Similarly, sweat is evaporated more rapidly when there is an appreciable air movement across the body, than when no such movement is present. Under those circumstances excess body heat is eliminated more efficiently. Short, stocky and obese individuals dissipate heat much less efficiently, both because of the increased body mass and the decreased skin surface area. More heat is produced in the greater body mass, and at the same time relatively less skin surface area is available for sweating and heat dissipation.

Age plays a significant role in the amount of heat stress that an individual can tolerate. This decreased tolerance to heat stress begins as early as the age of thirty-five years. After that age the amount of oxygen that is made available to the body is reduced by 25 to 30 percent. This results partially from a decrease in the functional output of the heart and circulatory system, and partially from the reduction in the efficiency of oxygen transport in the lungs. Obviously this deficit, in both of these components, is much more severe in smokers. The greater the age, the more pronounced these physiologic deficiencies become. With age the muscles of the heart, as with the muscles of the body in general, weaken and become less efficient. These changes and their resultant deficiencies are precisely the reason that professional athletes lose the ability to compete in strenuous sports during this same period in life.

The circulation becomes less efficient with age, partially as a result of the weakening of the heart and partially because of arteriosclerosis. The result is that the heat produced in the body as a result of metabolism and muscular activity is not as readily transported to the surface for dissipation. Another factor making older individuals more at risk for heat disorders is that there is a delay in the onset of sweating and a reduction in the amount of perspiration produced. Both of these changes are age induced. This results in greater heat retention within the body, and earlier onset of all of the heat disorders. The reduction in the efficiencies of these mechanisms also prolongs the recovery time for heat related disorders.

During periods of increased heat stress, with the accompanying increased perpiration, there is a significant increase in the amount of salt lost from the body. The resultant dilution of the body fluids results in a false signal from the region of the brain that normally conserves salt. The consequence is that the kidneys excrete additional quantities of salt as well as water. In order to avoid the serious consequences of these heat-induced imbalances, it is necessary to increase the salt intake prophylactically. This is best done with meals. Electrolyte solutions can be used during periods of heat exposure if necessary. Balanced solutions that are designed to replace all of the fluids and electrolytes that are lost during heat exposure are marketed. Tablets should be avoided since they irritate the stomach.

The quantity of salt supplementation needed is directly related to the amount of loss and can be calculated by experts using complex formulae. For recreational activities and tasks around the home such calculations are not practical, and are usually not necessary. In the extreme, as much as ten to fifteen grams of supplemental salt may be required over an eight-hour period. Caution must be exercised in consuming supplemental salt, however. It would be rare circumstances where this quantity would be needed at home.

Under normal conditions any excess of salt and water consumed is controlled and eliminated by the kidney. This requires normal conditions of kidney function and normal water intake. Kidney function is commonly reduced in diabetes, in high blood pressure and in older individuals. It may also be reduced as a result of other diseases and as a result of exposure to toxic drugs and chemicals. Diuretics, which are commonly taken for high blood pressure deplete the body of salt and fluid volume. As a consequence they render the individual more susceptible to heat disorders. Supplementation of salt requires adequate intake of water at the same time. Prophylactic salt supplementation carries a particular risk for those individuals who have high blood pressure, because salt has a very deleterious effect on blood pressure. In these instances the quantity of salt consumed should be monitored and balanced carefully.

Alcohol consumption greatly increases the susceptibility to all of the heat disorders. It suppresses the hormone in the body that regulates salt and water excretion through the kidneys, leading to excessive water loss and dehydration. Excessive alcohol consumption several days before exposure to heat may result in this deleterious effect. Alcohol should be avoided, therefore, whenever recreational activities or home projects are planned, especially during periods of prolonged hot weather.

Physical conditioning improves the efficiency of the circulation and of the function of the heart in general. It also improves lung capacity and the efficiency of lung function. This improves heat tolerance to a degree, but it does not eliminate the need for acclimatization. Exposure to heat should be undertaken in steps in order to permit time for the physiological adjustments that take place with prolonged exposure to heat. These include an increase in the capillaries and in circulation and an increase in oxygen transport in the lungs. This acclimatization generally takes about four to seven days. In anticipation of recreational activities that might involve heat stress, particularly strenuous activities such as running, these principles should be applied during preparation for the event.

## HEAT EXHAUSTION

This disorder is also called heat prostration, heat collapse and heat fatigue. It is the mildest form of heat disorder and the most common. It results from an excessive loss of fluid from the body after a prolonged exposure to high temperatures. It can occur indoors or outside. Although it occurs most frequently in individuals who are not acclimatized to the heat and who are involved in strenuous activities, it can happen to sedentary people. It is a common occurrence each summer, particularly during periods of high relative humidity. Strenuous exertion, poor ventilation and heavy clothing contribute to the development of this disorder. It is more common in and poses a greater risk for older individuals, especially those taking diuretics for high blood pressure. There is usually adequate warning through the development of increasing fatigue, weakness, anxiety and drenching sweats, but the symptoms may not be dramatic, and are often overlooked. Faintness usually develops following the above symptoms. Disordered mentation such as confusion may be seen. The body temperature is below normal, the skin is pale and clammy, the pulse is weak and slow and the blood pressure is lowered.

It is essential to recognize these early warning signs of heat exhaustion at the earliest possible moment, and to take steps to prevent progression to a more serious stage. These early steps include removal from the hot environment to a cooler one, even if only in the shade, or removal from a hot attic or roof. Discontinuance of physical activity, removal of heavy clothing and drinking cool fluids will all help to reverse this potentially serious condition. Once the heat exhaustion victim has progressed to the point where assistance is needed, these measures become more urgent. In addition to removing from the hot environment, the person should be made to lie flat or with the head slightly low.

## HEAT STROKE

This condition is also called sunstroke, but it is not necessary to be exposed to the sun to fall victim to this disorder. It is a stage beyond heat exhaustion and is life threatening. Aggressive measures are urgent. In this disorder, the body's temperature regulating mechanism fails. In most cases there is little or no perspiration, the skin is dry, hot and red. Some victims with fully developed symptoms continue to perspire, however. The pulse is rapid (160 to 180) and firm. Respirations are rapid and shallow. The blood pressure is usually low. Constriction of the blood vessels prevents the transfer of heat from the body core to the surface. The body core temperature rises rapidly to a level of 105 to 106 degrees Fahrenheit. If aggressive measures to reduce this are not taken, the temperature rise progresses to convulsions and death. Permanent brain damage may occur if the individual survives. Headache, weakness and dizziness are followed by a sudden loss of consciousness. Disorientation may be present and may progress to delirium.

Efforts to control the body temperature should be initiated immediately by immersing the victim in cool water or by wrapping him in cool moist blankets or cloth. It is essential that the body temperature be lowered as rapidly as possible. The victim should be hospitalized immediately. The outlook is less favorable for the aged, debilitated and alcoholics than is the case for young individuals in good health. Most heat related deaths are due to heat stroke. Individuals who have survived a previous episode of heat stroke are particularly at risk and should exercise the utmost care in avoidance.

Heat exhaustion and heat stroke occur with increased frequency during heat waves. Daily deaths due to these disorders double or triple during prolonged periods of high temperature. It is essential to decrease physical activities, increase fluid intake, especially water, and to stay in a cool environment. Fans and light, minimal clothing may be adequate in some cases. At temperatures of 95 degrees Fahrenheit and above, fans lose their effectiveness, however. Air conditioning can be life saving during very hot periods. If air conditioning is not available, spending a few hours at an air conditioned shopping mall during the middle of the day is helpful. Nursing home patients are a group of individuals who are particularly at risk during periods of prolonged heat. The majority of cases occur in elderly people who have preexisting diseases such as arteriosclerosis and heart disease, especially those taking diuretics.

## PRICKLY HEAT

Also called miliaria, this condition occurs when the ducts of the sweat gland become plugged with keratin and dead cells on the skin. The sweat retained in the glands bursts through the wall of the duct into the surrounding tissue. Here it causes inflammation, and sometimes infection. Frequent bathing, skin hygiene and clean clothing are the measures to take to prevent this condition.

# HYPOTHERMIA

This is a disorder that can occur in anyone with prolonged exposure to the cold. It occurs in the elderly, however, in circumstances where it might not be expected. Many of the aged die in their homes each winter, even when the temperature is only mildly cold, in the range of sixty-five degrees Fahrenheit. Among the factors accounting for this are impaired circulation induced by age, decreased vasomotor ability to compensate for exposure to lower temperatures, and a decreased perception of cold. Decreased heat production through metabolic channels and poor heat conservation of the body in this age group also contribute to the increased risk. The tendency for older people, especially those who live alone, to neglect regular and adequate nutrition also increases the risk in this age group. A greater awareness of these risk factors is needed, both by the aged and their families. It is urgent that this population and those who care for them fully understand the risks and how to avoid them.

Once the body core temperature falls below 95 degrees Fahrenheit, the definition point for hypothermia, it continues to fall insidiously until death results. (A rectal temperature reading normally gives an accurate assessment of the body core temperature.) This condition carries a mortality rate of approximately 50 percent. About 700 to 800 people die each year in the United States from this cause. The number has increased in recent years due to the increase in the aged population, and to the increase in the number of people living without shelter.

Evidence of impending hypothermia is fatigue, weakness, lack of coordination, apathy and drowsiness progressing to confusion. When the body core temperature falls below 90 degrees Fahrenheit, these symptoms progress to stupor and coma. Anyone who has been in a cold environment will have cold extremities, but older individuals who are at risk of hypothermia will present a cold abdomen that is not normally seen. The lack of shivering in this age group can be misleading. Shivering increases heat production in the body and is a natural defense mechanism in hypothermia. Its absence in this age group compounds the danger. The presence of hypothermia in these people may be overlooked since the standard thermometer measures only to 94 degrees, and it must be diligently shaken to get it to that level. Thermometers that measure lower are available, and should be used when checking for hypothermia. In rewarming older people suffering from hypothermia, it is important to not rewarm them too rapidly, since hypotension (low blood pressure) can result.

Alcohol increases the risk of hypothermia at any age. It interferes with the constriction of blood vessels that is the natural defense mechanism of the body in conserving heat. It also decreases the individual's perception of cold so that normal precautions are not taken. Alcohol should be avoided by everyone during activities that involve prolonged exposure to cold, such as skiing, camping and hiking. Drugs that depress the central nervous system such as tranquilizers, sleeping medications and so called "recreational drugs" may also increase the susceptibility to hypothermia. Hypothermia can occur under these altered circumstances when the outdoor temperature is only moderately cold.

Immersion in cold water brings about hypothermia much sooner due to the rapidity of heat loss from the body. A very lean person will suffer a life threatening lowering of the body core temperature sooner than will an obese individual. Heart irregularities are common with hypothermia and are a common cause of death. These are all the more serious by virtue of the fact that when the temperature of the heart muscle is lowered it responds much less readily to resuscitative measures.

## FROSTBITE

This affliction also can affect any age, old or young. The risk is greater in the aged and in the very young. There also is an increased risk in those individuals who have impaired circulation, such as with diabetes, heart disease and arteriosclerosis. The decreased perception of cold and the diminished efficiency of vasomotor control, as described above, account for the increased problem in the aged. The risk is also increased with the use of alcohol, impairment of consciousness from any cause, exhaustion and hunger. The windchill factor also influences the risk, and thus it is greater with wet clothing. Contact with metal greatly increases the risk of frostbite. Many B-17 gunners during World War II suffered frostbite of the fingers and hands when they removed their gloves to work on jammed machine guns.

With frostbite, ice crystals may form in the tissues, and the small blood vessels may thrombose (clot), leading to gangrene. Where the frost damage is superficial, the tissues will be firm, cold and white. The areas most commonly involved are the face, ears, fingers and toes. The skin may peel or blister one to two days after frostbite occurs. Pronounced permanent damage to the blood vessels may occur, with resultant hypersensitivity to cold.

Where the cold damage is deeper, a loss of feeling is noted in addition to the cold, hard, white tissues. These areas become red, blotchy, swollen and painful as they rewarm. If the damage is severe enough, gangrene results. The frozen tissues should be handled gently to avoid additional damage. The involved areas should be rewarmed as rapidly as practical, without further damaging the tissues by excess heat. Rewarming is best accomplished by immersion in warm water, starting at 60 to 70 degrees Fahrenheit. The temperature of the water can be gradually increased to 80 to 90 degrees Fahrenheit. It is important to keep in mind that these areas have no feeling, and the temperature of the water must be monitored for the victim.

Frostbite is frequently seen in hands and feet even though the body core temperature remains normal. If hypothermia is present also, the first priority should be to raise the core temperature. It accomplishes nothing to rewarm frozen feet and hands if the victim expires from hypothermia. Medical attention should be sought as soon as possible. Special techniques and equipment, such as peritoneal dialysis, intravenous solutions and monitoring of blood gasses, pH and potassium all may greatly improve survival. Cigarettes absolutely must be avoided during the recovery period. Infection and gangrene are common complications of this condition.

As mentioned earlier, the elderly are at increased risk of all of the temperature disorders, both elevated and lowered temperatures. This fact is due to physiologic changes of aging that reduce the efficiency of the body in temperature regulation. The mechanisms that increase heat production during cold exposure, both shivering and other physiologic mechanisms, are reduced in the aged. There is also a decrease in the sensory perception so that these individuals don't feel the temperature changes as readily as younger people do. The age at which these changes occur is variable. Certainly they have taken place by the age of eighty, but they can occur in the fifties in some individuals. Illnesses such as diabetes invoke these changes at a younger age. These changes take place gradually over time, not overnight.

Another physiologic change that takes place in the aged that accounts for the impairment of adjustment to temperature extremes is a reduced ability of the autonomic nervous system to bring about constriction and dilation of the blood vessels. Sweating, which is the major mechanism whereby the body dissipates heat, is markedly impaired in the aged. Sweating does not commence in older people until a higher temperature is reached, and the amount of perspiration is greatly reduced.

Illness and disease also contribute to these impairments in adjustment to temperature extremes. Diabetes, arteriosclerosis, heart disease and any chronic illness that results in debilitation increase the risk. Malnutrition and poor hydration are common in this age group. Malnutrition in particular reduces the heat production in the body. This coupled with the reduction of circulation resulting from arteriosclerosis greatly increases the risk from cold exposure. Also adding to this risk is reduced mobility brought about by arthritis, stroke, heart disease and degenerative joint disease, especially in the hip and knees.

Either heat or cold disorders frequently result in kidney failure which leads to death, even if the temperature disorder is successfully treated. Successful treatment of temperature disorders is much less likely in the elderly, however, than it is in younger, healthy victims. A high index of suspicion and observation during periods of temperature extremes is essential. This age group should avoid going outdoors in periods of cold. Adequate clothing is essential, especially a hat, for 30 percent of the body heat is lost through the head. During extended periods of heat, these people should avoid being out in the sun, they should wear light clothing and develop a habit of drinking adequate fluids on a regular basis, not responding merely to thirst. Fans and cool baths help avoid heat disorders.

## MALIGNANT HYPERTHERMIA

This condition occurs in individuals who are unfortunate enough to inherit genetic disorders that render them susceptible to most of the common inhalation anesthetics. These include ether, halothane and cyclopropane. The condition is also precipitated by succinylocholine chloride which is routinely used for muscle relaxation during surgery. The acute hyperthermia that is provoked by the administration of any of these medications invokes a serious medical emergency, and can result in death. A family history of such a disorder provides forewarning.

# XII

# Health Maintenance: Reducing Hazards

Good health is one of life's many elements that we best appreciate only after it has passed us by. Most of us come into this world with healthy bodies, and all of the opportunity that we need to maintain them that way. The destruction of health is almost always self-inflicted, as are most of our woes. The concept of the body as a temple, held by some, provides an excellent guide to the preservation of health. If we keep it clean, provide the proper nutrition and adequate rest that are essential to the body and avoid abuse of all substances, including food, we can be reasonably well assured of good health and longevity.

## NUTRITION

Good nutrition is one of the prime requisites for good health. This mandate is much more frequently deviated from in the extreme than on the short side. Unlike so many of the developing societies, the wealth and abundance of our society kills far more individuals than does starvation. Obesity and excessive consumption of animal fats and refined sugars delivers many people to an early grave, and much suffering along the way. Our bodies require certain raw materials in order to perform the essential tasks of growth and repair, and the warding off of disease. These raw materials include meat to provide the essential amino acids that the body cannot manufacture, a small quantity of fat to provide the body with the essential fatty acids that it cannot synthesize, and carbohydrates for energy. In addition to these three basic groups, certain vitamins and minerals are required.

All of this can be accomplished by the ingestion of approximately 1500 to 1800 calories per day for most people. The exact requirement depends upon the individual's ideal body weight and level of physical activity. All calories in excess of those required by the body for these essential functions are converted to fat in the storage depots. (You know where these are.)

Neglect of any of the essential basic materials carries the risk of developing a variety of disorders. The most efficient source, and the only complete source of protein is meat, eggs and milk. Protein from animal sources provides the body with the nine essential amino acids that the body cannot synthesize from other sources. All of the legumes are lacking in one or more of these essential building materials. With a careful balance of legumes it is possible to come close to providing a complete balance. In reality this seldom happens, and some vegetarians supplement their diet with eggs to assure against a deficiency of these essential nutritional elements.

Protein and the essential amino acids are the building blocks that the body uses in the manufacture of all the protein substances, including blood and the elements of the immune system that protect the body from disease. Neglect of this component of the diet can result in increased susceptibility to infections in general. Protein, along with carbohydrates, also provides fuel for energy. The amount needed depends on many factors, including illness or the state of health, and whether or not growth is still progressing. For the average adult, the intake of fifty grams of protein daily balances the protein that is used up in metabolic activities in the body. This assumes that a proper balance with fat and carbohydrates exists.

A minimum amount of fat is also needed to provide the body with the three essential fatty acids that the body cannot synthesize. Fat has had a bad press recently, and it is true that we have consumed far too much of it. We do, however, need about 30 percent of our daily calories in fat in order to provide these essential fatty acids. At that reduced level we are minimizing the risk of arteriosclerosis. A deficiency of the essential fatty acids shows up as a dry and scaly skin, and in infants and children in a deficiency in growth as well.

The official position of the American Medical Association is that, given a normal, adequate diet, supplemental vitamins are not necessary. It is not easy, however, to assure an adequate intake of vitamin C (ascorbic acid) in northern climates in the winter. The usual sources, citrus juices, cannot be relied upon if they have been allowed to thaw and then refrozen during shipment, as is often the case. Ascorbic acid is readily oxidized by heat and zinc in the coatings of containers and strainers. Fruit that reaches the table is seldom "tree ripened" and thus the vitamin C content is questionable. Ascorbic acid is easily synthesized and is reasonably inexpensive. A tablet containing 250 milligrams taken once or twice daily carries no risk, if taken with food to protect the stomach, and assures that the minimum daily requirement for vitamin C is met. This vitamin cannot be stored in the body, so a daily intake is necessary.

Taking one therapeutic strength vitamin from a reputable manufacturer (such as Theragran-M) daily does not carry a risk for the average individual. Such a practice insures that the minimum daily requirement of virtually all of the vitamins and minerals is met. One should be cognizant of the fact, however, that vitamins A and D can be easily overdosed, with serious consequences. Both of these vitamins are routinely added to several foods such as bread, milk, cereals and other foods and drinks, increasing the risk of excessive consumption. It is important to limit the intake of therapeutic strength vitamins to not more than one daily.

Vitamin D carries the smallest margin of safety, and therefore the greatest risk of overdose. No more than 400 units daily should be added to the diet. It is found in milk, bread and margarine and naturally in egg yolk, liver and salt water fish. It is also formed in the body as a result of exposure of the skin to the sun's ultraviolet irriadiation. Excessive doses can result in damage to the kidney and eye. Women taking calcium supplements should utilize the calcium products that do not contain vitamin D. Otherwise significant overdosage of this vitamin can occur.

Excessive doses of vitamin A also can result in damage to the eye, including hemorrhage, blurring of vision and double vision, as well as loss of eyebrows and eyelashes. Loss of appetite, dry, fissured skin, brittle nails, hair loss, inflammation of the gums and mouth, overgrowth of bone, liver damage and nervous system disorders are other side effects. Much larger doses of this vitamin are required to produce toxic effects than is the case with vitamin D, thus some less risk is involved. Sources of vitamin A include milk, butter, margarine, liver, carrots, sweet potatoes, other yellow vegetables and tomato juice. A number of cases of yellowing of the skin (carotenemia) have resulted from consuming excessive quantities of substances containing vitamin A, such as carrot juice.

Several metals and trace elements are essential dietary components, but these are toxic in excess, and excess is very easy to achieve with some. Serious illness has been observed as a result of selenium supplementation, which has gained popularity recently. This results in damage to the nervous system and loss of hair and nails. Chromium produces destruction of the tubules in the kidneys. Molybdenum can produce an anemia through poorly understood mechanisms. Several deaths from heart failure resulted from the addition of cobalt to beer to enhance foam formation. This practice has been discontinued. Iron, copper, magnesium, manganese and zinc are more forgiving but nonetheless can produce ill effects. A normal, well-balanced diet that includes cereals, nuts and meats will easily provide an adequate supply of all of these minerals except for iron. Iron is cheap and easy to acquire, since no prescription is required. It must be taken with prudence, however, for iron overload is possible, with toxic results. Many children have lost their lives to ingestion of iron tablets that were left within their reach.

## EXERCISE

Adequate and appropriate exercise is essential for the maintenance of muscle tone, to maintain bone density and to keep the heart and lung in good working order. Exercise need not be demanding nor extreme; one does not have to run eight miles each day to enjoy good health. Simply walking one to three miles daily, or at least every other day, is adequate for an individual of average activity. Some added benefits of running have been demonstrated for the heart, lungs and blood pressure, but again there is no added benefit beyond running one to three miles every other day. Running presents an added risk of disorders of the feet, knees and hip joints. This is particularly true for those individuals unfortunate enough to inherit a proclivity toward arthritis. Swimming is excellent exercise, with virtually no risk nor adverse effect (other than the risk of drowning), but it is not as readily available as is running or walking. Well-designed exercise bicycles provide good exercise for the cardiovascular system. These have the advantage of being available regardless of the weather.

## SLEEP

Requirements for sleep vary considerably from one individual to another, generally ranging from seven to nine hours nightly. Little is understood about the sleep process. It appears to provide the body with an opportunity for recovery and rejuvenation, which seems reasonable. Little is actually known about the physiology of

211

this activity, although it has been the subject of considerable study in recent years. Chronic neglect of this vital function does result in some definable disorders. This phenomenon has had some investigation among troops in wartime. An increase in the stress level and a decreased ability to deal with stress develop. Increased activity of the gastrointestinal tract, as is seen with stress in general, is observed, as well as a decrease in neuromuscular coordination. This is manifested by an increase in the number of stools, a stool of smaller caliber and perhaps a watery stool. Bloating and an increase in the amount of gas may be noticed along with this. It also may be accompanied by pain and cramping in the abdomen, or pain in the lower back. A stomach or duodenal ulcer may develop after protracted periods of stress.

An individual can ascertain his own sleep needs by simple observation. If a person feels tired and worn out throughout most of the day, and very sleepy in the early afternoon, it is likely that inadequate sleep has been experienced. This assessment should be made over a period of several days, for anyone can have a restless night, especially if severe thunderstorms pass through. As stated above, most people will require between seven and nine hours each night in order to function efficiently.

## HYGIENE

Cleanliness and personal hygiene are equally as important as nutrition in maintaining good health. Adequate nutrition provides the raw materials that the body needs in order to manufacture the various elements in the immune and defense mechanisms. Cleanliness and good hygiene lessen the demands on these defense mechanisms by reducing the number of microbial agents that gain entrance to the body. This frequently makes the difference between health and disease, particularly in the case of organisms that the body is less able to ward off. In the case of viral hepatitis, for instance, simple hand washing after handling soiled diapers may protect a person from contracting this disease. It will also help to avoid spreading it to other members of the family. A review of food-borne diseases in chapter VI will reinforce the importance of hand washing in the prevention of illness.

Hand washing mechanically removes disease causing microbial agents from the hands. Using a hand soap that contains an effective germicide such as triclocarban (Dial, Safeguard and Zest) greatly enhances the removal of bacteria and fungi. Some people develop a sun sensitivity when using these products, so this must be watched for. Use of Betadine skin cleanser (used by physicians in surgery, available in pharmacies) when handling fecal or infectious, contaminated material is even more effective. The use of one of these soaps is especially useful after changing diapers, as mentioned above. The hands can never be rendered sterile (that is why we wear gloves in surgery), but contaminating microorganisms that present a threat of disease can be removed by washing well with Betadine.

Washing the hands before eating is a mandate that dates back to biblical times, but it seems to have been forgotten in our reliance on miracle drugs. The limitations of these drugs are periodically demonstrated to us in dramatic fashion, and should serve to remind us that "an ounce of prevention is worth a pound of cure." When Moses was leading his people through the wilderness, he had no antibiotics. The rules for hygiene and a clean campsite that he had mandated were vital to survival. We are more fortunate, but the arrogance that has prompted complacency in cleanliness is ill advised. Many individuals in our society die as a result of infections each year in spite of the best efforts of medicine and miracle drugs.

Hand washing and personal hygiene were considered a basic part of the curriculum in elementary school when I was growing up. I was given a firm indoctrination at home by a mother who had received limited formal education. The commandments of Moses were apparently passed to her through the generations by her family. This is another of the basic responsibilities of parents that has been abdicated in our society. It should be taught to children virtually from birth, but we are much more anxious to potty-train and teach essentials such as shoe tying. It is especially distressing to observe the common practice of food handlers in restaurants of returning to their posts after a trip to the rest room without washing their hands. Many cases of diarrhea and other food-borne diseases are suffered by people each year because of this carelessness. Take note on your next trip to a public rest room of how many people walk out without washing their hands. Take particular note of your waiter/waitress.

Sharing of towels and washcloths is another violation of basic hygiene that frequently leads to the sharing of illnesses. This is especially risky when one member of the family has an overt infection, such as conjunctivitits (pink-eye). This bacterial infection is readily transmitted from one person to another. Other infections that may be transmitted in this manner may be less obvious, but

213

may be even more health threatening. Or particular importance is viral hepatitis, which is much more prevalent today than it was twenty years ago. There is a serious risk of spreading hepatitis A through the community use of towels and washcloths. Even more serious, because of the potential for serious sequelae, is hepatitis B. The latter can be spread from a carrier who has no apparent illness.

In 1986, in a case reported to the Centers for Disease Control, a three-year-old boy was diagnosed as having hepatitis B, an unusual disease in children under the age of fourteen years. Investigation by health authorities revealed evidence of hepatitis B infection in ten other family members. Nine family members shared four toothbrushes, and this appeared to be the means of transmission of the disease. The role that the sharing of towels and washcloths played in this episode cannot be separated from that of the toothbrushes. Sharing of razors and other toilet articles carries the same risk of transmission of disease, the most serious of which would be hepatitis A and B, and possibly AIDS.

## HEPATITIS

Hepatitis A is spread from humans almost exclusively through the fecal–oral route. About 24,000 cases are reported to the Centers for Disease Control each year. Many cases are not reported. If all sewage were properly treated, and if everyone practiced good personal hygiene such as hand washing, we would not have this large number of cases. Hepatitis A is commonly spread within households and in institutions such as nursing homes when a case is present. It is most commonly spread by contamination of food, or by sharing towels or toilet articles in these circumstances.

Hepatitis A is also spread by contamination of water, milk and shellfish. All of the shellfish that is harvested from the coastal waters, especially among the eastern seaboard and Mexico, must be considered contaminated. This contamination has come about as a result of the widespread practice of dumping untreated sewage into the coastal waters of our continent. The existence of this disease in our society at present levels is a national disgrace. It is a graphic demonstration of the deterioration in our public health and personal hygiene practices. Many cases of hepatitis A occur as a result of eating improperly cooked oysters and clams from these regions. This is a serious illness that usually lasts for about six weeks. There is no antibiotic or other remedy for it. Fortunately, virtually all healthy people recover from this disease. There is no carrier state for hepatitis A.

Hepatitis B is a more serious disease in that it has a far more severe impact upon the liver. A percentage of individuals suffer a chronic stage that can result in death. Some people suffer a particularly severe case of acute hepatitis B that results in death in a matter of a few months. There is a carrier state with this form of hepatitis, and these individuals can transmit the disease to others throughout their lifetime. Cancer of the liver is another complication of this form of hepatitis. About 90 percent of the people with this disease recover. The course is more prolonged, however, and more severe in the elderly and in those with underlying disease such as diabetes, anemia and heart disease.

Currently, the most common method of transmission of hepatitis B is through contaminated needles. Since the advent of disposable needles over twenty years ago, such transmission does not occur through legitimate needle use, except for accidental needle sticks of doctors and nurses. The explosion of drug abuse as a recreation in our society, and the concomitant sharing of contaminated needles, accounts for the great majority of cases today. The other primary method by which this disease is spread is through sexual transmission. Unlike hepatitis A, hepatitis B is not commonly spread through the feces. The semen and saliva are infectious, however, and sexual contacts of people who either have active disease or who are carriers present a very real risk of contracting the disease.

The groups of people who are at a high risk of contracting hepatitis B are:

Spouses of acute cases and carriers
Sexually promiscuous individuals, especially male homosexuals
Health-care workers exposed to needles or blood products
Individuals who receive transfusions
Hemophiliacs, through blood products
Residents and staff of institutions: prisons, nursing homes, mental institutions

Hepatitis B is not transmitted through gamma globulin nor through RhoGAM (for Rh negative pregnant women). The processing of these products inactivates the virus. Unfortunately this is not the case for whole blood and some blood products, notably the factor VIII and IX products that are essential to hemophiliacs.

Physicians have known for years that a small percentage of cases of hepatitis are caused by agents other than the viruses that cause type A and B. These cases have been classified as non-A, non-

215

B hepatitis. A pathogen that has been labeled the Delta agent causes some of these cases. It has not been identified. This is a much more serious disease, with a higher incidence of death. It is spread primarily by needles, and is limited to individuals who are exposed to blood and blood products. It is thus seen in hemophiliacs and drug addicts. Very recently an additional agent has been identified that is believed to be responsible for most cases of non-A, non-B hepatitis. It has been labeled the hepatitis C agent.

Repeated tonsil and other mouth infections have been traced to toothbrushes. This can be prevented by soaking the toothbrush is a solution of household bleach for thirty minutes. One tablespoonful of bleach in a glass of water is sufficient. This should be done at least on a weekly basis. The household bleach must be fresh, since it is not stable and loses strength over a period of time. This means that if your jug has been sitting around for a while, it should be tossed and replaced with a fresh one. You also should make your purchase at a store where there is a high enough rate of turnover to assure freshness.

Frequent (and adequate) laundering of towels, washcloths, bed linen and clothing also serves to reduce the risk of and frequency of infections and illness in general. This may be required after one usage if soilage occurs. It should be kept in mind that, as with the washing of hands, laundering becomes much more urgent after soilage by fecal material or by secretions from an obviously infected source, such as a family member with hepatitis. In order to accomplish the destruction of disease causing microbes, hot water and an effective laundry detergent, in adequate concentration, are needed. Badly soiled loads will need a larger measure of detergents than the same quantity of clothing that is less heavily soiled.

In dealing with clothes or bedding that have been contaminated by materials with the potential for causing disease, household bleach is very effective in killing most organisms. The organic matter, such as blood, feces and tissue must be removed by laundering first to assure effectiveness. Clothing and bed linen that is soiled by blood or by feces by a family member who is suffering from a communicable disease such as hepatitis should be laundered with adequate detergent and hot water to remove this soilage. They then should be run through another wash cycle with detergent, hot water and bleach. Bleach and most antimicrobial agents will not work in the presence of such organic material. Lysol (a mixture of cresols) in a 5 percent solution is effective in destroying virtually all microbial agents even in fecal contaminated materials. Diapers that have been contaminated by a patient with hepatitis may be soaked in a solution of Lysol for sixty minutes prior to laundering in order to inactivate the virus. Disposable surgical gloves should be worn when handling any contaminated diapers or bed linen.

Dentures should be scrubbed daily to remove adhered debris and microbial growth. They then should be soaked in a solution of household bleach, one tablespoonful in eight ounces of water for thirty to sixty minutes. This will control the yeast and other organisms that tend to grow on these appliances. This practice is especially important for diabetics and for everyone after eating foods containing sugar. Dentures appear to be impervious. In reality microorganisms readily set up shop on their surface and in the many crevices that are present.

In no area of the house is cleanliness more urgent than in the kitchen. Frequent hand washing is a must with food handling. It should not be done by the clock nor on a fixed schedule, rather it should be done as often as needed. After handling eggs or poultry, for instance, anything touched by the hands must be considered contaminated by Salmonella (see chapter VI). The household cook should wash the hands immediately after handling poultry, or any raw meat, and wash the faucet handles. This may seem obsessive until you have suffered through an acute Salmonella diarrhea.

Keeping all counter tops, handles (refrigerator, stove, microwave) and tables clean and free of food residues is also essential in the prevention of illness. Bacteria multiply rapidly in these residues, particularly at room temperature. (Whether or not an individual succumbs to a bacterial diarrhea frequently depends upon the number of organisms ingested.) We are fortunate in that the hand- and dish-washing detergents (and detergents in general) that we have available to us today are very effective in accomplishing this microbial destruction. They are much more effective surface active agents than formerly available, and thus more effective in disrupting the bacterial capsules. This renders the organisms incapable of reproducing and causing disease.

Proper refrigeration of food (see chapter VI) cannot be stressed too strongly. Those who had the dubious privilege of living with the iceboxes and winter window storage boxes should have an appreciation for the modern refrigerator and freezer that most people take for granted. Food cannot be left sitting at room temperature after it has been prepared or after a meal without risking illness. Some bacteria multiply rapidly at room temperature, increasing the risk of food-borne illness. Other bacteria produce potent toxins at room temperature, causing serious and very unpleasant sickness. Adequate cold temperatures diminish these bacterial activities. For refrigeration this requires a maximum temperature of 38 to 40 degrees Fahrenheit. Freezers should be kept at a temperature of zero degrees Fahrenheit or below. For most refrigerators that are manufactured for home use, this will require a setting close to the maximum. Every refrigerator should have an accurate thermometer in it to monitor the temperature. This was installed by the manufacturers in days past. Rapid cooling of some disease causing bacteria can destroy up to 90 percent of the organisms.

One of the most effective means of spreading disease is by coughing or sneezing. The photograph of a sneeze that has been published in books for the past thirty years is a dramatic demonstration of this potential. The disease containing droplets are disseminated over a wide area, to be deposited into the innermost reaches of the lungs of anyone breathing the contaminated air. The most notorious disease spread in this fashion is tuberculosis, but it is not alone. Many bacterial and viral infections can be spread from person to person in this manner. Older people, people with chronic illnesses and people with suppressed immune systems are particularly vulnerable to infections from this source. Covering the mouth and nose with a tissue to prevent this air-borne dissemination is another common sense practice that seems to have fallen by wayside. Many of the cases of colds, influenza and bronchitis that are suffered each year result from this carelessness.

## TOBACCO

Second only to imprudent eating and drinking practices, cigarette smoking is the single most damaging behavior in our society. The destruction of health from this widespread practice includes not only lung and bladder cancer, but emphysema, chronic obstructive lung disease, heart disease and other vascular disease. The tobacco plant contains cancer causing agents such as nitrosonornicotine and related compounds even before burning. This is attested to by the significant incidence of mouth cancer associated with the use of smokeless tobacco, even in young men. The death in recent years of a high school athlete as a result of the use of smokeless tobacco is a grim testimonial to this danger.

Tobacco smoke contains an even more diverse complex of carcinogens, cancer accelerators and cancer promoters. About forty of these agents have been identified. These include several polycyclic aromatic hydrocarbons and phenolic compounds. The great increase in lung cancer in men since 1930 is associated with the introduction of manufactured cigarettes in 1915. Women picked up the habit in earnest in the early 1940s, during World War II, and the lung cancer incidence in women related to this cigarette smoking began to increase in 1960.

The serious consequences of smoking, and of the use of smokeless tobacco, have gained widespread recognition in recent years. Significant progress has been achieved finally in eliminating this health hazard. Public laws are beginning to free individuals from being forced to inhale the noxious and very toxic products of smoking. It is a sad commentary on the citizens in our society that such laws have become necessary.

## SCABIES

The "seven year itch" is caused by a mite that burrows underneath the skin where it deposits eggs for 30 to 60 days. Sensitization to the mites and their excrement causes an intense, severe itching that is worse at night and after a hot bath. The most common sites for these burrows, and the first to appear, are between the fingers on the back of the hand, and on the inner surface of the wrists. As the infestation progresses, it spreads to other areas of the body. The face and head and the palms of the hands are usually not involved in adults but may be in children. The larva from the hatched eggs mature to adults on the skin surface in about two weeks, and then continue the cycle. Individuals with poor personal hygiene habits suffer heavier infestations than do people who are more fastidious in their bathing and laundry habits.

Scabies is transmitted from person to person, frequently as a result of sharing beds and clothing. Mere skin contact with an infested person is enough to contract the disease, as many dermatologists can attest to. This disease, as with all of the diseases that are caused by mites that feed on man, is directly related to low levels of hygiene and cleanliness. It is more common in regions with a hot climate where water is scarce. Frequent and regular laundering of clothing and bedding destroys the organism and reduces the frequency and intensity of the disease. During the past fifteen to twenty years it has spread from an uncommon disease among the middle class in the United States, to the status of a disease that is seen regularly by physicians. Secondary bacterial infections result from scratching, and streptococcal infections thus acquired have caused serious kidney damage in a number of individuals.

The organism can be eradicated readily by lindane or crotamiton, if the instructions of the physician are followed diligently. Benzyl benzoate, 25 percent, also is still used by some physicians, and is recommended by the World Health Organization. The itching may persist for several weeks after the destruction of the parasites, and should be treated with antihistamines. Repeated application of lindane or crotamition will not relieve the itching and it may lead to sensitivity. Such practice should be avoided. Cortisone cream may spread any secondary bacterial infection that has developed and should be avoided.

Everyone in the household who harbors the parasite, every sexual contact, everyone who shares a bed with the victim, must be treated at the same time. Even individuals who have had only casual physical contact with the infested person may need treatment. All clothing and bed linen must be well laundered, with detergent and hot water. Fabrics that cannot be laundered must be dry cleaned. Reinfestations are common as a result of failure to follow these dictums, and this is one disease that no one wants to repeat.

## PEDICULOSIS

Three varieties of lice are seen in humans, and all are transmitted from human to human. They feed on the blood of man, and live out their thirty-day life cycle either on the body or in the clothing. Head lice are seen predominately among school children, and are about two to three millimeters in length. Body lice are seen primarily among the homeless and individuals of extremely low levels of sanitation. This louse actually lives in the seams of clothing that is worn next to the skin, and it and its ova can be seen there. Laundering the clothing with adequate detergent and hot water obviously will destroy these. Pubic or crab lice are most commonly a sexually transmitted disease, although they can be acquired readily from infested clothing and bedding. When they are acquired sexually, the possibility of any of the other sexually transmitted diseases exits, and these should be tested for. Pubic lice are about five millimeters in length and almost as wide.

As with scabies, all clothing and bed linen must be laundered thoroughly. Combs and hairbrushes can be disinfected by boiling.

These human infestations also can be eradicated by carefully following the physician's instructions for using lindane (Kwell) in adults, crotamiton in children. Pyrethrins with piperonyl butoxide (Rid) are also effective in all forms of pediculosis, and these present less risk of toxicity to the nervous system than does lindane. We have the technology and knowledge to eliminate these scourges of mankind completely, but that would require cooperation and cleanliness on the part of all. We had the same opportunity to eliminate syphilis and gonorrhea from the face of the earth after World War II when both diseases were easily cured with penicillin. Man is his own worst enemy.

Body lice transmit epidemic typhus, relapsing fever (see chapter IX) and trench fever. Trench fever, so named because of its prevalence among troops during wartime, is endemic in Russia, Poland, Tunisia and Mexico. It is caused by a rickettsia that the louse transmits from one human to another. It cannot exist without lack of cleanliness and hygiene in human populations.

## BEDBUGS

These are wingless insects about four to five millimeters in length, that hide in the mattress seams, furniture or even wallpaper during the day, and feed on humans at night. Sensitivity to the saliva may develop in some individuals and this produces itching. Disease is not transmitted by these bugs, but anemia can result from persistent feeding of the parasites. Bathing and laundering of both clothing and bed linen on a regular basis can help to eliminate these creatures. Good hygiene along with modern plumbing and appliances have given us great freedom from this bane of mankind.

Sulfur dioxide fumigation through the burning of sulfur was a popular remedy in past years. The fumes (sulfur dioxide) are toxic to humans and must be avoided. Fumigation by hydrocyanic acid was also used in the past by professionals, but was dangerous to handle or even to be around. These techniques have been supplanted by the pesticides, several of which are effective. The organophosphates are effective but they cannot be taken to bed with you. The mattress and bedroom can be sprayed with an aerosol containing pyrethrin and piperonyl butoxide, making certain that you stay out of the room for at least thirty minutes after spraying. A freshly laundered mattress cover will then help to prevent skin contact with the pyrethrin.

# CONTACT LENSES

The loss of sight is one of the greatest tragedies that can befall a person. This happens far more often than it should as a result of neglect of proper care among diabetics and patients with glaucoma. The extremely widespread popularity of contact lenses has given us an additional risk that is causing loss of vision unnecessarily. This loss is unnecessary because it can be prevented in every instance if instructions are followed and if lenses are properly cared for. These precautions are almost universally neglected and abused because they require a significant investment in time and effort on a daily basis. No one should decide to acquire contact lenses until after they have thoroughly reviewed the procedures that are mandatory for the maintenance and care of these devices. No parent should permit a teenager to get contact lenses until these requirements are reviewed, and until the parent feels certain that the child will comply with them.

The chief risk entailed in wearing contact lenses is damage to the cornea, the clear covering over the center of the eye. The damage may be caused by scratching the cornea during insertion of the lens, but more frequently corneal damage is caused by deposits on the contact lens. The hemoglobin in blood serves as an efficient system for the transport of oxygen to all of the living tissues of the body, except for the cornea. The cornea is provided with no circulation, no blood vessels, and no hemoglobin. It must obtain the oxygen that ever living tissue requires from the air through the tears, and must expel carbon dioxide the same way. This latter substance renders the surface of the cornea acidic, which is damaging to contact lenses. A buffering solution is inserted with these lenses to protect them from this acidic environment.

The cornea actually uses oxygen at a fairly rapid rate, making this method of oxygen transport all the more remarkable. The original hard lenses interfered with this function seriously, and that feature accounted for most of the problems that wearers experienced. If this oxygen deprivation continues long enough, neovascularization, a growth of blood vessels into the cornea, can occur. This can result in impairment of vision. Soft contact lenses have a water content of as much as 80 perecent, and thus they carry oxygen to the cornea much more efficiently. This eliminated many of the problems that were associated with hard lens use.

The down side of this feature of soft lenses is that the high water content results in the retention of many different chemicals in the lens. This includes those chemicals that are used for cleansing and disinfection. It also provides a better media in which microorganisms can multiply. These lenses further are characterized by the buildup of protein deposits from the tears. These deposits cause irritation of the cornea and sensitivity reactions in the inner lining of the upper lid. For these reasons, cleansing and purging of the lenses become even more urgent.

Soft contact lenses must be cleaned daily. The deposit of protein materials begins almost immediately after insertion of the lens. In addition to the irritation of the cornea and the sensitivity reaction of the lids, these deposits can ruin the contact lens. A daily cleaner solution is designed to remove these protein deposits, but it does not disinfect the lens. This requires a second step. Prior to progressing to the second step it is essential to remove all of the cleaning solution by thorough rinsing. If this is not done, the daily cleaner solution that is retained in the contact lens can irritate the cornea and damage the lens. After rinsing the lens thoroughly, disinfection is then carried out. Classically this has been accomplished by boiling for thirty minutes, which effectively destroys all of the microorganisms that have accumulated in the lens. It is important to clean and disinfect the lens case also, otherwise the lenses will become contaminated again when they are placed in the case.

Chemical disinfectants have become popular as a replacement for boiling. While less troublesome, they are not as effective as boiling. Hydrogen peroxide has enjoyed popularity in the past, and is fairly effective. Standard hydrogen peroxide loses its strength on the shelf, however, and for this reason stabilized solutions have been developed. It is important to use only fresh 3 percent hydrogen peroxide solution sold for this purpose, or a similar stabilized solution. It is fairly effective in sterilizing contact lenses, if they have been thoroughly cleansed of organic deposits. Hydrogen peroxide is totally ineffective as an antiseptic in wounds because it is decomposed and inactivated by the tissue enzymes almost immediately. If this occurs while disinfecting your lens, there is no way for you to know, unless you do a culture.

Hydrogen peroxide has the advantage of not leaving a residue buildup in contact lenses. It must be thoroughly rinsed out of the lens, however, or a painful eye will result. Other chemical disinfectants are being investigated. Poly-amino-propylbiguanide has been marketed, and others will follow. One hindrance is the cost of investigation and approval by the Food and Drug Administration. This process takes years in addition to the high cost. The other obstacle is the same one that has prevented the use of many effective germicides in medicine in general. Many substances that kill microorganisms have similar deleterious effects on the tissues of the body. Phenol, while very effective in destroying bacteria, cannot be used in the eye. The same can be said about tincture of iodine.

Some preservatives in the various solutions also cause irritation of the eye. Thimerosal, which has been commonly used as a preservative in saline and other solutions, causes widespread irritation of the eye due to the development of a sensitivity. This problem is compounded by the fact that the contact lens takes up and retains the thimerosal. Some manufacturers have replaced this preservative with other less sensitizing substances, but it remains in some products as of August, 1989. *Caveat emptor*. Read the label.

An enzyme cleaning solution is used weekly to remove any residual protein deposits that are not removed by the daily cleaner. For all of these processes and for all of these solutions, the directions from the manufacturer should be read carefully and adhered to strictly. Only the solutions that are specified for your lenses must be used. Most are not interchangeable. Ignoring this caveat risks damage to the contact lens, the eye or both. Efforts to conserve solutions and money have led many people to mix their own saline solution from salt tablets. This practice has led to serious infections in the eye. Any infection in the eye is a very serious matter, but the infections that result from home brewed saline solutions involve Acanthamoeba. This is a protozoan that has not been associated with infections previously. This organism is widespread in soil and in water all around us, including the water from your faucet. It does not cause disease ordinarily. Heat sterilization as described will kill this organism and its cysts. Other means of sterilization will not assure the destruction of Acanthamoeba.

Only sterile saline solutions should be used in caring for contact lenses. Hands should always be washed carefully before handling lenses, not only to avoid contamination of lenses with microorganisms, but also to remove all hand cream, cosmetics and other greases. Some soaps leave a residue of lanolin or other oleaginous substance on the hands that then contaminates the contact lens. This financial disaster can be avoided by using only pure soap such as Ivory or Neutrogena before handling lenses. Contact lenses can also be destroyed by the oils in hair conditioners and hair rinses. Eye doctors who examine contact lenses see such contamination frequently.

Infections by Acanthamoeba are particularly worrisome because we have no medication that is effective in destroying the organism. Antibiotics are effective in controlling most bacterial infections, but we do not have comparable agents for infections caused by protozoa. Acanthamoeba can also be acquired by wearing contact lenses in the swimming pool, in hot tubs and by placing the lenses in the mouth. The mouth and saliva are far from sterile and saliva makes a poor wetting agent. These infections threaten blindness or even the loss of the eye. Random testing has demonstrated that every sample of homemade saline solution that was examined was contaminated by bacteria, fungi or Acanthamoeba. The water that comes from your faucet is not sterile. Neither is the distilled water that you buy in the supermarket.

During the past decade new materials have been developed for hard lenses that permit the transportation of oxygen through them to the cornea. These are called rigid gas permeable lenses. The newer polymers for these lenses are also more resistant to protein deposits than previous materials, and much more so than soft lenses. These lenses still require a longer period of adaptation than do soft lenses. Since they lack the high moisture content of soft lenses they do not dry out and change shape, as soft lenses tend to do. Visual correction may be better as a result. These lenses are also easier to keep clean, and they last longer. They are much more expensive, however, and they require more care and expertise in fitting. They also require different solutions for care and maintenance than those used with soft lenses.

Individuals with allergies are destined to have more problems with contact lenses than people who are not thus plagued. They also cannot be worn in certain occupational settings, such as dusty atmospheres and laboratories where chemical vapors are encountered. Most people can discipline themselves to not wear their lenses at work where they know that a risk exists. It is a great temptation to forget about contact lenses when sawing or grinding jobs need to be done in the home workshop, however. Contact lenses should not be worn when working with household ammonia, oven cleaners or wall and tile cleaners either. Any cleaner that gives off vapors that irritate the nose, throat or eyes may collect in the contact lenses. Any irritation or problem that is not readily resolved by removal and cleaning of the lens, or any problem that recurs when the lens is reinserted, should be taken to the doctor for examination.

# Glossary

| | |
|---|---|
| **Acute** | Of sudden onset, relatively short duration and usually severe. |
| **Aerosol** | Very small solid or liquid particles that remain suspended in the air for some time. |
| **Amino acids** | The basic structural groups of which proteins are composed. |
| **Arteriosclerosis** | Thickening and hardening of the walls of the arteries. |
| **Carcinogenic** | Causing cancer. |
| **Caveat** | A warning. Let him beware. |
| **Caveat emptor** | Let the buyer beware. One buys at his own risk. |
| **Chronic** | Persisting for long periods. |
| **Compound** | A substance that is made up of two or more chemical elements. |
| **Defoliate** | To cause the leaves of a plant or tree to drop prematurely. |
| **Dinoflagellate** | A minute marine plantlike protozoan. |
| **Endemic** | Present at all times. |
| **Epidemic** | A disease attacking many people in a community or region at one time. Not normally present, or present in small numbers. |
| **Eutectic mixture** | That mixture of two or more substances which has the lowest melting point. |
| **Excrement** | Feces. |
| **Excreta** | Waste materials excreted by the body, e.g., urine and feces. |
| **Fibrosis** | The formation of fibrous tissue, tissue that contains fibers, replacing the normal cells. |
| **Flatulence** | Gas in the stomach and intestines. |
| **Gastrointestinal tract** | The stomach and intestines. |
| **Heterozygous** | Carrying only one dominant gene for a particular trait. |

227

| | |
|---|---|
| Homozygous | Carrying both genes for a particular trait, thus assuring expression of the trait. |
| Hydrocarbon | Chemical substances composed soley of hydrogen and carbon molecules. |
| Hygiene | The science of health and prevention of disease: cleanliness. |
| Infestation | The establishment of parasites on the body, usually on the skin. |
| Ingestion | Taken into the body through the mouth. |
| Keratin | A tough, very insoluble protein of which hair, nails and horns are composed. |
| Labyrinth | The inner ear. |
| Limestone | Calcium carbonate. Much of it formed by the remains of sea animals, e.g., mollusks and coral. Marble was formed from limestone by heat and pressure. |
| Microbial agent | One of the microorganisms, usually one that causes disease. |
| Micrometer | Formerly micron. A unit of measure, one millionth of a meter. |
| Microorganisms | Bacteria, viruses and protozoa that can be seen only with a microscope. |
| Morbidity | Sickness. The condition of being ill. |
| Mutagen | A substance that induces genetic mutation in plants or animals. |
| Necrosis | Death of tissue: decay. |
| Organic compounds | Substances that contain carbon in the molecular structure. |
| Pandemic | A widespread epidemic, usually throughout a continent. Involving several countries rather than one singly. |
| Particulate | A very small, separate particle that remains suspended in the air. Includes fog, mist, smoke, smog, fume (welding) and dust. |
| Personal hygiene | Cleanliness: sanitary behavior. |
| Phenolic | Of or containing phenol, a strong and corrosive substance derived from coal tar. Also a substance with a chemical structure similar to phenol. |
| Phytoplankton | Planktonic plant life. |
| Plankton | Passively floating minute plant and animal life in water. |
| Porphyria | A metabolic disorder characterized by the excretion |

|  |  |
|---|---|
|  | of porphyrins in the urine and by a serious sensitivity to the sun. It may be inherited or acquired by exposure to certain chemicals. |
| **Protozoa** | Minute single-celled organisms, the simplest forms of the animal kingdom. |
| **Respirable particles** | Particles that remain suspended in air, that are small enough to pass into the lungs when they are inhaled. Generally up to five micrometers. |
| **Rickettsia** | Nonfilterable microorganisms somewhere between the bacteria and the viruses in size, structure and organization. |
| **Silica** | Silicon dioxide. Most of the earth's crust is composed of this substance, including quartz, flint, granite and sand. |
| **Silicates** | Combined forms of silica, including asbestos, mica and talc. |
| **Spirochaete** | A spiral, motile bacteria. Members of this group cause syphilis, yaws, relapsing fever and Lyme disease. |
| **Systemic** | Affecting the body (or plant) as a whole rather than a single organ. A systemic pesticide is taken up by the plant and distributed throughout the plant and its fruit. |
| **Teratogen** | An agent that produces physical defects in the fetus. |
| **Toxicity** | The degree of poisonous or harmfulness of a substance. |
| **Zygote** | A cell formed by the fertilization of an ova by a sperm cell. |

# Index

233

234

235